EPISCOPAL CONFERENCES

HISTORICAL, CANONICAL, AND THEOLOGICAL STUDIES

Publications of the Woodstock Theological Center

Archbishop: Inside the Power Structure of the American Catholic Church, Thomas J. Reese, S.J., Harper & Row Publishers, Inc., 1989

The Catholic Challenge to the American Economy: Reflections on the U.S. Bishops' Pastoral Letter on Catholic Social Teaching and the U.S. Economy, edited by Thomas M. Gannon, S.J., Macmillan Publishing Company, 1987.

The Ethics of Discourse: The Social Philosophy of John Courtney Murray, J. Leon Hooper, S.J., Georgetown University Press, 1986.

Between God and Caesar: Priests, Sisters and Political Office in the United States, edited by Madonna Kolbenschlag, *Woodstock Studies 8*, Paulist Press, 1985.

Tracing the Spirit: Communities, Social Action and Theological Reflection, edited by James E. Hug, S.J., *Woodstock Studies 7*, Paulist Press, 1983.

Inequality and the American Conscience, Christopher Mooney, S.J., *Woodstock Studies 6*, Paulist Press, 1983.

Human Rights in the Americas: The Struggle for Consensus, edited by Alfred Hennelly, S.J. and John Langan, S.J., Georgetown University Press, 1982.

Human Rights and Basic Needs in the Americas, edited by Margaret E. Crahan, Georgetown University Press, 1982.

Above Every Name: The Lordship of Christ and Social Systems, edited by Thomas E. Clarke, S.J., *Woodstock Studies 5*, Paulist Press, 1980.

Claims in Conflict, David Hollenbach, S.J., *Woodstock Studies 4*, Paulist Press, 1979.

Personal Values in Public Policy, edited by John C. Haughey, S.J., *Woodstock Studies 3*, Paulist Press, 1979.

The Faith That Does Justice: Examining the Christian Sources for Social Change, edited by John C. Haughey, S.J., *Woodstock Studies 2*, Paulist Press, 1977.

Religious Freedom 1965-1975: A Symposium on a Historic Document, edited by Walter J. Burghardt, S.J., *Woodstock Studies 1*, Paulist Press, 1976.

EPISCOPAL CONFERENCES

HISTORICAL, CANONICAL, AND THEOLOGICAL STUDIES

Edited by
Thomas J. Reese, S.J.

GEORGETOWN UNIVERSITY PRESS
WASHINGTON, D.C.

Library of Congress Cataloging-in-Publication Data

Reese, Thomas J., 1945-
    Episcopal conferences.

    Includes index.
    1. Episcopal conferences (Catholic)   I. Title.
BX837.5.R44   1989   262'.3   89-16784
ISBN 0-87840-493-7

TABLE OF CONTENTS

Preface

In the Catholic church, Roman officials perform many useful functions. One of their contributions to the academic community is to highlight certain topics as important for the church and therefore worthy of study. At one time, a statement by a Vatican official might have ended debate in the church. Today, however, the maxim *Roma locuta est, causa finita est* (Rome has spoken, the case is finished) yields to *Roma locuta est, causa incepta est* (Rome has spoken, the project begins). By issuing an *instrumentum laboris* or working paper, Rome is inviting not only bishops but the scholarly community to participate in discussions and debates that will clarify issues so that the truth can be found. This collection of essays is a response to the Vatican invitation to examine the theological and juridical status of episcopal conferences.

My interest in episcopal conferences began when, as associate editor of *America*, I followed the development of the peace pastoral by the National Conference of Catholic Bishops (NCCB). The conference and its pastoral were front-page news across the country, thanks in part to attacks on the letter by the White House and conservative Catholics.[1] More importantly for our purposes, the pastoral had also been questioned by some European theologians and bishops. In order to discuss these differences, the NCCB drafting committee met in Rome in January 1983 with Vatican officials and representatives from the European episcopal conferences. The minutes of that meeting reported that Cardinal Joseph Ratzinger, prefect of the Congregation for the Doctrine of the Faith, stated that "A bishops' conference as such does not have a mandatum docendi. This belongs only to the individual bishop or to the college of bishops with the pope."[2]

When I saw this quotation, I recognized that it could be used by the bishops' opponents to undermine the teaching authority of the peace pastoral and any other statement issued by the conference. I immediately contacted Avery Dulles, S.J., and suggested that he write a letter to *America* responding to Cardinal Ratzinger's comments which I had quoted in an article reporting final passage of the peace pastoral.[3] After discussions back and forth

---

1. Thomas J. Reese, "Nuclear Weapons: The Bishops' Debate," *America* 147 (December 18, 1982): 386-89.

2. Jan Schotte, "A Vatican Synthesis," *Origins* 12 (April 7, 1983): 692.

3. Thomas J. Reese, "The Bishops' 'Challenge of Peace,'" *America* 148 (May 21, 1983): 395.

with Avery, the proposal grew from a letter to an op-ed piece, and finally to an article.[4]

Cardinal Ratzinger continued to raise questions about episcopal conferences in an interview that received wide circulation.[5] The status of episcopal conferences was therefore put on the agenda of the 1985 extraordinary synod. At the synod, Bishop James Malone, then president of the NCCB, called for a study of the theological and juridical status of episcopal conferences, a request that was incorporated into the final report of the synod.[6]

Interestingly, the report did not say who was supposed to do this study. When Cardinal Godfried Danneels, the relator for the synod, was asked who would do the study, he responded that anyone could do it: the episcopal conferences, theologians, Vatican agencies. He invited everyone to go to work on the topic.

Sad to say, after taking the initiative in calling for the study, the American bishops then dropped the ball in the Vatican court and went home. The NCCB committees and staff devoted no time to the project, nor did they contract with American scholars for research on this topic which was of such vital interest to their teaching authority. They simply waited for the Vatican to do the study for them.

The Vatican study was released in early 1988 with a letter from Cardinal Bernardin Gantin, prefect of the Congregation for Bishops.[7] He called the document an *instrumentum laboris*, a working paper, and requested corrections

---

4. Avery Dulles, "The Teaching Authority of Bishops' Conferences," *America* (June 11, 1983): 453-55.

5. Joseph Ratzinger with Vittorio Messori, *The Ratzinger Report*, trans. Salvator Attanasio and Graham Harrison (San Francisco: Ignatius Press, 1985).

6. Synod of Bishops, "Final Report," *Origins* 15 (December 19, 1985): 444-50.

7. "Theological and Juridical Status of Episcopal Conferences" (Vatican City: Congregation for Bishops, July 1, 1987, photocopy). Also printed as "Draft Statement on Episcopal Conferences," *Origins* 17 (April 7, 1988): 736.

Since this *instrumentum laboris* was released with a January 12, 1988, cover letter by Cardinal Bernardin Gantin, prefect of the Congregation for Bishops, many refer to it as the congregation's document. According to Archbishop Jan Schotte, secretary general of the synod of bishops, the *instrumentum laboris* was actually done under the direction of a postsynodal commission composed of five members: Cardinal Gantin, Cardinal Ratzinger, Cardinal Jozef Tomko, prefect of the Congregation for the Evangelization of Peoples, Cardinal D. Simon Lourdusamy, prefect of the Congregation for the Oriental Churches, and himself.

and emendations from bishops and episcopal conferences before the end of the year.

As soon as the working paper was available, the Woodstock Theological Center brought together a team of prominent American ecclesiologists who went to work analyzing and discussing the document. Avery Dulles, Joseph Komonchak, Ladislas Orsy, and James Provost were members of this original group. Komonchak, Orsy, and Provost also took part in an international symposium at Salamanca on episcopal conferences that occurred right before the *instrumentum laboris* was released.[8]

The Vatican *instrumentum laboris* was a great disappointment. Although the document had been completed as early as July 1987 and was not released until January 1988, the English translation was poorly done and appeared rushed. The released text contained whiteouts, crossed out words, misspellings, typos, and handwritten corrections. Worse yet, the theological reasoning was onesided, inconsistent, and lacked any historical sense.[9] Large sections of the document were lifted from articles or editorials in *Civiltà Cattolica*. As one professor commented, "If this paper were turned in by a graduate student, I would not give it a 'C' grade." Many theologians considered the *instrumentum laboris* so poorly done that they did not want to waste their time commenting on it.

Encouraged by the Woodstock Center, Dulles, Komonchak, Orsy, and Provost pursued the issue in a series of articles that were published in *America*.[10] Copies of this issue of *America* were distributed by the Woodstock Theological Center to all the U.S. bishops and to episcopal conferences around the world. Correspondence indicated that the articles were helpful to

---

8. For their reports on the meeting, see Ladislas Orsy, "Episcopal Conferences: Report on a Meeting," *America* 158 (February 6, 1988): 119-21, and Joseph A. Komonchak and James H. Provost, "Meeting in Salamanca: Ready for Rome, Defining Episcopal Conferences," *Commonweal* (February 26, 1988): 102-105. For the papers given at the conference, see Hervé Legrand, Julio Manzanares, and Antonio García y García, eds., *The Nature and Future of Episcopal Conferences* (Washington, DC: The Catholic University of America Press, 1988) or see *Jurist* 48 (1988): 1-412.

9. See article by Joseph Komonchak in this volume.

10. Avery Dulles, "The Mandate to Teach," *America* 158 (March 19, 1988): 293-95; Ladislas Orsy, "Some Questions from History," 299-301; Joseph A. Komonchak, "Bishops, Conferences and Collegiality," 302-304; James H. Provost, "Questions of Communion and Collegiality," 296-98.

bishops preparing responses not only in the United States but in the Antilles, Australia, Brazil, Canada, Ecuador, Mexico, New Zealand, Paraguay, the Philippines, South Africa, southeast Asia, Venezuela, and other parts of the world. One conference told the Vatican that the *America* articles "represent what is the basic view of our seminary professors as well as the general consensus of the Bishops of this Conference." In less than a year, the articles were also being cited by scholars writing in Belgium,[11] Canada,[12] Germany,[13] India,[14] and Italy.[15]

With the completion of these initial responses to the *instrumentum laboris*, the Woodstock Theological Center expanded its research group to include more theologians, canonists, and historians in order to do a more scholarly and extensive analysis of the theological and juridical status of episcopal conferences. We decided to expand our research beyond the *instrumentum laboris* to include aspects of the question that had not yet been considered. The result of this research is this collection of essays.

The Woodstock Center and I are very grateful to the outstanding scholars who generously gave of their time and energy for this project, not only in writing their own articles but in critiquing and commenting on drafts of each other's papers. An entire weekend in December 1988 was devoted to a discussion of the papers by the participants together with invited guests who included Donald E. Heintschel, associate general secretary of the NCCB/USCC, Michael J. Buckley, S.J., staff to the NCCB Committee on Doctrine, James L. Connor, S.J., director of the Woodstock Theological Center, and other Woodstock fellows. This was truly a collaborative effort. Some of these scholars also helped the special committee of former NCCB

---

11. David Seeber, "Episcopal Conferences: the view of the Congregation for Bishops," *Pro Mundi Vita Studies* 7 (January 1989): 6.

· 12. Sr. Susan Wood, "The Theological Foundations of Episcopal Conferences and Collegiality," *Studia Canonica* 22 (1988): 328 and 337.

13. Walter Kasper, "Nochmals: Der theologische Status der Bischofskonferenzen," *Theologische Quartalschrift* 168 (1988): 238. Herman J. Pottmeyer, "Was ist eine Bischofskonferenz," *Stimmen der Zeit* 206 (July 1988): 446.

14. Felix Wilfred, "Episcopal Conferences--Their Status," *Vidyajyoti* 52 (October 1988): 479, 482, 486, 487.

15. Giuseppe Ruggieri, "Le conferenze episcopali viste da Roma: Collegialità affettiva ma non effettiva," *Il Regno-Attualità* 33 (giugno 15, 1988): 299.

presidents who drafted the NCCB response to the *instrumentum laboris* which was approved in November 1988.[16]

The collection of articles is divided into three parts, with an introduction by Joseph A. Komonchak, professor of theology at the Catholic University of America. He places our research in the context of the debates on episcopal conferences that began at Vatican II and have continued ever since.

Part 1 uses historical scholarship to look at episcopal conferences and their predecessors. Brian E. Daley, S.J., professor of church history at the Weston School of Theology, takes us to the patristic period of the church to examine regional councils and how they interacted with the church of Rome. Elizabeth K. McKeown, professor of church history in the theology department of Georgetown University, and Gerald P. Fogarty, S.J., professor of history and religious studies at the University of Virginia, Charlottesville, bring us back to the twentieth century with descriptions of the origins and development of the National Catholic Welfare Council, the predecessor of the NCCB.

Part 2 presents papers of a more analytical nature. Since I am a political scientist, my article examines the NCCB/USCC as a consensus-making institution by looking at the procedures used by the conference assembly in approving statements. Thomas J. Green, professor of canon law at the Catholic University of America, investigates the treatment of episcopal conferences in the 1983 Code of Canon Law. Joseph Komonchak then returns with a detailed analysis of the Vatican *instrumentum laboris*.

Finally, part 3 examines episcopal conferences from a theological perspective. Avery Dulles, S.J., holder of the Laurence J. McGinley Chair in Religion and Society at Fordham University, examines the doctrinal authority of episcopal conferences. Ladislas Orsy, S.J., professor of canon law at the Catholic University of America, also explores the teaching authority of bishops' conferences. Michael A. Fahey, S.J., professor of ecclesiology and dean of the faculty of theology at the University of St. Michael's College, Toronto, examines the pertinence of Eastern church synodal practices for Western episcopal conferences. James H. Provost, professor of canon law at the Catholic University of America, discusses episcopal conferences as manifestations of *communio*.

---

16. National Conference of Catholic Bishops, "Response to Vatican Working Paper on Bishops Conferences," *Origins* 18 (December 1, 1988): 397-402.

This study of episcopal conferences would have gone nowhere without the generosity of these scholars who gave time and energy to this task in the midst of their many other commitments. Thanks are also due to foundations and individual contributors who recognized the importance of this project and gave it their support, especially the U.S. Catholic Conference, the Raskob Foundation, the Cambridge Center for Social Studies (a funding arm of the Jesuit Conference), and another foundation that prefers to remain anonymous. I am also grateful to David Staples, who oversaw production of the book, and David Collins, S.J., who helped in editing and research. John Breslin, S.J., director of the Georgetown University Press, and his staff saw to the speedy printing and distribution of the text.

As a fellow of the Woodstock Theological Center, I am especially grateful for the encouragement and assistance of our director, James L. Connor, S.J. The Woodstock Theological Center is an independent research center based at Georgetown University in Washington, D.C. Sponsored by the Maryland and New York Provinces of the Society of Jesus, the center is committed to research on contemporary problems in the light of the Christian faith. A list of Woodstock publications is on page ii.

In many ways, this project on episcopal conferences is a model for future collaboration between the center and the academic community. By identifying an important issue and providing logistics and funding, the center has brought together the best scholarly minds to work on a topic of critical importance to the church. Interaction between the center's research fellows and outside scholars has produced results that would otherwise have taken years to realize if it had been done at all. The center has also taken responsibility not only for encouraging the research, but for disseminating its results to both the hierarchy and the academic community. We look forward to many more such productive and fruitful endeavors.

Thomas J. Reese, S.J.
Woodstock Theological Center
Georgetown University

Joseph A. Komonchak

Introduction: Episcopal Conferences under Criticism

When the Second Vatican Council began to discuss giving episcopal conferences a common juridical form and authority, it initiated a debate which, far from dying out, has in recent years increased in intensity. The extraordinary session of the synod of bishops in 1985 included a discussion of the nature and role of the conferences which ended in a proposal for a fuller and deeper study of their theological status and especially of their teaching authority. Subsequently, a Vatican commission was appointed to examine these issues; and in 1988, after a year's work, it distributed a working-paper (*instrumentum laboris*). The paper's generally negative conclusions have so far only provoked further discussion.

This collection of essays may be read as an American contribution to the contemporary discussion. I would like here to offer a context for understanding the debate by briefly reviewing the history of episcopal conferences and the conciliar debate, and by describing the chief criticisms which they have received since Vatican II.

The Emergence of Episcopal Conferences

The history of episcopal conferences is generally considered to have begun in the first half of the nineteenth century.[1] When the bishops of Belgium met in 1830 to deal with the issues posed by the revolution which

---

1. By far the most comprehensive and detailed history is by Giorgio Feliciani, *Le conferenze episcopali* (Bologna: Il Mulino, 1974), which gives the earlier bibliography on 41 n. 6. Earlier examples and forms of nonconciliar meetings of bishops are now also attracting scholarly attention; see, for example, Antonio García y García, "Episcopal Conferences in Light of Particular Councils during the Second Millennium," in *The Nature and Future of Episcopal Conferences*, ed. Hervé Legrand, Julio Manzanares, and Antonio García y García (Washington, DC: The Catholic University of America Press, 1988), 57-67, esp. 64-67.

took place earlier that year, they established a model of episcopal consultation and collaboration which was to be imitated in many European countries, in Latin America, in Australia, and in missionary countries throughout the nineteenth century. A few of these meetings were initiated by the local bishops, but Popes Pius IX and Leo XIII encouraged bishops to meet often to promote common attitudes and practices. A very broad range of concerns marked the agendas of these regional and national meetings, as the bishops attempted to deal with the century's rapid social, economic, political, and cultural changes. During the twentieth century, conferences were established in many other countries and on every continent. The 1959 *Annuario Pontificio* lists for the first time the forty-two conferences existing on the eve of the Second Vatican Council.

The relationship between episcopal conferences and particular councils is a matter of some debate. In fact, episcopal conferences began to appear at a time when the practice of holding particular councils had fallen into near desuetude.[2] While the conferences did not enjoy the legislative authority of the councils, they were often urged for the same motives, were assigned the same topics, and performed many of the same functions as the councils.[3] Despite the fairly consistent wish of the popes that the conferences not substitute for councils, the more ancient institution for episcopal collaboration did not in fact revive. Conferences became, as Feliciani explains, "the ordinary and privileged instrument for the *consensio episcoporum* on the local level, so much so that their traditional merely consultative character was called into question." Nevertheless, the popes down to Pius XII resisted proposals to give the conferences any general juridical status, initially perhaps out of a fear of nationalism, and later out of a reluctance to introduce a new intermediary structure between Rome and the individual bishop.[4] The role which the conferences, with Rome's powerful support, were by then playing, however, made it inevitable that the question of their theological and juridical status would be posed at Vatican II.

---

2. See Eugenio Corecco, *La formazione della Chiesa cattolica negli Stati Uniti d'America attraverso l'attività sinodale* (Brescia: Morcelliana, 1970), 71-84.

3. See Feliciani, *Le conferenze episcopali*, 133-35, 165-70, 279, 305, 383.

4. See Feliciani, *Le conferenze episcopali*, 304-306.

Vatican II

Episcopal conferences became an important *fact* at Vatican II on its first working-day, when the proposal of Cardinals Achille Liénart and Josef Frings was accepted to postpone the election of conciliar commissions until the various conferences could meet and draw up lists of candidates. From that point on, the conferences became an important instrument for the exchange of information and for the construction of opinion among the bishops of particular nations or regions.

Before the issue of conferences' juridical status had been determined, *Sacrosanctum Concilium* (the constitution on the liturgy) began to assign them a certain decision-making authority for the adaptation of the liturgy. The conferences became a topic in their own right at the second session of the council,[5] when the bishops took up a draft document on "Bishops and the Governance of Dioceses." Two questions chiefly occupied them: the theological basis for the conferences and their juridical authority. The first of these was essentially whether conferences could be considered expressions or exercises of episcopal collegiality. One group of bishops argued that collegiality refers only to acts of the whole college, including its head, which affect the universal church. In its strict theological sense, collegiality could not be used for any other exercises of authority.

Opposing this all-or-nothing interpretation, another group of bishops argued from history for a more elastic notion of the nature and exercises of collegiality. Throughout history, collegiality had been expressed in many different ways and degrees, and episcopal conferences could be considered particularly appropriate expressions of it in today's world.

As several bishops noted at the time, the question turned on the meaning of episcopal collegiality itself. Given the several divergent meanings of the term, even when applied to the whole college, the conciliar commission decided to leave the issue unresolved. Because of the differences of opinion, "the conciliar commission considered it better to present only the historical

---

5. See Feliciani, *Le conferenze episcopali*, 353-443; Remigiusz Sobanski, "The Theology and Juridic Status of Episcopal Conferences at the Second Vatican Council," in *The Nature and Future of Episcopal Conferences*, 68-106; Angel Antón, "The Theological 'Status' of Episcopal Conferences," ibid., 185-219.

and pastoral basis, referring to the need to act today in a communion of charity and love, other reasons being sketched in the theological draft or *passim* in this draft."[6] This decision was reflected first in the brief historical comment which introduces the section of *Christus Dominus* (the decree on bishops) on "synods, councils, and especially episcopal conferences" (*CD* 36-38) and in the definition of a conference as "a form of assembly in which the bishops of a given country or region exercise their pastoral office jointly (*coniunctim*) in order to enhance the Church's beneficial influence on all men, especially by devising forms of the apostolate and apostolic methods suitably adapted to the circumstances of the times" (*CD* 38:1). As Feliciani notes, this decision left the decree on bishops more cautious than *Lumen Gentium* or Pope Paul VI himself on the question of relating the conferences to collegiality.[7]

The other warmly debated question was whether to assign legislative authority to the conferences. Some of the strongest defenders of the collegial character of the bishop's office, such as Cardinal Frings, were among those who opposed this proposal. To introduce a level of hierarchical authority between the monarchical bishop and the universal primate would, it was feared, do injury to one or the other, or indeed to both, and might open the way to a revival of ecclesiastical nationalism. On the other hand, a majority appeared to be in favor of a limited legislative role for the conferences; and it was this opinion which prevailed in the final text of *Christus Dominus*.

A particular form of this second debate concerned the question of the magisterial competence of the conferences which was explicitly stated in notes accompanying the early drafts of the decree on bishops. The arguments on this issue were similar to those concerning legislative authority and the division of numbers was approximately the same. The final text of *Christus Dominus* did not include the explanatory notes, but they were dropped simply for brevity's sake and not because the council wished to deny conferences magisterial authority.[8]

---

6. *Acta Synodalia Sacrosancti Concilii Vaticani II*, vol. 3/2 (Vatican City: Typis Polyglottis Vaticanis, 1974), 53 (my translation).

7. See Feliciani, *Le conferenze episcopali*, 377.

8. See Julio Manzanares, "The Teaching Authority of Episcopal Conferences," in *The Nature and Future of Episcopal Conferences*, 234-63, esp. 239-43; and Avery Dulles' article in this volume.

Developments after Vatican II

Since the council, episcopal conferences have grown in number and in significance for the life of the churches. The *Annuario Pontificio* now lists over a hundred of them, and what was said ten years after the council has been reinforced since the promulgation of the new Code of Canon Law: "Today there is hardly any significant question relating to the apostolate and to ecclesiastical governance whose solution does not require a consultation or an intervention of this new institution."[9] The author of this remark surveyed the practical developments and concluded that the fears expressed at the council with regard to the conferences had not been realized. He noted, on the other hand, that the theological and juridical questions left open by the council's texts had still not been resolved in any sort of consensus.

That episcopal conferences were central topics of discussion at the two extraordinary sessions of the synod of bishops indicates that not all elements of their development have been unanimously considered positive. Paul VI had apparently already been intending to devote a session of the synod to episcopal conferences, but their differing responses to *Humanae Vitae* gave a special urgency to his calling the synod of 1969 to discuss the question of their relationship with the Holy See and with each other. The debates at this synod, just as those at Vatican II, concentrated on the nature of collegiality and the relevance of the principle of subsidiarity, and questioned the doctrinal authority of the conferences. The synodal debates did not resolve the theological questions, but the recommendations endorsed by the synod reaffirmed their practical importance.

In the years that followed, the conferences became increasingly important elements in the church's structures. Simultaneously, attacks on the theological status of the conferences increased, especially before and during the synod of 1985. At this synod itself many reports and interventions stressed the positive contribution of the conferences to the life of the churches throughout the world. The synod therefore asked the pope for a fuller and deeper study of the conferences and especially of their magisterial role. In 1988, the Congregation

---

9. Julio Manzanares, "De conferentiis episcopalibus post decem annos a Concilio Vaticano II," *Periodica* 64 (1975): 588-631, at 596 (my translation). See also the article by Thomas Green in this volume.

for Bishops sent out the first result of the study undertaken at Pope John Paul's request in the form of a working paper on the theological and juridical status of episcopal conferences.[10]

To provide a context for the debate engendered by this Roman text, it will be useful to review the criticisms directed in recent years at the development of episcopal conferences, which, by and large, have been taken over in the *instrumentum laboris*.

The Critique of Episcopal Conferences

Put most simply, the criticisms claim that two fears expressed at Vatican II have been fulfilled: Episcopal conferences have come to pose threats to the authority of both the individual bishop and the pope.

According to critics, the authority of the individual diocesan bishop is being threatened by the size, organization, and prominence of the conferences which so outweigh him that his freedom to exercise his own ministry is being compromised even in areas where the conferences do not possess legislative competence. The *locus* of the church's self-realization is thus in danger of shifting away from the diocese and its parishes to a national center. The episcopal conferences achieved a decentralization with reference to Rome, but a centralization with reference to the dioceses.

The reasons for the shift are varied. There have always been and are today some bishops who welcome being relieved of responsibilities by the actions of a superior institution. And the national character of conference structures and activities can deflect attention away from regional and diocesan concerns. In addition, the episcopal conferences can grow in bureaucratization, a most paradoxical phenomenon in the church after a council which so stressed the communion and participation of all the members of the church. A multiplication of offices, the introduction of new types of professional

---

10. The typed copy received by the U.S. bishops was published as "Draft Statement on Episcopal Conferences," *Origins* 17 (April 7, 1988): 731-37. Recognizing the inadequacy of the English translation provided, Archbishop John May, president of the NCCB, requested and received a copy of the original Italian text of the document. This has since been published in *Il regno-documenti* 23 (1988): 390-96. (Note: All citations of the *instrumentum laboris* are from my own translation of the Italian original, but the references are to the pages and columns of the *Origins* version.)

experts, and a tendency towards uniform practices and regulations are among the elements of this development. Confusion often arises within the episcopal conferences themselves, and particularly between their general assemblies and the administrative bodies which prepare and implement their agenda. The individual bishop often finds himself facing, therefore, not only the general assembly of his fellow bishops, but the commissions and staff of the central national bureaucracy.[11]

The effect of these developments is sometimes expressed in the statement that before episcopal conferences we had bishops without an episcopate; now we have an episcopate without bishops.[12]

These fears and criticisms were summarized shortly after the 1969 synod by Henri de Lubac:

> Too elaborate an organization of these regional groups of bishops risks doing harm to the personal initiative of each of them, absorbing him in specialized tasks which take him away from his diocesans, laity or priests, sometimes paralyzing him in his essential ministry, perhaps even dulling his consciousness of his personal obligations as much with regard to the total catholicity as in the government of his own Church. What would tend to prevail in this case would be an impersonal, anonymous leadership, developing into a bureaucracy; it would by that very fact be a theoretical, abstract teaching of neutral tone, without human warmth, in which the faithful would no longer recognize the voice of their pastor. Finally, just as some bishops were reproachable not long ago for fleeing their responsibilities by hiding behind a Roman congregation, it could be feared that a number might again and even more be prompted to flee them today by taking refuge behind some national commission or other, whether this commission be instituted in virtue of a conciliar decree or

---

11. Tendencies towards bureaucracy were already noted by René Laurentin on the eve of the 1969 synod; see René Laurentin, *Enjeu du deuxième Synode et contestation dans l'Église* (Paris: du Seuil, 1969), 129-30. For a critique of this phenomenon, see James Hitchcock, *Catholicism and Modernity: Confrontation or Capitulation?* (New York: Seabury, 1979), 96-125, and F.-X. Kaufmann, *Kirche Begreifen: Analysen und Thesen zur gesellschaftlichen Verfassung des Christentums* (Freiburg: Herder, 1979), 136-46.

12. Cardinal Gouyon, "Les rélations entre le diocèse et la Conférence Épiscopale," *L'Année Canonique* 22 (1978): 1-23.

of a Roman recommendation. The temptation might even be stronger, the pressure being more immediate. Jacques Maritain recently recalled, and no subtlety of the theological or, as they say, "pastoral" order could obscure the pertinence of his remark: "A bishop is by divine mandate the pastor of his diocese; it is for him alone, on his responsibility before God, to make decisions concerning the souls entrusted to him. If he became, as it were, not *de jure* but *de facto*, the executive agent of a commission, would it not be his very mission as a successor of the apostles and the evangelical prescription itself which would be injured?"[13]

In the year before the synod of 1985, these fears were echoed in Cardinal Joseph Ratzinger's famous book of interviews. Whereas once he argued strongly for the need to overcome a monarchical vision of the episcopal office, which was interested in collegiality only when it did not affect a bishop's "rights," now he believes it necessary to remind bishops that they have an inalienable responsibility which they cannot relinquish to a larger group. Psychologically, "in many episcopal conferences, the group spirit and perhaps even the desire for a quiet, peaceful life or conformism lead the majority to accept the positions of active minorities bent upon pursuing clear goals." This might even be considered "a clear sociological law," which also operated at Vatican II, where it is estimated that only ten percent of the bishops ever spoke from the floor. Similarly, in the conferences there is a tendency on the part of many bishops simply to depend on drafts prepared by commissions or staffs. A desire for agreement can also produce flat statements without the decisiveness which may be required. Truth is not something that can be "created through ballots. . . . Truth can only be found, not created."[14] Highly

---

13. Henri de Lubac, *The Motherhood of the Church followed by Particular Churches in the Universal Church* (San Francisco: Ignatius Press, 1982), 267-69. This text appeared in French in 1971.

14. Cardinal Joseph Ratzinger with Vittorio Messori, *The Ratzinger Report: An Exclusive Interview on the State of the Church* (San Francisco: Ignatius Press, 1985), 61-62. In Germany in the 1930s, he added, "the really powerful documents against National Socialism were those that came from individual courageous bishops. The documents of the conference, on the contrary, were often rather wan and too weak by comparison to what the tragedy called for. . . ." On the attitudes and actions of the German bishops' conferences during this period, see Feliciani, *Le conferenze episcopali*, 233-38.

organized bureaucracies, like those he knew in Germany, do not leave enough room for individual initiatives and original ideas coming from remarkable personalities. "The saints were all people of imagination, not functionaries of apparatuses. . . . And the Church, I shall never tire of repeating it, needs saints more than functionaries."[15]

Hans Urs von Balthasar echoed the theme even more vigorously:

> Let us read the Gospel again: Jesus always designated persons for service, not institutions. The persons of bishops belong to the fundamental structure of the church, not bureaucratic offices. There's nothing more grotesque than to think of a Christ who would want to establish committees! We have to rediscover a Catholic truth: in the church everything is personal, nothing should be anonymous. Instead, today so many bishops are hiding behind anonymous structures. Committees, subcommittees, all kinds of groups and offices.[16]

An editorial in *Civiltà Cattolica* published six months before the 1985 synod repeated these criticisms,[17] and they were echoed when the *instrumentum laboris* warned of the dangers that episcopal conferences run:

> a) their being transformed into bureaucratic, decision-making structures which, by restricting the possibility for bishops to express their own thoughts and of engaging in dialogue with their confreres, may lead to the view that the individual bishops are mere executors of the conferences;

---

15. Ratzinger, *The Ratzinger Report*, 67; see also 43-44, with regard to new spiritual movements in the church: "What is striking is that all this fervour was not elaborated by any office of pastoral planning, but somehow it sprang forth by itself. As a consequence, the planning offices--just when they want to be very progressive--don't know just what to do with them. They don't fit into their plan."

16. Hans Urs von Balthasar with Vittorio Messori, *Un Papa nutrito di preghiera per questa Chiesa offesa e ferita* (Milano: Avvenire, 1985), 11 (my translation).

17. "Conferenze episcopali e corresponsabilità dei vescovi," *Civiltà Cattolica* 136/2 (1985): 417-29, and 422-25, where Maritain, de Lubac, and Gouyon are all cited. At the meeting of the college of cardinals just before the 1985 synod, Jerome Hamer repeated his 1976 observations on the conferences; see *Synode Extraordinaire: Célébration de Vatican II* (Paris: du Cerf, 1986), 600-602.

b) that, by the weight of frequent decisions coming above all from their permanent organs and the commissions within them, the conferences coerce the psychological freedom of the bishops, who might thus be led to see the episcopal conferences as a sort of super-government of the dioceses and might sacrifice to it their right and duty to resolve in communion with their own prebyterium the problems of their particular Churches.[18]

With regard to papal authority, on the other hand, the fear is that the conferences might cause a revival of nationalism in the church. Cardinal John Wright expressed this fear at the 1969 synod,[19] and his warning was echoed soon after by de Lubac.[20] In his survey of the results of ten years' experience of episcopal conferences, Julio Manzanares saw no evidence of a threat to the unity of the church.

The contrary seems true, since the episcopal conferences clearly have been an effective instrument for calm and moderation whenever difficulties and tensions have arisen in the application of the Council's principles for renewal. Unless someone still thinks that unity is identical with uniformity and that all who are working for the prescribed adaptation of religious life to the genius and traditions of peoples are weakening the unity of the Church.[21]

The warnings continued to be made, however, usually without specific examples being offered. Cardinal Jerome Hamer echoed de Lubac's fear in 1976, 1983, and 1985.[22] Cardinal Ratzinger in turn reminded his interviewer that "it is a matter of safeguarding the very nature of the Catholic Church,

---

18. "Draft Statement on Episcopal Conferences," 735A.

19. See Giovanni Caprile, *Il Sinodo dei Vescovi: Prima assemblea straordinaria (11-28 ottobre 1969)* (Rome: Ed. "Civiltà Cattolica," 1970), 120-21.

20. Henri de Lubac, *The Motherhood of the Church*, 270-73.

21. Manzanares, "De conferentiis episcopalibus," 598.

22. Jerome Hamer, "Chiesa locale e comunione ecclesiale," in *La chiesa locale: Prospettive teologiche e pastorali*, ed. A. Amato (Rome: Libreria Ateneo Salesiano, 1976), 44. The argument is repeated verbatim in Jerome Hamer, "La responsabilité collégiale de chaque évêque," *Nouvelle Revue Théologique* 105 (1983): 641-54, and in *Synode Extraordinaire*, 602.

which is based on an episcopal structure and not on a kind of federation of national churches. The national level is not an ecclesial dimension."[23] Once again, just before the 1985 synod, the *Civiltà Cattolica* editorialist resumed the theme, quoting Wright, de Lubac, Hamer, and Ratzinger.[24] Likewise the 1988 *instrumentum laboris* fears "the emergence of ecclesiastical instances which would claim an undue autonomy from the Apostolic See and would thus end up by setting themselves against it and its doctrinal and disciplinary directives."[25]

The two fears of infringing on episcopal and papal rights came together in the question of the teaching authority of episcopal conferences. Already implicit in the discussion of the responses to *Humanae Vitae*, it was urged particularly strongly as the U.S. bishops were working on their peace pastoral. Criticisms were raised both about the process used in preparing that document and about certain positions proposed for adoption in the early drafts, some of which appeared to differ both from papal statements and from the positions of other episcopal conferences, particularly in Europe.[26] Cardinal Ratzinger strongly voiced his view: "No episcopal conference, as such, has a teaching mission; its documents have no weight of their own save that of the consent given to them by the individual bishops."[27] The question was raised at the 1985 synod which called for further study of it. While this was underway, *Civiltà Cattolica* published an article denying a magisterial role to the conferences.[28] A doctoral dissertation defended at the beginning of 1987 at the Gregorian University reached the same conclusion, but sparked a vigorous debate

---

23. Ratzinger, *The Ratzinger Report*, 60.

24. "Conferenze episcopali e corresponsabilità dei vescovi," 425-27.

25. "Draft Statement on Episcopal Conferences," 735A.

26. See Archbishop Jan Schotte's report on the Vatican consultation in January 1983 as the U.S. bishops were preparing their pastoral letter on nuclear arms, "A Vatican Synthesis," *Origins* 12 (April 7, 1983): 692, where Cardinal Ratzinger is reported as having said, "A bishops' conference as such does not have a *mandatum docendi*. This belongs only to the individual bishop or to the college of bishops with the pope."

27. Ratzinger, *The Ratzinger Report*, 60. See, two years earlier, his comment: "bishops' conferences do not have any teaching authority and cannot as conferences make teaching binding," in Joseph Ratzinger, *Church, Ecumenism and Politics: New Essays in Ecclesiology* (New York: Crossroad, 1988), 58.

28. Giandomenico Mucci, "Le conferenze episcopali e l'autorità del magistero," *Civiltà Cattolica* 138/1 (1987): 327-37.

between two of the university's professors.[29] While this debate was in course, the *instrumentum laboris* also concluded that the conferences do not, as such, have any magisterial authority.[30] Even those who have supported the magisterial role of the conferences have raised questions about the number of documents being issued by conferences and their offices, about the confusion which often arises between types of statements, and about a tendency of some conferences to intrude into social and political matters with what they consider the comparative neglect of the bishops' proper religious responsibilities.[31]

In the critical literature here summarized it is obvious that there are both empirical and theological questions at stake. Empirically, the authors cited do not offer any evidence about how widely their fears have been realized nor any specific examples. The comments on episcopal conferences made by bishops themselves at the synods of 1969 and 1985 were sometimes critical, but the latter synod particularly gives a much more positive picture than that of the critics.[32]

Theologically, the most recent literature on the conferences does not reveal great progress beyond the stage of the debate at the council and in the synod of 1969. The basic issues still are the meaning of episcopal collegiality and whether the conferences can be considered an exercise of collegiality or not. The arguments for and against remain largely the same ones defended at those two meetings. What has changed is that some of the most prominent defenders of the collegial character of the conferences during the conciliar debate have now changed sides. The most prominent of these, Jerome Hamer and Joseph Ratzinger, now occupy important posts in the Roman curia. It may

---

29. The dissertation was by James P. Green, *Conferences of Bishops and the Exercise of the "munus docendi" of the Church* (Rome: Gregorian University, 1987). Disagreements among his readers led them to engage in a public debate on the issue which has since been published: Gianfranco Ghirlanda, "De Episcoporum Conferentia deque exercitio potestatis magisterii," *Periodica* 87 (1987): 573-604; and Francisco J. Urrutia, "De exercitio muneris docendi a Conferentiis Episcoporum," ibid., 605-36.

30. "Draft Statement," 735B-C.

31. See, for example, Avery Dulles, "Bishops' Conference Documents: What Doctrinal Authority?" *Origins* 14 (January 24, 1985): 528-34; "What is the Role of the Bishops' Conference," *Origins* 17 (April 28, 1988): 789-96; "The Teaching Authority of Bishops' Conferences," in *The Reshaping of Catholicism: Current Challenges in the Theology of Church* (San Francisco: Harper & Row, 1988), 207-26.

32. See the pre-synodal reports and the interventions found in *Synode extraordinaire*.

be of some interest, then, to trace the course of their shift in position on these issues.

In the midst of the debate at Vatican II, Hamer published a brief article whose conclusion was much quoted:

> There are not two collegialities: the one exercised at the universal level and the other manifested on the scale of some region. There is only one collegiality, but which knows infinitely varied modalities. . . . In short, the episcopal conferences, demanded by the development of the world, do not constitute simply a practical arrangement, but are truly a possible expression and an appropriate manifestation of the solidarity of the episcopal body, which is a reality of divine right in the church of Christ.[33]

Ratzinger was actively involved in the conciliar debates on collegiality. In a 1964 lecture in Rome, after providing an acute criticism of the differing ideas of collegiality which were vying at the council, he declared his preference for the patristic over the modern notion, argued that episcopal conferences are related to the ancient church's synodal structure, saw them "as an expression of the collegial structural element" in the church's constitution, and even imagined that they might in the future give rise to new "patriarchal areas."[34] Later in the same year, Ratzinger put the issues quite clearly:

> The opinion is often encountered that the bishops' conferences lack all theological basis, that therefore they cannot act in a way that would oblige the individual bishop, and that the notion of collegiality can only be applied to the common action of the entire episcopate. Here again we have a case where a one-sided and unhistorical effort at systematizing breaks down.

---

33. Jerome Hamer, "Les conférences épiscopales, exercice de la collégialité," *Nouvelle Revue Théologique* 85 (1963): 966-69 (my translation).

34. Joseph Ratzinger, "Konkrete Formen bischöfliche Kollegialität," in Johann Christoph Hampe, *Ende der Gegenreformation?* (Stuttgart: Kreuz-Verlag, 1964), 155-63 (my translation). See also, from the same year, "Primat und Episkopat," in *Das neue Volk Gottes: Entwürfe zur Ekklesiologie* (Düsseldorf: Patmos, 1969), 121-46, esp. 142-43, where he offered these ideas as a way of overcoming the church's image of a centralized state and as missionary and ecumenical imperatives.

Obviously, the *"suprema potestas in universam Ecclesiam,"* which canon 228, 1 of the code ascribes to the ecumenical council, applies only to the college of bishops as a whole in union with the bishop of Rome. But in the church is it always a question of the *suprema potestas*? That would remind us, in a fatal way, of the disciples' dispute about their own rank. We should rather say that the concept of collegiality, alongside the office of unity which belongs to the pope, also signifies a many-sided and changeable element which is a fundamental part of the church's structure, but can be realized in many different ways. The collegiality of bishops expresses the fact that there must be an ordered plurality in the church (under and in the unity guaranteed by the primacy). Bishops' conferences are therefore one of the many forms of expression of collegiality, which finds partial realization in them, while on the other hand having a reference to the whole.[35]

By 1976, however, Hamer's view had changed.[36] "The episcopal college," he now argued, "is situated along the line of the local collaboration of several particular churches; it is not a reduced form of the episcopal college." Its actions are "collective" rather than "collegial" and have authority only in virtue of the authority of the universal church. Truly collegial actions can only be posed by the whole college. But ordination does communicate to the bishop "an orientation of collegial spirit, an openness of spirit and a readiness for collegiàl realizations, activity in solidarity, a concern for the universal church, which the council called 'collegial sentiment.'" "All the forms of collaboration

---

35. Joseph Ratzinger, "The Pastoral Implications of Episcopal Collegiality," in *The Church and Mankind*, vol. 1 of *Concilium* (Glen Rock: Paulist Press, 1964), 63-65 (translation slightly revised in light of original in *Das neue Volk Gottes*, 222-23). At the end of the third session of the council, he wrote, "The collegiality of the bishops, as a medium for achieving unity and plurality and as an expression of the upbuilding of the one Church of God from the many local Churches, supplies the normal pattern of orderly life in the Church. This collegiality can take many forms. The early Church established the various synods and instituted the patriarchate; today the same reality takes a new form in bishops' conferences." See Joseph Ratzinger, *Theological Highlights of Vatican II* (New York: Paulist Press, 1966), 129-30.

36. I have not been able to make use of Jerome Hamer, "Esercizio del potere, unità nella libertà e servizio alle comunità locali: Il significato delle conferenze episcopali," in *Crisi del potere nella Chiesa e risveglio comunitario* (Milan, 1969), 190ff, cited in Feliciani, *Le conferenze episcopali*, 471 n. 36.

among bishops depend on this collegial sentiment. On this grounds it can and must be said that the episcopal conference, without having the power to pose collegial acts, is nonetheless a real manifestation of the collegial sentiment," that is, of the personal attitude of each bishop, which grounds "a secondary and derivative sense" of collegiality.[37]

Ratzinger's shift in position became widely known in his famous interview: "We must not forget that the episcopal conferences have no theological basis, they do not belong to the indispensable structure of the Church as willed by Christ; they have only a practical, concrete function." Now it is the individual bishop's role which needs to be strengthened: "It must once again become clear that in each diocese there is only one shepherd and teacher of the faith in communion with the other pastors and teachers and with the Vicar of Christ. The Catholic Church is based on the balance between the *community* and the *person*, in this case between the community of individual particular churches united in the universal Church and the *person* of the responsible head of the diocese."[38]

Along with this shift in concern, Ratzinger's later writings reveal an important shift with regard to the relationship between the universal church and the particular churches. No longer mentioned are his earlier proposals for establishing new and autonomous patriarchal areas, related to the episcopal conferences, replacing the vision of a church marked by a uniform canon law, liturgy, and system for appointment of bishops with one that sees the one church existing in the many churches, each of these with its own form. Instead we find regular warnings against assigning such a priority to the local church communities that the universality of the church is considered a secondary dimension, the result of a confederation of the local churches. A christologically centered and eucharistically based ecclesiology--this remains a constant in Ratzinger's thinking--will not permit this view: The one Christ is present and active in all the eucharistic assemblies which thus are from the beginning and at their heart the one and universal Body of Christ. A rather different

---

37. Hamer, "Chiesa locale e comunione ecclesiale," 41-43 (my translation). The identical arguments are repeated in "La responsabilité collégiale de chaque évêque," 641-54, and in *Synode Extraordinaire*, 600-602, where, however, he does not repeat his remarks about this "secondary and derivative sense" of collegiality.

38. Ratzinger, *The Ratzinger Report*, 59, 60.

view of the ecclesiology of the ancient church is now offered by Cardinal Ratzinger:

> This romantic idea of the particular Church, which is supposed to be a recovery of the structure of the ancient Church, contradicts both the historical reality of the ancient Church and the concrete experiences of history, which certainly ought not to be blindly overlooked in such considerations. The ancient Church certainly did not know an exercise of the Roman primacy in the sense of Roman Catholic theology of the second millennium; but it was well acquainted with living forms of universal Church unity which not only had the character of manifestations but were constitutive of the being-Church of the individual Churches. In this sense there always was a priority of the universal Church to the particular Church.

In discussing the ancient church, he does not make a single reference to particular councils, and regional groupings of churches are only mentioned in order to stress how, without the papal primacy, they inevitably give in to "the negative 'law' of particularizing tendencies."[39] Now, collegiality basically means

---

39. Ratzinger, *Church, Ecumenism and Politics*, 74-77. For the historical priority of the universal church, see also his speech to the college of cardinals in 1985:

> If on the one hand it must be said that the church is not a papal monarchy, on the other hand neither can it be considered a confederation of particular churches whose unity results only as something secondary from the addition of individual churches, so that the ministry of unity would consist only in moderating the agreement of the churches. As in a body the unity of the organism precedes and sustains the individual organs, because the organs would not exist if the body did not, so also the unity of the catholic church precedes the plurality of particular churches which are born from this unity and receive their ecclesial character from it. This temporal order is stated in many ways in the New Testament writings. It is enough to cite some examples. According to St. Luke's narrative in the Acts of the Apostles, the church began on the day of Pentecost in the community of Christ's disciples speaking in all languages. Here St. Luke, indeed the Holy Spirit, is intimating that the catholic, universal church, our mother, existed before the individual churches were born, which arise from this one mother and always are referred to her.

Joseph Ratzinger, "De Romano Pontifice deque Collegio Episcoporum" (Rome: 1985, photocopy), 3 (my translation).

"transcending the local horizon in what is common to catholic unity," so that "particularizations basically contradict the idea of collegiality."[40] Collegiality is concretely exercised by each bishop especially by his ruling well his particular church and by his reference to the whole church; it is no longer said to have partial, regional manifestations or expressions.

In 1985, as the International Theological Commission was completing its booklet on the church, Ratzinger secured the introduction of a paragraph on episcopal conferences which acknowledged their pastoral usefulness but denied that they could be called collegial:

> Episcopal collegiality, which succeeds to the collegiality of the Apostles, is *universal*. In relation to the *whole* of the church, it belongs to the *totality* of the episcopal body in hierarchical communion with the Roman pontiff. These conditions are fully verified in an ecumenical council and can be verified in a united action of the bishops throughout the world according to what is set down in *Christus Dominus* 4 (see *Lumen Gentium* 22). To some degree they can also be verified in the synod of bishops, because "representing the whole catholic episcopate, it at the same time indicates that all bishops participate in hierarchical communion in the concern for the whole church" (*CD* 5; see *LG* 23). On the other hand, institutions such as episcopal conferences (and their continental groups) belong to the organization and to the concrete or historical form of the church (*iure ecclesiastico*). If words such as "college," "collegiality," "collegial" are applied to them, they are being used in an analogous and theologically improper sense.[41]

This conclusion has since been cited and adopted by the *instrumentum laboris*.[42]

---

40. Ratzinger, *Church, Ecumenism and Politics*, 13-14.

41. Commissio Theologica Internationalis, *Themata Selecta de Ecclesiologia* (Vatican City: Libreria Editrice Vaticana, 1985), 34 (my translation). For the controversial history of this paragraph, see Giuseppe Ruggieri, "Le conferenze episcopali viste da Roma: Collegialità affettiva ma non effettiva," *Il regno-Attualità* 33 (1988): 297 n. 2.

42. "Draft Statement on Episcopal Conferences," *Origins* 17: 733B. The Roman text is not entirely consistent, however, stating elsewhere that episcopal conferences are "true, but partial" expressions of collegiality.

I know of no place where either Hamer or Ratzinger has attempted to explain the paths of or reasons for their considerable shift in the evaluation of episcopal conferences. Neither has explicitly repudiated the earlier writings, but it is difficult to agree with Manzanares, who for this reason thinks that the later writings must be reconciled with the earlier ones.[43] They do not appear to be reconcilable.

One may at least note that there is a certain literary genealogy, most obvious in the case of Hamer, who regularly refers to the chapter which in 1971 Henri de Lubac devoted to episcopal conferences.[44] After noting that the conferences play a role today analogous to that played by various forms of particular synods in the ancient church and can rightly be considered "one of the possible variants of collegiality" (quoting Ratzinger and Hamer), de Lubac argued: "Nevertheless, strictly speaking, that is, in its full meaning, based on Scripture, episcopal collegiality, which succeeds to that of the Twelve, is essentially universal,--and, on the other hand, a collective act is not in itself a collegial act." Thus the council did not say that in their conference bishops carry out their responsibility 'collegially,' but that they carry it out 'conjointly.'" Their immediate purpose is practical and local and therefore cannot be considered collegial.

> The point of view adopted by the Council, as we can see, is essentially pragmatic. Some bishops would have preferred a more precise bond indicated in the texts between this institution of episcopal conferences and the faith-principle of collegiality or the unity of the episcopate. The Council disregarded this. It did so because, in reality, even if bonds of what could be called appropriateness do indeed exist between this institution and this principle, the *doctrinal* bond, properly speaking, does not exist--or at least it is only indirect, insofar as the members of these conferences can together extend their concern beyond the area in which they exercise their usual activity. A principle of divine right is one thing,

---

43. Manzanares, "The Teaching Authority of Episcopal Conferences," 257 n. 109. Here I agree with Charles Murphy, "Collegiality: An Essay Toward Better Understanding," *Theological Studies* 46 (1985): 38-49.

44. Henri de Lubac, *The Motherhood of the Church*, 257-73. I have occasionally improved the translation by reference to the French original.

an institution of ecclesiastical right, suggested by the circumstances of time and place, is quite another. . . . *Lumen gentium* is as clear as possible in this regard. It recognizes no intermediary of a doctrinal order between the particular Church and the universal Church.[45]

De Lubac has here adopted the position of the *Nota praevia* defining strictly collegial actions as exercises of the whole college alone. He verges on the opinion that the use of *coniunctim* in *Christus Dominus* 38:1 was meant to exclude collegiality as a basis for the conferences.[46] He works with a very strict division between what is of divine right in the church and what is of ecclesiastical right. His article thus had the effect of considerably limiting the theological significance of the conferences.

Back behind de Lubac's chapter, moreover, there is another significant publication which appeared shortly after the council and has been constantly cited since.[47] Willy Onclin distinguished there a "direct and formal" collegiality which is only exercised by the whole college of bishops for the sake of the whole church. Indirectly, however, "collegiality is expressed in certain actions which do not emanate from the college as such, but from individual bishops or groups of bishops in the service of various particular Churches." After discussing several instances of this, Onclin considered the sort of "joint activity" of bishops which once was organized in local councils but now will be strengthened by episcopal conferences. These represent a collective exercise of the authority which each bishop has in his own diocese. The article ended with a paragraph which has been widely quoted ever since:

> . . . when bishops meet in local councils or episcopal conferences, they are not the representatives of the college of bishops. They are not exercising there the authority which they all, united in the college, possess with regard to the universal Church, but the authority with which they

---

45. Ibid., 264-65.

46. Hamer explicitly draws this conclusion in "Chiesa locale e comunione ecclesiale," 42, and repeats it in later articles. The chief historians of the conciliar debates argue, however, that this vague adverb was chosen precisely in order to leave *open* the question of the collegial character of the conferences.

47. Willy Onclin, "Collegiality and the Individual Bishop," in *Pastoral Reform in the Church*, vol. 8 of *Concilium* (New York: Paulist Press, 1965), 81-91.

are invested as heads of their particular Churches. Thus, the decrees of
particular councils and the decisions of episcopal conferences are not,
either directly or indirectly, acts emanating from the college of bishops,
but measures taken by bishops collectively exercising the powers they
have in their own particular Churches.

But de Lubac and many people after him fail to quote the very next paragraph
of Onclin's article:

> Yet the bishops' duty to make collective use of their individual episcopal
> authority in order to ensure the common good of a group of particular
> Churches implies that they are responsible for particular Churches other
> than their own and for the government of these Churches. Local councils
> and episcopal conferences may therefore be considered the juridical
> expression of the bishops' responsibilities as members of the college of
> bishops and of their concern for all the Churches. As such they are a
> manifestation of episcopal collegiality.[48]

Comparing the two articles, one senses that de Lubac has constricted
Onclin's position. Onclin certainly distinguishes between "direct and formal"
and "indirect" exercises of collegiality, but so far from considering the latter
to be merely "collective" as opposed to "collegial" actions, his chief concern
is to vindicate them as manifestations of collegiality. Onclin does *not*
counterpose "joint" and "collegial" acts, but is still working with the broad and
variegated notion of collegiality which can be found in the conciliar texts.

It is, however, de Lubac's use of Onclin's article which has been widely
accepted and repeated in the recent literature on episcopal conferences.
Hamer regularly cites both authors. De Lubac's article underlies, even verbally
at times, the argument of the International Theological Commission. Both
authors are important sources for the series of articles which *Civiltà Cattolica*

---

48. Onclin, "Collegiality and the Individual Bishop," 90-91.

devoted to the conferences,[49] and these, finally, supplied crucial elements and often the very words for the argument of the recent *instrumentum laboris*.[50]

The result is a document whose chief positive description of the nature and sphere of competence of episcopal conferences is the sentence that they "are organs useful for examining, debating, and coordinating vast ecclesial problems at the national or supra-regional level."[51] For the rest, the *instrumentum laboris* is mainly concerned with warning against the dangers that the episcopal conferences will infringe the authority and freedom of either bishops or the pope and with setting out the things which the conferences are *not*. Thus they "were not instituted for the pastoral governance of a nation nor to substitute for the diocesan bishops as a sort of superior and parallel government, but to help them in the fulfillment of some common tasks"; they do not represent the episcopal college,[52] and so their decisions "are never *acts of the college*."[53] "It is thus not exact to speak of a collegial exercise of episcopal power in the case of the episcopal conference."[54] They "do not, as such, enjoy the *munus magisterii*," do not "constitute a doctrinal instance; they have no competence to establish doctrinal and moral contents," and they "cannot substitute for the individual bishop."[55]

The document produced in response to the 1985 synod's call for a fuller and deeper study of episcopal conferences, then, is little more than a concentrated expression of the chief warnings and criticisms which have

---

49. See the three unsigned editorials, "La dottrina dell'episcopato prima e dopo la 'Lumen Gentium,'" *Civiltà Cattolica* 136/1 (1985): 313-24; "Conferenze episcopali e corresponsabilità dei vescovi," 136/2 (1985): 417-29; "Il Sinodo dei Vescovi come sviluppo della collegialità episcopale," 136/4 (1985): 105-17; and three articles by Giandomenico Mucci, "Il principio di sussidiarietà e la teologia del collegio episcopale," 137/2 (1986): 428-42; "Le conferenze episcopali e l'autorità del magistero," 138/1 (1987): 327-37; "Concili particolari e conferenze episcopali," 138/2 (1987): 340-48. Internal evidence suggests that Mucci was also the author of the editorials.

50. The dependence of the *instrumentum laboris*, particularly in sections II, IV, and V, on the *Civiltà Cattolica* articles is so great that the latter can be recommended as the best commentary on the Roman text.

51. "Draft Statement," 735A.

52. Ibid., 734C.

53. Ibid., 735B.

54. Ibid., 734C.

55. Ibid., 735C.

surrounded this institution since the council debated it and decided to give it juridical form and authority. If there may be some benefit in having in one place a compendium of criticisms, one may be forgiven for thinking that the synod of 1985 had something else in mind when it made its suggestion.

The Current Debate

The discussions of the nature and role of episcopal conferences especially over the last five years address a mixture of practical and theological issues. As often happens in ecclesiastical discussions, there is a tendency for the two kinds of issues to be confused. This almost always has unfortunate effects. When the practical questions are invested with ultimate significance, with wild charges that it is the very nature of the church which is at stake, it becomes very difficult to address them in and for themselves. In turn ecclesiology runs the danger of being degraded into an ideology, a defense of personal or group biases. Neither side in the debate about episcopal conferences is exempt from either danger.

These are not circumstances in which it is appropriate to attempt an authoritative resolution of the question of the nature and role of the conferences. What would be more helpful is a serious effort to sort out the issues, to investigate what precisely are the practical problems as encountered by individual bishops or by Roman authorities, to address them practically, as, for example, by reforms in the statutes, to identify the basic ecclesiological issues, to clarify them historically and theologically, and to work towards a genuine ecclesial consensus. This is a considerable agenda, which it will take time to meet. The authors and editor of this volume hope that it will make its own contribution to that effort.

Part I:

Historical

Studies

Brian E. Daley, S.J.

Structures of Charity: Bishops' Gatherings and the See of Rome in the Early Church

BRIAN DALEY is associate professor
of historical theology at the Weston School
of Theology, Cambridge, Massachusetts

In institutions with a long tradition, history can be a powerful means to inspire and legitimate change. Thus when the Second Vatican Council, in its Decree on the Pastoral Office of Bishops in the Church (*Christus Dominus*), formally encouraged bishops to work together in national and regional bishops' conferences, it began by recalling similar gatherings at the origins of Christian history. "From the earliest ages of the Church," the council declares, "bishops in charge of particular churches, inspired by a spirit of fraternal charity and by zeal for the universal mission entrusted to the apostles, have pooled their resources and their aspirations in order to promote both the common good and the good of individual churches. With this end in view synods, provincial councils and, finally, plenary councils were established in which the bishops determined on a common program to be followed in various churches both for teaching the truths of the faith and for regulating ecclesiastical discipline."[1]

In a way characteristic of many decrees of Vatican II, the document immediately applies this historical observation to its own pastoral concerns: "This sacred Ecumenical Synod expresses its earnest hope that these admirable institutions--synods and councils--may flourish with renewed vigor so that the growth of religion and the maintenance of discipline in the various churches may increasingly be more effectively provided for in accordance with the needs of the times."[2] *Christus Dominus* then proceeds--without further juridical

---

1. Austin P. Flannery, ed., *Documents of Vatican II* (Grand Rapids: Eerdmans, 1975), 586.
2. Ibid.

distinction between the various types of bishops' gatherings--to lay down the guidelines for the contemporary Roman Catholic institution of episcopal conferences.[3]

Because of the importance of this early Christian parallel as a model for the increased collaboration between bishops, it is important to include some reflections on the patristic theory and practice of regional bishops' gatherings in any study of the draft statement on episcopal conferences, or *instrumentum laboris*, recently circulated by the Vatican Congregation for Bishops.[4] And since a key concern of that document is to define more closely the relationship of the teaching and pastoral role of episcopal conferences to that of the Holy See,[5] I will consider the relations between these local gatherings in the church's early centuries and the bishops of Rome, as well as the various expectations popes and assembled bishops had of each other. The subject is enormously complex, and the amount of relevant patristic evidence and modern scholarly discussion dauntingly vast.[6] All I can do here is summarize the main fruits of research on popes and bishops in the early church, insofar as it concerns the issues at hand, and to point out the contribution that a sense of our origins might make--in the spirit of *Christus Dominus* 36--to the new dialogue on episcopal conferences to which the *instrumentum laboris* invites us.

---

3. Ibid. 37-38. *Codex Iuris Canonici* (1983), cans. 439-59, draws a clear distinction, not found in the conciliar text, between "plenary councils" of all the particular churches in the region of a bishops' conference, summoned for stated purposes with the approval of the Holy See, and the permanent institution of episcopal conferences.

4. For the text, see *Origins* 17 (April 7, 1988): 731-37.

5. For the document's concluding call for "clarifications" of the legislative power and pastoral authority of episcopal conferences with reference to the authority and magisterial function of the pope and the universal college of bishops, see *Origins* 17: 736f.

6. See especially H.-J. Sieben, "Das Nationalkonzil im frühen Selbstverständnis, in theologischer Tradition und in römischer Perspektive," *Theologie und Philosophie* 62 (1987): 526-62; "Concilium Perfectum. Zur Idee der Sogenannten Partikularsynode in der Alten Kirche," *Theologie und Philosophie* 63 (1988): 203-29; and "Episcopal Conferences in Light of Particular Councils during the First Millenium," in H. Legrand, J. Manzanares, and A. García y García, eds., *The Nature and Future of Episcopal Conferences* (Washington, DC: Catholic University of America Press, 1988), 30-56.

Synods in the Early Church

The classical "model" of the church found in early Christian documents, from the time of Ignatius of Antioch (around the year 115) until at least the mid-fourth century, is that of the local community gathered around the Eucharistic table and presided over by a single bishop.[7] So Vatican II cites Cyprian of Carthage as its authority for recognizing the ecclesiological priority of the "particular church," and for describing the role of the local bishop as sign and guarantee of the church's unity at its most fundamental level.[8] But while a sense of the obligation of bishops to communicate with each other and to support each other in their leadership is clear even in the earliest patristic works,[9] there is no documentary evidence for formal gatherings of bishops until the last forty years of the second century.

Those decades, which first witnessed a sense of need among orthodox leaders to specify the authentic sources of faith in a Christian biblical canon, were also apparently the time of the first Christian synods. They were summoned first, in the 160s, to deal with the threat to church order posed by the Pentecostal Montanist sect,[10] and later, around 197, to resolve the bitter dispute among the churches over the dating of the Paschal festival.[11] These

---

7. For the earliest clear expressions of this "Eucharistic"--and episcopal--ecclesiology, see Ignatius, Letters to the Ephesians, 5f.; Trallians, 2f.; Philadelphians, 2; Smyrnaeans, 8f.; Polycarp, 1.

8. See *Lumen Gentium* 23: "The individual bishops are the visible source and foundation of unity in their own particular Churches, which are constituted after the model of the universal Church; it is in these and formed out of them that the one and unique Catholic Church exists." (Flannery, *Documents*, 376). The council cites, as authority for this statement, Cyprian, Epistula 66.8 and 55.24 (*Corpus Scriptorum Ecclesiasticorum Latinorum* [CSEL] [Vienna, 1855 seqq.], 3.2: 733, 642).

9. See, in addition to the passages in Ignatius' letters already cited, I Clement 1 and 44 (written in Rome, probably about the year 96); here, however, the episcopal function in the community seems to have been exercised by a board of elders rather than by a single leader.

10. Some kind of gathering of anti-Montanist bishops from Thrace, Asia Minor, and Syria seems to be suggested by Eusebius, *Historia Ecclesiastica* 5.19; cf. 5.16. On the synods held during the controversy over the celebration of Easter, see J. A. Fischer, "Die Synoden im Osterfeststreit des 2. Jahrhunderts," *Annuarium Historiae Conciliorum* 8 (1976): 15-39.

11. See Eusebius, *Historia Ecclesiastica* 5.23-25, which lists gatherings of bishops in the provinces of Asia (the west coast of Asia Minor), Palestine, Rome, Pontus (northeastern Asia Minor), southern Gaul, Osrhoene (eastern Syria), and Achaea (southern Greece).

were questions of Christian self-definition, questions of what traditions of faith and worship were normative in the communities that claimed apostolic origin; for that reason, apparently, they were also questions on which most bishops did not feel qualified to act alone.

In the centuries that followed, synodal gatherings of bishops to deal with issues of common pastoral concern were a regular and indispensable feature of church life, the ordinary institutional expression of the cohesion of local Eucharistic communities in a universal body. The first ten volumes of Giovanni Domenico Mansi's monumental collection of Christian conciliar documents gives evidence for over four hundred synods and meetings of bishops, Eastern and Western, known to have been held between the mid-second century and the pontificate of Gregory the Great.[12] Presumably there were many more, whose traces have vanished. Most were small local or provincial gatherings, others included all the bishops of a larger political region or "diocese," and a few were attempts to gather representatives from the whole Christian world, under imperial sponsorship, to deal with questions of "ecumenical" or universal import for the faith.

The regularity with which Christian bishops met for business seems to have varied according to need, political circumstances, and the ability of church leaders to overcome collective inertia. At least five synods are attested for Rome and eight for the province of Africa between 250 and 260, for instance: a time of strong leadership by Cyprian of Carthage and his Roman counterparts, and a time when the growing Christian communities, although still persecuted by a hostile Roman state, openly faced crucial questions of faith and discipline. The evidence suggests that meetings were normally much less frequent during periods of repression or social unrest. But with the public support--legal, financial, and moral--that followed the "peace of Constantine," regular gatherings of Christian bishops soon came to be recognized as an important means of preserving ecclesial and political unity. Meetings were so frequent that the pagan historian Ammianus Marcellinus wryly observed that

---

12. J. D. Mansi, ed., *Sacrorum conciliorum nova et amplissima collectio*, 31 vols. (Florence-Venice, 1757-98; impr. and cont. Paris, 1899-1927), 1-10. Mansi includes material of varying value, and both his texts and his chronology are often in need of correction; still, the collection provides the most complete conspectus of synodal evidence available. For a useful summary of the extant legislation of synods in the patristic period, see J. Gaudemet, *Les sources du droit de l'Église en Occident du IIe au VIIe siècle* (Paris: Cerf, 1985), 37-56, 103-21.

the public transportation system, during the reign of Constantius II (337-61), was paralyzed by Christian bishops traveling to and from their synods at the imperial expense![13]

The fifth canon of the Council of Nicaea ordained that the bishops of each civil province should gather in synod twice a year--once before the beginning of Lent and once in the autumn--mainly to insure common treatment of those excommunicated by their local bishops.[14] This legislation was repeated by later gatherings[15] and urged, within their own spheres of influence, by a number of the more determined fifth- and sixth-century popes[16]-- a fact which suggests that bishops needed constant prompting to remain in such frequent and demanding contact.

In 393, Bishop Aurelian of Carthage, the outstanding leader of the African church in Augustine's day, presided over a "plenary council of all Africa" at Hippo Regius, which reaffirmed the Nicene requirement and started an important series of regular meetings that was to last until the Vandals invaded North Africa in the mid-420s.[17] Some of these were devoted to routine

---

13. Charles U. Clark, ed., *Ammiani Marcellini Rerum Gestarum Liber*, vol. 1 (Berlin: Weidmann, 1910), 250.

14. G. Alberigo, ed., *Conciliorum oecumenicorum decreta (COD)*, 3rd ed. (Bologna: Istituto per le Scienze Religiose, 1972) 8.15-33.

15. See can. 20 of the collection usually attributed to the "Dedication" Synod of Antioch (341): Mansi, 2.1316f.; Eduard Schwartz, however, suggested a date as early as 328 for these canons: "Zur Geschichte des Athanasius, VIII: Von Nicaea bis zu Konstantins Tod," *Gesammelte Schriften*, vol. 3 (Berlin: De Gruyter, 1959), 216-30. See also can. 19 of the Council of Chalcedon (451): *Conciliorum oecumenicorum decreta* 96.1-20; can. 37 of the "Apostolic canons" (from Syria, c. 380; *Apostolic Constitutions* 8.47.37): F. X. Funk, ed., *Didascalia et Constitutiones Apostolorum*, vol. 1 (Paderborn: Schöningh, 1905), 572.

16. See, for example, Leo the Great, Ep. 14.8 (J.- P. Migne, ed., *Patrologia Latina* [*PL*], 217 vols. and 4 index vols. [Paris, 1878-90], 54.673f.: insisting on semi-annual synods for the provinces of Illyricum); Ep. 16.7 (*PL* 54.702f.: requiring one synod a year for all the bishops of Italy and Sicily); Gregory the Great, Ep. 1.1 (*Corpus Christianorum, Series Latina* [*CCL*] [Turnhout-Paris, 1953, seqq.] 140 1.10-13: bishops of Sicily should meet once a year); Ep. 4.9 (*CCL* 226.37-42: bishops of Sardinia should meet twice a year, according to the canons); cf. Appendix I (*CCL* 140A.1094.52-56: abolishing custom of an annual synod at Rome for all bishops of Italy and Sicily).

17. See *Breviarium Hipponense*, can. 5, *CCL* 149 34.20-27. Munier presents evidence for thirteen such "general" or plenary African councils between 393 and 427; twelve other local synods for the province of Proconsular Africa are known to have been held in Carthage alone during this same period, as well as seven in other cities. See ibid., xx-xxxvi.

business: jurisdictional disputes and appeals from disciplined clerics. Others dealt with the burning theological and ecclesiological issues of the day, Donatism and Pelagianism. Beginning with the synod of Orléans in 511, the bishops of Frankish Gaul also held, at diminishing intervals, a series of synods in various cities that came to play an important role as legislative gatherings in the Christianization of the Frankish kingdoms.[18] Similarly, the bishops of Visigothic Spain began, with the Synod of Tarragona in 516, a series of meetings that were to become more frequent and more important with the conversion of King Reccared from Arianism to orthodox faith in 589.[19] From the end of the fourth century, then, bishops' gatherings at what we might call--with some risk of anachronism--the national level were a recognized, if not an absolutely regular, part of the structure of the Western church.

The agenda at these early Christian bishops' meetings included the whole range of what are today termed "faith and order" issues. Some, for instance, attempted to formulate common policy on the reconciliation of "lapsed" Christians or the recognition of heretical baptisms (as in the African and Roman synods of the 250s). Others dealt with the response of the local churches to heresy, recognized or suspected: to various forms of Arianism (as in most Eastern and Western synods between 325 and 381), to Origenism (as at provincial synods held in Alexandria and Jerusalem in 400),[20] to Pelagianism (as at the extraordinary synod of Aquileia in 442, as well as at the regular pan-African synods between 416 and 419), to Priscillianism (as at Saragossa in 380 and again, somewhere in Spain, in 447),[21] to "monophysite" or anti-Chalcedonian Christology (as at the somewhat expanded local synod of

---

18. *Concilia Galliae 511-695*, CCL 148A. Cf. O. Pontal, *Die Synoden im Merowingerreich* (Paderborn: Schöningh, 1986).

19. See. J. Vives, *Concilios Visigóticos e Hispano-romanos* (Barcelona/Madrid: CSIC, 1963). Cf. J. Orlandis, "Die Synode im katholischen Westgotenreich," in J. Orlandis and D. Ramos-Lisson, eds., *Die Synoden auf der Iberischen Halbinsel bis zum Einbruch des Islam (711)* (Paderborn: Schöningh, 1981), 95-396.

20. For the documents on Origenism produced by these synods, see Jerome, Epp. 92-93, *CSEL* 55: 147-56.

21. See Mansi, 3.633-36; 6.491. Cf. Leo the Great, Ep.15.17 (*PL* 54.690 C6 - 692 B3); on the genuineness of this letter and its theological importance, see J. Ruiz-Goyo, "Carta dogmatica de San Leon Magno a Santo Toribio, Obispo de Astorga," *Estudios Eclesiásticos* 15 (1936): 367-79.

Constantinople of 536),[22] even to the aberrant doctrines of minor figures like Bonosus of Nis (condemned, at synods held in Capua in 389 and Thessalonica in 390, for denying Mary's permanent virginity).[23]

Through provincial and regional synods, too, until the mid-fifth century, the complex process of the reception of major, imperial councils as "ecumenical" (i.e., representative of universal faith) was carried on. In the midst of the violent controversies that followed the Council of Chalcedon, for instance, Emperor Leo I, in 458, specifically asked provincial synods throughout the Eastern Empire to meet and consider whether or not they still wished to adhere to the Chalcedonian Christological formula.[24] Such gatherings had also been the pattern of local response to the Council of Nicaea (325).[25] And through negotiations between the provincial synods of the Antiochene and Alexandrian churches, the unfinished Christological business of Ephesus was finally resolved in 433.[26] More often, provincial synods dealt with a host of

---

22. E. Schwartz, ed., *Acta Conciliorum Oecumenicorum (ACO)* (Berlin, 1914 seqq.), 3.27-119.

23. Mansi, 3.683-6, 689f.

24. For an abbreviated collection of the responses of these synods, known as the *Codex Encyclius*, see *ACO* 2.5:9-98. See T. Schnitzler, *Im Kampfe um Chalcedon. Geschichte und Inhalt des Codex Encyclius von 458*, vol. 16 of *Analecta Gregoriana* (Rome, 1938); A. Grillmeier, "Auriga mundi. Zum Reichskirchenbild der Briefe des sog. Codex Encyclius (458)," in *Mit Ihm und in Ihm* (Freiburg: Herder, 1975), 386-419. For a discussion of the whole process of reception, see "Konzil und Rezeption. Methodische Bemerkungen zu einem Thema der ökumenischen Discussion der Gegenwart," ibid., 303-34.

25. See E. Schwartz, "Vom Nicaea bis zu Konstantins Tod," *Gesammelte Schriften*, vol. 3 (Berlin: De Gruyter, 1956-63), 188-264. In a letter written to Eusebius of Antioch and his provincial clergy in 340, Pope Julius I insists that the Council of Nicaea had in fact ordained "that the decisions of one synod should be examined in another": Athanasius, *Apologia contra Arianos* 22.1, in *Athanasius' Werke*, H. G. Opitz, ed. (Berlin/Leipzig: DeGruyter, 1938) 2.1:103.23-27. He is probably thinking of some sort of appeal process for disciplinary decisions; none of the extant canons of Nicaea, however, establish such a procedure.

26. Cyril of Alexandria, Letter to John of Antioch, Ep. 39 (*ACO* I 1.4.15.22-20.13; see 16.21-25). By the time of the "Three Chapters" controversy that followed the Second Council of Constantinople (553), local synods had apparently ceased to be the ordinary vehicle for reception. Pope Pelagius I, in a letter written in the spring of 559, even argues that it has never been canonically acceptable for local synods to pass judgment on universal ones: "Nec licuit aliquando nec licebit particularem synodum ad diiudicandum generalem synodum congregari. Sed quotiens aliqua de universali synodo aliquibus dubitatio nascitur, ad recipiendam de eo quod non intellegunt rationem, . . . ad apostolicas sedes pro percipienda ratione conveniunt." Ep. 59 in *Pelagii I Papae Epistulae*, P. M. Gassó and C. M. Battle, eds. (Montserrat, 1956) 158.35-40.

practical and disciplinary issues, like appeals by clerics against the decisions of local bishops,[27] boundary disputes,[28] and the recognition of the orders of priests converted from schismatic churches.[29] Occasionally, special regional gatherings of bishops were summoned to engage in dialogue with bishops of such schismatic churches, in the hope of restoring communion.[30]

A synod of African bishops meeting in Carthage in 390 described its purpose simply but comprehensively: it was summoned "for the faith and for the advantage of the church".[31] Other gatherings of bishops saw their common purpose to be the achievement of church unity, a unity which is the concrete and institutional realization of the charismatic gift of love. From the time of Cyprian, in fact, the *raison d'être* of local synods was assumed to be not simply the resolution of conflicts and the enactment of canonically binding decisions, but the achievement of a consensus on faith and pastoral practice that was itself the work of the Spirit, a consensus that bound the bishops of a region not only to each other but to the whole tradition that went before them.[32] Unity of this kind, expressed in the event and the work of a synod, was "the common link of charity, . . . the bond uniting our mother, the Catholic church."[33] In passages like these, as I shall emphasize again later, *caritas*

---

27. See, for example, can. 7 of the Council of Carthage of 390 (*CCL* 149.15); can. 8 of the Council of Hippo of 393 (*Breviarium Hipponense*, can. 8 [*CCL* 149.35f.]).

28. See, for example, can. 8 of the Cyrillian "council" at Ephesus (July 31, 431) (*ACO* 1: 1.3.28); can. 11 of the Council of Carthage of 390 (*CCL* 140.17f.).

29. See cans. 8-11 of the Council of Nicaea, on the procedure for recognizing the orders of schismatic or "lapsed" clergy who are reconciled with the Catholic church: *COD* 7ff.; can. 37 of the Council of Hippo of 393 (*CCL* 149.43f.) and can. 3 of the Council of Carthage, September 401 (*CCL* 149.200), determining a similar policy for Donatists. Both of the latter councils were plenary councils of the African church.

30. Such, for example, were the large *collatio* of Catholic and Donatist bishops held in Carthage in 411 and reported on by Augustine in his *Breviculus* (S. Lancel, ed., *Sources Chrétiennes* [*SC*] [Paris: Cerf, 1972-75], 194, 195, 224; also *CCL* 149A); the meeting of six orthodox and six monophysite bishops in Constantinople in 532 (*ACO* IV 2.169-84; cf. Sebastian Brock, "The Conversations with the Syrian Orthodox under Justinian [532]," *Orientalia Christiana Periodica* 47 [1981] 87-121); and the Spanish synod of Arian and Catholic bishops of 587, preparing for the reception of Reccared into Catholic communion (Mansi, 9.971f.).

31. *CCL* 149.12. Cf. Possidus, *Vita Augustini* 21 (*PL* 32.51).

32. See Sieben, "Episcopal Conferences," 31ff.

33. Letter written to Pope Sylvester by the synod of Western bishops, meeting at Arles in 314 (C. Munier, ed., *Concilia Galliae, 314-506* [*CCL* 148:4.8f.]).

clearly means more than warm feelings: it is the very stuff of a unity given by the Spirit and safeguarded by the charism of episcopal office; it is the foundation of church order, the heart of Christian communion.

Bishops and the Papacy

A central issue raised by early synodal practice, directly relevant to any consideration of the contemporary role of Roman Catholic episcopal conferences, regards the relationship between such gatherings of bishops and their wider concern for the universal church, especially as that universal horizon was represented by the bishops of Rome.

Collegiality and Communion

Catholic theology since *Lumen Gentium*--including the theology of the recent *instrumentum laboris*--has tended to discuss this complex of issues in terms of the *communion* of local communities that comprises the universal church, and of the "collegiality" or collective responsibility of bishops which realizes and expresses that communion. Both concepts find their model and source in the theology and practice of the early church and have been exhaustively discussed in the years since Vatican II.[34] I can only touch summarily on them here.

The classic patristic exponent of the collegial conception of episcopal office is undoubtedly St. Cyprian. Writing in a time of considerable tension and discord within the worldwide Christian community, due to persecution from without and varying pastoral responses to that persecution from within, Cyprian is a passionate defender of the importance of "normal" church govern-

---

34. A classic account of the early church's understanding of this communion is Ludwig Hertling, *Communio. Church and Papacy in Early Christianity*, trans. J. Wicks (Chicago: Loyola University Press, 1972). On early conceptions of episcopal collegiality, see J. Lécuyer, *Études sur la Collégialité épiscopale* (LePuy/Lyon: Mappus, 1964); L. Mortari, *Consecrazione episcopale e collegialità. La testimonianza della chiesa antica* (Florence 1969); Y. Congar, "La collégialité de l'épiscopat et la primauté de l'évêque de Rome dans l'histoire (brève esquisse),"*Angelicum* 47 (1970): 403-29; P. Zmire, "Collégialité épiscopale dans l'église d'Afrique," *Recherches Augustiniennes* 7 (1971): 3-72; K. Stockmeier, "Primat und Kollegialität im Lichte der alten Kirche," *Theologisch-praktische Quartalschrift* 121 (1973): 318-28.

ment for concord and continuity in the gospel tradition. For him, this government rests on the irreducible authority of the local bishop within his own church, and the practical unity of bishops in their concern for all the churches. "God is one," he writes to the people of Carthage in 251, "and Christ is one and the church is one, and there is one teaching authority (*cathedra*), founded on Peter by the voice of the Lord. No other altar can be built, no new priesthood come into being, besides the one altar and the one priesthood. Whoever gathers elsewhere, scatters."[35] Both Jesus' words to Peter in Matthew 16:18 and his commission to the Twelve in John 20:21ff. are, in Cyprian's view, a clear indication that bishops are, "by divine law,"[36] the foundation of church structure and the guarantee of its apostolic continuity. And Peter's response to Jesus in John 6:68, "Lord, to whom shall we go?" not only reveals to Cyprian that "the church does not abandon Christ," but that "the bishop is in the church and the church in the bishop, and if anyone is not with the bishop he or she is not in the church."[37]

So, for Cyprian, it is the unity of bishops which guarantees the worldwide unity of the church, since "the church which is universal and one is not split or divided, but is everywhere connected and joined together by the glue of bishops in union with each other."[38] "As there is one church founded by Christ, though divided into many members throughout the whole world," he writes to the Numidian bishop Antonianus late in 251, "so the episcopate is one, though spread out in the harmonious diversity of many bishops. . . ."[39] Such unity does not necessarily imply that each bishop follows exactly the same pastoral policies, he assures Antonianus: "while the bond of concord remains firm and the indivisible mystery of the catholic church endures, each individual bishop determines and pursues his own course of action, ready to give account for his policy to the Lord."[40] But the Lord's commission of one apostle, Peter, as "rock" of the church implies, for Cyprian, that teaching authority in the church

---

35. Ep. 43.5 (*CSEL* 3.2:594.5-8).

36. Ep. 33.1 (*CSEL* 3.2:566.2-13); cf. Ep. 73.7 (*CSEL* 3.2:783.12-23).

37. Letter to Florentius [254], Ep. 66.8 (733.2-6).

38. Ep. 66.8 (8-11). Cf. Letter to Pope Stephen [c. 254], Ep. 68.3 (746.3ff.).

39. Ep. 55.24 (*CSEL* 3.2:642.12-15).

40. Ep. 55.21 (639.4-7). On the responsibility of each bishop to God alone, see also Letter to Magnus [255], Ep. 69.17 (765. 23f.) and 72.3, to Stephen [256] (778.4f.).

is one.[41] Like the single sunlight, which shines in many rays, or a single supply of water flowing in many streams, "episcopal authority is one, of which each part is held by individuals as belonging to a single whole."[42] And the implication of this collective authority is that each bishop also bears a responsibility for what happens in the wider church, beyond the borders of his own diocese. So Cyprian writes to Pope Stephen about 254, urging him to intervene in the church of Arles and have the people there elect a new bishop to replace Marcianus, who has joined with the Novatianists; "for even though we shepherds are many, we tend one flock, and we must gather and nourish all the sheep whom Christ has sought out by his blood and his passion. . . ."[43]

Cyprian's appeal to Stephen to act in the case of the bishop of Arles points to the other much-discussed aspect of his conception of the communion of bishops: his view of the leadership or "primacy" of the bishop of Rome. Although the chief role of Peter in the New Testament, in Cyprian's view, is to symbolize the one ministry of leadership given to all the apostles and their successors,[44] the present bishop of the church of Peter--Rome--clearly exercises a ministry of unification that is in some way analogous to Peter's. The "chair of Peter," in the famous phrase of one of his letters to Cornelius of Rome, is the "first church, from which the unity of the episcopate arises."[45] To be in communion with the bishop of Rome is to "endorse firmly and to maintain both the unity and the charity of the catholic church."[46] Like Irenaeus at the end of the previous century,[47] Cyprian seems to see the "primacy" or "priority" of the Roman church, and therefore of its bishop, in its role as

---

41. See the much-discussed passage, *De ecclesiae catholicae unitate* 4f., in both its "first" and "second" editions: M. Bévenot, *Cyprian. De Lapsis and De Ecclesiae Catholicae Unitate* (Oxford: Clarendon Press, 1971), esp. xi-xv and 63f.

42. *De unitate* 5 (Bévenot 64): "Episcopatus unus est cuius a singulis in solidum pars tenetur."

43. Ep. 68.4 (*CSEL* 3.2:747.20ff.). Cf. Ep. 68.3 (*CSEL* 3.2:746.5ff).

44. So *De Unit.* 4 (Bévenot 60-64).

45. Ep. 59.14 (*CSEL* 3.2:683.10f.): schismatics have dared to send formal letters "ad Petri cathedram atque ad ecclesiam principalem unde unitas sacerdotalis exorta est. . . "

46. Letter to Cornelius, Ep. 48.3 (*CSEL* 3.2:607.16ff.). See also Letter to Antonianus [251] Ep. 55.1: in assuring Cornelius of his agreement in faith, Antonianus has let him know that he, Antonianus, is in communion with him, "that is, with the universal church."

47. See especially the frequently quoted passages *Adversus Haereses* 3.3.2 and 3.4.1 (*SC* 34).

normative bearer of the apostolic teaching.[48] Cyprian believes the bishop of Rome should use the authority of his position aggressively when the good of the wider church demands it, as his correspondence on Marcianus of Arles reveals. He also seems to recognize the right of bishops to appeal to the Roman see for a reconsideration of judgments made against them by their confreres, though he clearly hopes this will be a rare practice.[49]

It is impossible to find in Cyprian's writings a coherent and detailed theory of the relationship of the pastoral authority of each Catholic bishop to that of the bishop of Rome. What one does find, in the midst of his advocacy of the importance of bishops, is a delicate balance between a sense of their autonomy and collective responsibility, on the one hand, and a clear, if less frequent, admission of the special leadership to be exercised by the bishop of Rome, on the other. This balance forms an essential part of the conception of *communio* which was to be normative in the Western church from Cyprian's time on: the understanding that each local church, sacramentally realized as the Body of Christ in the Eucharistic celebration of bishop, clergy and people, joined the universal or "catholic" communion of churches by mutual hospitality and mutual assurances of continuity in the faith of the Apostles, and that communion in faith and charity with the bishop of Rome was an indispensable criterion for achieving that universal bond.[50]

---

48. See, for example, Ep. 59.14 (*CSEL* 3.2:683.13f.): the faith of the Romans was praised by the Apostle Paul because "infidelity could gain no access to them."

49. Ibid.; see also Ep. 59.9 (676.2ff.), where he explains that he has not informed Cornelius earlier of the excommunication of the heretical bishop Felicissimus because he did not think it was "the kind of matter which ought to be brought to your notice at once and quickly, as something great or dangerous (*quasi magna aut metuenda*)." In Ep. 67, disavowing Pope Stephen's reinstatement of the deposed Spanish bishops Basilides and Martial, Cyprian and the African bishops do not argue against the right of such an appeal to Rome, but maintain that Stephen has made a faulty judgment (see esp. c. 6: ibid. 739f.).

50. See, for example, Optatus of Mileve, *Contra Parmenianum* 2.2 (*CSEL* 26:36): *commercium formatarum*, the exchange of letters of communion, with the bishop of Rome assures union with the whole church *in una communionis societate*; Theodosius I, Decree of Feb. 27, 380 (*Codex Theod.* 16.1.2): the *religio* preached by St. Peter and preserved by Pope Damasus and Patriarch Peter of Alexandria is normative for all nations; Letter from Council of Aquileia to the Emperors Gratian, Valentinian II, and Theodosius I (Ambrose, Ep. 5 *extra collectionem* [Ep. 11]; *CSEL* 82:184.47-50): from the church of Rome, "totius orbis Romani caput"; and from its tradition of faith, "in omnes venerandae communionis iura dimanant"; and in the early sixth century (515), the profession of faith required by Pope Hormisdas from Eastern bishops wishing

Spheres of Papal Jurisdiction

The exercise of pastoral care and jurisdiction--in however wide or narrow a sense both words are taken--by the bishops of Rome developed rapidly in the two centuries that followed the peace of Constantine. Again, I can hardly do more here than sketch out some of the major lines of that development, as it is related to the growing understanding of the relationship between the popes and local councils in those centuries. However, the readiness of the popes of this period to act outside the local church of Rome, and the self-understanding with which they acted, varied noticeably with regard to the different parts of the Christian world. Language, historical connections between various churches, and the varying acceptance of a Christian imperial ideology in East and West conspired together to introduce variety in the way Roman ecclesiastical leadership was understood and exercised in different parts of the post-Constantinian Empire. One can distinguish at least three "spheres" in which differing degrees of papal influence were exercised: Italy and the adjoining islands, other parts of the Latin-speaking West, and the Eastern churches.[51]

1) The area in which the Roman bishops understandably exercised the strongest influence among their colleagues was Italy itself, along with Sicily, Sardinia, Corsica, and the smaller islands of the Tyrrhenian Sea: the churches Rufinus of Aquileia called the "suburbicariae ecclesiae."[52] This "super-metropolitan" or (in later language) patriarchal jurisdiction was confirmed by the Council of Nicaea as an "ancient custom," and guaranteed there to the bishops of Alexandria and Antioch as well as the bishop of Rome.[53] From the

---

to put an end to the Acacian schism (*Collectio Avellana* 116b; *CSEL* 35:521.27ff.): ". . . ideo spero ut in una communione vobiscum, quam Sedes Apostolica praedicat, esse merear, in qua est integra et vera christianae religionis et perfecta soliditas. . . ."

51. The most convenient and reliable summary of the data on these Roman "spheres of influence" is still P. Batiffol, *Cathedra Petri* (Paris: Cerf, 1938), esp. 41-79. For a discussion of the broader lines of church organization as it developed in this period, see C. Vogel, "Unité de l'église et pluralité des formes historiques d'organisation ecclésiastique du IIIᵉ au Vᵉ siècle," in Y. Congar and B. D. Dupuy, eds., *L'épiscopat et l'église universelle* (Paris: Cerf, 1964), 617-36.

52. Rufinus, *Historia ecclesiastica* 10.6 (*Die Griechischen Christlichen Schriftsteller der ersten drei Jahrhunderte* [*GCS*] [Leipzig, 1897 seqq.], 2:967.1); see Batiffol 43.

53. Council of Nicaea, can. 6 (*COD* 8f.). For the role of metropolitan bishops in confirming

mid-fourth century, when the emperors sponsored Arian bishops in Milan and other northern Italian sees, this patriarchal sphere of influence was restricted to Italy south of the Apennines and the islands. Nonetheless, it remained the most clearly defined area of papal authority through the time of Gregory the Great. Within it, fifth- and sixth-century popes took the responsibility, usually through legates, to oversee the administration of vacant sees and to supervise the election of bishops by the local clergy and people.[54] Their consent to each elected candidate in the region was required,[55] and they would usually ordain those approved.[56] The popes also acted as judges of all formal charges brought against Italian bishops. The more assertive among them, such as Innocent I or Leo, even took steps to unify both the orthodoxy and the liturgical practice of the local churches in the region along Roman lines.[57]

2) A wider region in which the bishops of Rome also exercised growing influence in this period was the whole West of the Roman Empire: the Latin-speaking regions of Europe west of the Rhine and south of the Danube, North Africa west of the Libyan desert, and the Balkan region west of Thessalonica. Even in the time of Cyprian, as we have seen, the bishops of Rome were acknowledged to have the right and even the responsibility to involve themselves in disputes in the churches of Gaul and Spain, at least in extraordinary circumstances. The Synod of Arles, summoned by Constantine from all the

---

episcopal elections and ordinations, see can. 4 (ibid. 7). The Roman bishops never accepted the title of "patriarch" for either their Italian or their wider Western areas of influence; see M. Maccarrone, *La Dottrina del primato papale dal IV all' VIII secolo nelle relazione con le chiese occidentali* (Spoleto 1960), 93. On the early development of this patriarchal jurisdiction of the bishops of Rome, see P. Hinschius, *System des katholischen Kirchenrechts mit besonderer Rücksicht auf Deutschland* (repr. Graz: Akademische Druck- und Verlagsanstalt, 1959), 1.552-60.

54. See Batiffol 44 for examples; cf. Gregory the Great, Epp. 1.55 (*CCL* 140.67f.); 1.56 (*CCL* 140:68); 1.79 (*CCL* 140:86f.); 7.38 (*CCL* 140:502f.); 10.7 (*CCL* 140A.832f.). Pope Leo I insisted on the importance of the participation of all the clergy and people in the election of their bishop: "he who is to preside over all should be chosen by all" (Ep. 10.6 [*PL* 54.634 A9f.]). Possidius reports that Augustine, too, thought that the consensus of the faithful and local custom should always be followed in ordaining bishops: *Vita Augustini* 21 (*PL* 32.51).

55. See Council of Nicaea, can. 6.

56. See Batiffol 44 for examples.

57. On issues of faith, see Leo, Ep. 7.1 (*PL* 54.620 B8ff.), in which he invites the bishops of Italy to help oppose Manichaeism "in consortium nostrae sollicitudinis". For liturgical standardization, see the famous letter of Innocent I to bishop Decentius of Gubbio: Ep. 25 (*PL* 20.551-61); Leo, Ep. 96 (*PL* 54.945); Ep. 168 (*PL* 45.1209 ff.).

Western provinces to deal with the Donatist schism in Africa, reported its decisions at length to Silvester, bishop of Rome, who did not attend, so that he could communicate them to the other churches.[58] The Council of Serdica (343), an exclusively Western gathering after the Eastern delegations had withdrawn over a doctrinal dispute, confirmed the right of bishops deposed by local synods to appeal to the bishop of Rome and *his* synod, who could, if it seemed justified, require the local synod to give the appellant a second hearing.[59] The Western Emperor Gratian gave this arrangement the force of civil law by a decree of 378,[60] and his successor Valentinian III, responding to a dispute between Pope Leo and Hilary, metropolitan of Arles, in 445, simply laid it down for the Western Empire that "whatever the authority of the Apostolic See has sanctioned or shall sanction shall be law for all."[61]

Since the time of Pope Damasus in the 370s, the bishops of Rome had adopted the curial style of issuing rescripts in response to disciplinary or doctrinal questions from bishops outside Italy, letters that were presumed to have the same legal force as the decisions of local synods.[62] Pope Siricius, in 386, sent to the African bishops nine canons enacted by a Roman synod, one of which required that no bishop be ordained without the knowledge of the Roman see. Presumably, the Africans were expected to observe this procedure in the same way as the Italians. The justification given in Pope Innocent I's letter to Decentius of Gubbio, is Rome's historic "priority" in faith: since all the churches in Italy, Gaul, Spain, Africa, Sicily, and the islands were either founded by Peter or by his successors, those churches should be ready to recognize Rome as "the source of their customs (*caput institutionum*)."[63]

---

58. *CCL* 148.4-22.

59. Can. 3B. C. H. Turner, ed., *Ecclesiae occidentalis monumenta iuris antiquissima* (Oxford: Clarendon Press, 1913), 460ff. See H. Hess, *The Canons of the Council of Sardica* (Oxford: Clarendon Press, 1958), 109-27; K. M. Girardet, "Appellatio. Ein Kapitel kirchlicher Rechtsgeschichte in Kanones des vierten Jahrhunderts," *Historia* 23 (1974): 98-127; H.-J. Sieben, "Sanctissimi Petri apostoli memoriam honoremus. Die Sardicensischen Appellationskanones im Wandel der Geschichte," *Theologie und Philosophie* 58 (1983): 501-34.

60. *PL* 13.586 B4 - 587 A5.

61. Transmitted as Leo, Ep. 11 (*PL* 54.638 B6ff.).

62. See Batiffol 56, and the letter of Pope Siricius, Damasus' successor, to Bishop Himerius of Tarragona in *Coll. Avellana* 40 (*CSEL* 35.90f.).

63. Ep. 25 (*PL* 20.552 B12).

One important means by which the Roman bishops of the fifth and sixth centuries secured their influence in the more distant regions of the West was the appointment of one of the region's bishops--usually the metropolitan of a major provincial see--as their personal legate or vicar. In 385, Pope Siricius delegated to the bishop of Thessalonica the power of confirming, in his name, all episcopal elections in the imperial prefecture of Illyricum (mainland Greece), always a sensitive border region, linguistically and politically, between East and West.[64] Pope Zosimus (417-18) conferred a similar role--though without the title--on the bishop of Arles for southern Gaul, a practice formalized by Pope Vigilius I in the next century (545). Pope Simplicius commissioned the bishop of Seville as his vicar in Spain in the 470s, and Gregory the Great not only regularly appointed a Sicilian bishop to act as his vicar in the island, but sent his disciple Augustine to Britain in 596, to organize church life there on Roman lines as primate of the English.

These vicars were not meant to usurp the functions of local leadership, or to deprive the local churches of their self-government. As Leo I made clear to Anastasius, his vicar in Illyricum, his role was to see that the canons and traditions of the local church were observed.[65] He was to convoke semi-annual synods, to judge disputes among the metropolitans of the region which they were unable to resolve among themselves, to prevent those metropolitans from unduly dominating church life in their provinces, and to serve as a channel of information to and from the pope.[66] Leo rebukes Anastasius sharply, in a later letter, for being overly authoritarian himself in his oversight of the Illyrian region and for failing to observe the rules of subsidiarity.[67] Still, Leo's strong sense of a God-given responsibility to be, for the universal communion, "the guardian of the Catholic faith and of the legislation of our ancestors,"[68] led him even to send a special vicar to Mauretania, where the Roman bishops had never exercised the same pastoral supervision as in Europe, to inquire into

---

64. This arrangement was confirmed by Innocent I (415), Celestine I (423/4), Sixtus III (437), Leo I (444) and Boniface II (532). On the institution of apostolic vicars, see Maccarrone, *La Dottrina*, 95-98.

65. "Propter custodiam regularum": Ep.6.2 (*PL* 54.617 B13f.).

66. Ep. 13.1f. (*PL* 54.664f.).

67. Ep. 14.1f. (*PL* 54.668-72). On Leo's sense of the importance of subsidiarity, see P. A. McShane, *La Romanitas et le Pape Léon le Grand* (Tournai/Montréal: Desclée, 1979), 301-305.

68. Letter to the Council of Chalcedon, Ep. 114.2 (*PL* 54.1031 A12f.).

reports of the uncanonical election of bishops there.[69] For him and for other fifth-century popes, the institution of a personal vicar among regional hierarchies of the Latin West was a concrete way of demanding accountability from local bishops for their canonical practice, and of expressing the universal pastoral oversight that the popes considered theirs by ancient tradition.[70]

3) Much less clearly defined was the claim of the bishops of Rome to a right of pastoral supervision in the churches of the Greek-speaking East. As a rule, the popes of the early post-Constantinian period were far less ready to intervene in doctrinal or disciplinary disputes in the Eastern churches than they were in the West; yet a growing, if cautious, sense of the concrete and worldwide consequences of the Petrine legacy is evident in their correspondence.

This is shown in the willingness of bishops of Rome to receive appeals, in extraordinary cases, from Eastern bishops who had been deposed from their sees by local synods or even by Eastern patriarchs.[71] In 340, Julius I had argued to his brother in the see of Antioch that Athanasius, as bishop of another Apostolic church (Alexandria), should not have been deposed without the consent of all Christian bishops, and that the ancient canons gave Rome the right to be first judge in cases concerning the see of Alexandria.[72] John

---

69. Ep. 12 (*PL* 54.645-56); see esp. section 1, where Leo explains he has sent his legate, Bishop Potentius, to look into the situation "pro sollicitudine quam universae ecclesiae ex divina institutione dependimus."

70. So Leo, Serm. 5.2 (*CCL* 138 22.26-23.30). "Quamvis enim singuli quique pastores speciali sollicitudine gregibus suis praesint, sciantque se pro commissis sibi ovibus reddituros esse rationem, nobis tamen cum omnibus cura communis est, neque cuiusquam administratio non nostri laboris est portio." Cf. his explanation of the hierarchical structure of pastoral care (*sollicitudo*) in his corrective letter to Anastasius of Thessalonica, Ep. 14.11 (*PL* 54.676 A6 - B13).

71. For a discussion of all the cases of such appeals prior to the Council of Chalcedon, see P. Batiffol, "Les recours à Rome en Orient avant le concile de Chalcédoine," *op. cit.* 215-48; cf. also the articles of Girardet and Sieben cited above (n. 59).

72. Athanasius, *Apologia contra Arianos* 35 (Opitz 113.5-9). The Greek historian Sozomen, writing of these events a century later, says Julius protested the deposition of Athanasius "because there is a sacerdotal canon (*nomos hieratikos*) which declares that whatever is enacted without the sanction of the bishop of Rome is null and void." *Hist. Eccl.* 3.10.1 (*GCS* 50: 113.3ff.). Julius' letter simply refers to the practice of referring controverted cases to Rome as a "custom (*ethos*)." Sozomen's language may reflect the more extensive claims of his papal contemporary, Leo.

Chrysostom, under attack from enemies in Constantinople and from the hostile Theophilus of Alexandria, appealed to Pope Innocent I in 404, as well as to the bishops of Aquileia and Milan, to use their influence to get him a fair trial. Innocent responded by protesting vigorously to the Emperor and by refusing to recognize John's successor.[73] Pope Sixtus III, in 437, informed bishop Proclus of Constantinople that Idduas, the bishop of Smyrna, had appealed to Rome a sentence passed against him at Constantinople, but that he, Sixtus, had endorsed the decision.[74] After the "Robber Synod" of Ephesus in the summer of 449, the three Eastern bishops who had been deposed at that contentious gathering by Dioscorus of Alexandria--Flavian of Constantinople, Eusebius of Dorylaeum, and Theodoret of Cyrrhus--all appealed to Pope Leo to overturn the decision at a synod held under his presidency at Rome, recognizing his "apostolic authority" as holder of the see of Peter.[75] A century and a half later, in 593, Gregory the Great wrote to John the Faster, patriarch of Constantinople, sarcastically rebuking him for feigning ignorance about two disciplined clerics who had subsequently appealed to Rome: "If you do not observe the canons, and wish to overturn the statutes of our ancestors, *I* do not know who *you* are!"[76] John eventually wrote to Pope Gregory about the

---

73. For John's letter, see Palladius, *Dialogue on the Life of Saint John Chrysostom* 2 (*PG* 47.8-12). Although no direct reply to it from Innocent is extant, we have his letter of protest to bishop Theophilus of Alexandria over the affair (Ep. 5 [*PL* 20.493-96]) and his letter to the clergy and people of Constantinople (Ep. 7: *PL* 20.501-508), as well as his reply to a later letter from John, written in exile (Ep. 12: *PL* 20.513f.).

74. Ep. 9.3 (*PL* 50.613 A15 - B5).

75. So Flavian: "I had good cause for referring my present situation to your Holiness, and for using an appeal to your apostolic authority, asking that it should reach out to the East and come to the help of the pious faith of the holy Fathers. . ." (*ACO* 2:2.1.77.9ff.; trans. J. Stevenson, *Creeds, Councils and Controversies* [London: SPCK, 1966] 311 [altered]); Theodoret: "I await the sentence of your Apostolic see. I beseech and implore your Holiness to help me in my appeal to your fair and righteous tribunal. . . I await your decision. If you bid me abide by the sentence of condemnation, I abide, and henceforth I will trouble no one. . . ." (Ep. 113 [*SC* 111: 64.5ff., 22ff.]; tr. Stevenson, *SC* 111: 314 [altered]); Eusebius: "In the past and from the beginning the Apostolic throne has been accustomed to defend those who suffer evil, and to help those who have fallen among inescapable disputes. . . The reason is that you hold to the right path and preserve your faith in our Lord Jesus Christ unshaken, and also that you show an undisguised charity towards all the brothers and sisters, all who have been called in the name of Christ." (*ACO* 2:2.1.79.20-25)

76. Ep. 3.52 (*CCL* 140.198.44ff.). In defense of his adoption of liturgical practices from the

case, and at least one of the clerics was later exonerated by the Roman synod.[77]

These instances, comparatively rare, of appeals to the popes for help, in major disciplinary disputes, by bishops of the Eastern churches, show at least traces of an ancient tradition recognizing the authority of Roman decisions even outside the Latin West. Papal letters from the fourth and fifth century occasionally show a similar willingness to make the Roman voice heard in doctrinal controversies in the East. Anastasius I writes to bishop John of Jerusalem during the dispute in Palestine over Origenism in 400-401, expressing his concern to preserve the gospel faith "among all my peoples" and to stay in touch, by letter, with "the parts of my body in all the various places of the earth."[78] Celestine I writes to the clergy of Constantinople in August 430, as the Nestorian controversy is gaining momentum: "Since you are our flesh and blood, I am rightly concerned lest the influence of a bad teacher turn your faith, which is proclaimed everywhere, from the path of truth."[79]

After his own strenuous diplomatic labors in securing the Christological settlement at Chalcedon, Pope Leo writes to Maximus, patriarch of Antioch, congratulating him on victory and thanking him for his readiness to keep Leo informed of the affairs of his church. As bishop of one of the three ancient Apostolic churches, "it is right, after all, that you should be a colleague with the Apostolic See in this concern."[80] When other bishops of East or West, even the bishops of Antioch or Alexandria, act together to preserve the gospel tradition, they do it, in Leo's view, as participants in the most fundamental pastoral responsibility of the bishop of Rome, his "care for all the churches."[81]

Constantinopolitan church, Gregory later remarked to John, bishop of Syracuse, that such internationalism was hardly inappropriate: "Who doubts that (that church) is subject to the Apostolic See? The most pious Lord Emperor and our brother, the bishop of that city, constantly admit this!" (Ep. 9.26 [*CCL* 140A.587.43-46])

77. See Gregory, Ep. 5.44 (*CCL* 140.336.209ff.); Ep. 6.14-17 (*CCL* 140.382-87).

78. Ep. 1 (*PL* 20.72 A8-11).

79. Ep. 14 (*ACO* I 2.15.16ff.).

80. Ep. 119.3 (*ACO* II 4.73.32).

81. See, for instance, Leo, Ep. 7.1 (*PL* 54.620B), inviting the bishops of Italy to share his concern to oppose Manichaeism; also Ep. 92 (*PL* 54.1024 A11-14); Ep. 93 (*PL* 54.1025 A14-B12); Ep. 83 (ibid. 919 C2-5). It is noteworthy that when the Council of Chalcedon wrote, as a group, to Pope Leo to inform him that it had confirmed the patriarchal status of the see of Constantinople as "second" after "the elder, royal Rome" (can. 28), it began the letter by

In the mid-sixth century, the Emperor Justinian's determination to unite the Christian world, after almost a century of Christological schism, led him to cultivate cordial relations with a succession of popes, and to affirm strongly their claim to universal pastoral leadership. "Everything that pertains to the state of the churches we hasten to bring to your Holiness's notice," he wrote to Pope John II in 533, "because we have always been deeply concerned to preserve the unity of your Apostolic See and the state of the holy churches of God. . . . Therefore we have been eager to subject and unite all the bishops of the entire Eastern region to your Holiness. . . . Nor do we allow any current matter which pertains to the state of the churches, however clear and obvious it may be, not to be brought to your Holiness' notice, since you are the head of all the holy churches."[82] Justinian arranged for the visits of three popes to Constantinople,[83] where they were received--sometimes graciously, sometimes violently--as heads of the universal communion of churches. In the end, Justinian treated the popes, too, chiefly as means towards his dream of a reunited Empire. But the rhetoric with which he addressed them, and the legal security, however tenuous, which he gave to their jurisdictional claims simply confirmed a direction of papal self-understanding which had been developing in the Western church for more than a century, and laid the groundwork in civil law for the medieval papacy.

---

acknowledging, "You are the interpreter to all of the voice of blessed Peter," and by thanking him for leading the council to its doctrinal decisions "as head among the members": Leo, Ep. 98.1, 4 (ACO 2:3.2.93.20f, 95.29f. [Latin]; ACO 2:1.3.116.26f., 118.32f. [Greek]).

82. Letter of June 6, 533 in Collectio Avellana 84 (CSEL 35.322.10-14, 15f., 21-24; Codex Justiniana 1.1.8). Cf. Novella 131.2, of March 14, 545 (R. Schoell and G. Kroll, ed., Corpus Iuris Civilis 3 [Berlin: Weidmann, 1972] 655.9-15), in which Justinian confirmed both the "first place" among bishops held by the bishops of "old Rome," and the "second place" granted to the bishops of Constantinople, the "new Rome," by the 28th canon of Chalcedon.

83. John I in 526, who was received in Constantinople as senior patriarch when Justinian was the main advisor to his uncle, the aging Emperor Justin I; Agapitus I in 536, who oversaw the deposition of Patriarch Anthimus and ordained his successor, Menas; and Vigilius, who was kidnapped after a liturgy in Rome in 545, brought to Constantinople by the imperial police, and kept under virtual house arrest there for nine years, so that he would give his approval to Justinian's agenda for the reunification of the churches. On Justinian's policy towards the papacy, see P. Batiffol, "L'empereur Justinien et le siège apostolique," op. cit. 249-317; F. Dvornik, Byzantium and the Roman Primacy (New York: Fordham, 1966), 71-88.

Popes and Local Synods

Against this background of an increasingly articulated papal claim to worldwide pastoral responsibility, the relationship of popes to local episcopal gatherings during the late patristic period can be sketched briefly.

1) First, local bishops' synods were simply a fact of life in the early church, from the second century onwards. In the absence of modern means of rapid and detailed communication, the normal way for the bishops of a province or region to deal with common problems was for them to meet in synod. Such gatherings were therefore the first and most obvious way for the leaders of the churches to express and realize the *pax, concordia,* and *caritas* that form the human reality of ecclesial communion.[84]

2) The efforts of the popes--especially those with a strong sense of universal leadership like Leo and Gregory--were often directed towards encouraging bishops to observe the canonical requirement of regular provincial and regional meetings. Leo strongly urged his vicar in Illyricum to make sure the bishops of the region met in semi-annual provincial synods,[85] and insisted that the metropolitans there send at least two or three bishops from their provinces to annual regional gatherings. If a bishop should miss such synods frequently and without a grave excuse, "let him know that he must face judgment."[86] The bishops of Italy were to gather twice a year at Rome, and the bishops of Sicily were to join them for their September meeting (on the anniversary of Leo's election), to "act together in the presence of the blessed apostle Peter, so that all his (i.e., Peter's!) canonical decrees and constitutions should remain in full force among the Lord's priests."[87] Gregory the Great, at the end of the sixth century, reinforced the requirement of semi-annual (in Sardinia and Italy) or annual (in Sicily) provincial meetings of bishops,[88] and obliged the Sicilian bishops to attend a pan-Italian synod at Rome

---

84. See, for example, Leo, Ep. 6.5 (*PL* 54.619); Ep. 94.1, to the Council of Chalcedon (*PL* 54.1027 ff.); Gregory the Great, Ep.1.1 (*CCL* 140.1f.).

85. Ep. 6.5.

86. Letter to the metropolitans of Illyricum, Ep. 13.2 (*PL* 54.665 B5f.).

87. Ep. 16.7 (*PL* 54.702 C4 - 703 A3). The Apostle's presence is understood, of course, to be personified in Leo himself.

88. Ep. 1.1 (*CCL* 140.1f.); Ep. 2.41 (*CCL* 140.129f.); Ep. 4.9 (*CCL* 140.225f.); Appendix 1

every five years.[89] The difficulties and dangers of ancient travel, as well as the universal human resistance to meetings, apparently made such reminders necessary.

3) The purpose of these meetings, in the minds of fifth- and sixth-century popes, was first of all disciplinary: to resolve disputes between bishops in an orderly way, corresponding to what we would today call the principle of subsidiarity.

Leo writes to Anastasius of Thessalonica that the semi-annual synods of each province in Illyricum are to act as courts for all cases between "the various ranks (*ordines*) of the church." If the provincial synod, under the metropolitan bishop, cannot reach a consensus, the case is to be referred to the regional synod, presided over by Anastasius as papal vicar. Only if that regional gathering is unable to reach consensus is the case to referred to Rome.[90] But doctrinal concerns, when they arise, are to be referred first to regional synods as well. Leo reminds Proterius, the new bishop of Alexandria, in 454, of the importance of holding regular provincial synods, as required by ancient custom, especially in the face of resistance to the Chalcedonian definition.[91] And he urges the bishops of the provinces of Aquileia[92] and northern Spain[93] to summon extraordinary synods to deal, respectively, with Pelagianism and Priscillianism in those regions. As in the days of Cyprian, popes and bishops of the fifth and sixth centuries assumed that local synods were competent to reach final decisions in matters of faith as well as pastoral practice, provided they reached a consensus that harmonized with the church's apostolic tradition.

4) Until at least the mid-fifth century, the Roman bishops apparently never claimed that the decisions of synods--whether provincial, regional, or international--depended for their validity on either formal or informal papal approval. Communication of such decisions to the pope seems, however, to

---

(*CCL* 140A.1092ff.).

89. Ep. 7.19 (*CCL* 140.470).

90. Ep. 14.7 (*PL* 54.673 C4 - 674 A8); cf. Ep. 13.2 (*PL* 54.665 A4 - B6). On the ancient canonical principle that only a lack of local consensus justified the involvement of a "higher" instance in a regional dispute, see Sieben, "Episcopal Conferences," 34ff., 51.

91. Ep. 129.3 (*PL* 54.1077 B13 - 1078 A1); cf. Ep. 129.1 (*PL* 54.1075f.).

92. Ep. 1.2 [442] (*PL* 54.594f.).

93. Ep. 15, to Turribius of Astorga (ibid., 680). On this letter, see above, n. 21.

have been expected. The synod of Arles in 314, as I have mentioned, carefully informed Pope Silvester of its decisions on the Donatist schism, and expected him to inform the wider Christian communion. Pan-African synods meeting in 393 (Hippo) and 397 (Carthage) developed a policy for recognizing the orders of Donatist bishops who joined the Catholic communion, which was not to be confirmed and put into practice until the main centers of the *transmarina ecclesia* (Rome and Milan) had been consulted.[94] Although we have no direct record of the replies of those churches, an address of Aurelius of Carthage to the African synod of 401 refers to the reservations Pope Anastasius and his Roman synod had expressed about the plan,[95] and the Africans apparently modified it to some extent as a result of these reservations.

Pope Leo began to claim more formal rights of confirmation. His letter to the bishops of the province of Mauretania in 444, demanding that they correct reported abuses in the election of bishops, ends with the request that a report of all the synod's decisions be sent to him, "so that it might also be confirmed by our judgment."[96] The letter sent by Leo and his Roman synod to Emperor Theodosius II in the fall of 449, arguing to the invalidity of the "Robber Synod" held in Ephesus that summer, implied, discreetly but unmistakably, that papal approval is a necessary part of the valid ecclesial reception of any synodal decrees.[97] And his firm rejection of canon 28 of Chalcedon, which confirmed the patriarchal privileges of Constantinople, within its region, as "equal" to those of Rome and "second after her," is based

---

94. See *Breviarium Hipponense*, can. 37 (*CCL* 149.44.228f.); *Codex canonum ecclesiae Africae*, prologue to acts of Synod of Carthage, June 16, 401 (*CCL* 149.194.411-19). On the issues involved in these consultations on the reconciliation of Donatists, see W. Marschall, *Karthago und Rom. Die Stellung der nordafrikanischen Kirche zum apostolischen Stuhl in Rom* (Päpste und Papsttum 1; Stuttgart: Hiersemann, 1971) 114-22.

95. *Codex canonum ecclesiae Africae*, prologue to acts of Synod of Carthage, Sept. 13, 401 (*CCL* 149.199.568-74).

96. Ep. 12.13 (*PL* 54.656 A15f.). The full text of this passage is illuminating: "Si quae vero aliae emerserint causae quae ad statum ecclesiasticum et ad concordiam pertineant sacerdotum, illic (i.e., in a provincial synod) sub timore Domini volumus ventilentur, et de componendis atque compositis omnibus ad nos relatio plena mittatur, ut ea quae iuxta ecclesiasticum morem iuste et rationabiliter fuerint definita, nostra quoque sententia roborentur."

97. Ep. 44.1 (*ACO* II 4.20.6-11); see M. Wojtowytsch, *Papsttum und Konzile von den Anfängen bis zu Leo I (440-461)* (Päpste und Papsttum 17; Stuttgart: Hiersemann, 1981) 327f.

on a direct claim of responsibility to preserve "the rules sanctioned by the fathers . . . for the government of the whole church."[98]

From Leo's response to these conciliar actions, it was only a short step to Gregory the Great's claim that papal consent was necessary if the decisions of local synods--even that of Constantinople--were to have force,[99] and to his declaration that the acts of Eastern synods which recognized the bishop of Constantinople as "ecumenical patriarch," according to the wishes of the incumbent, were null and void.[100] Like Leo, Gregory saw his special office in the universal church to be that of defending "the statutes of Gospels and canons, and the truth of humility and uprightness."[101] But he interpreted this responsibility for tradition with a breadth and self-confidence that was to reach its full development in the Carolingian and medieval papacy.[102]

5) Along with this sketch of the developing relations between popes and local synods, what can be said about the *theological* understanding of the role of such gatherings, and of their relationship to the Petrine ministry, during the later patristic period? There is little direct discussion of the subject in patristic literature, just as there is little direct reflection in the West on the nature of the church and its structures before the twelfth century. However, it is possible to see the outlines, at least, of an emerging theology of synods in the writings of the leading Western Christian thinkers of the period--especially in the works of Augustine, Leo, and Gregory the Great.

Augustine was less enthusiastic than many of his contemporaries about the normative value for faith of conciliar decrees. As his biographer Possidius

---

98. Ep. 104.3, to the Emperor Marcian (22 May, 452: *ACO* 2:4.56.24f.); cf. Ep. 105.3, to the Empress Pulcheria (same date: *ACO* 2:4.58.33-59.1). Cf. Wojtowytsch 342-50.

99. See Ep. 9.157 (*CCL* 140A.715.50f.): ". . . sine apostolicae sedis auctoritate atque consensu nullas, quaeque acta fuerant (sc., in a local synod), vires habeant," In his letter to the Frankish Queen Mother Brunhild, Gregory asks for her help in convening a Frankish council which "we have decided (*decrevimus*)" should be held, and delegates Bishop Syagrius of Autun to organize it (Ep. 9.214: ibid. 774.51-54; cf. Epp. 215-216: ibid. 775-79).

100. Ep. 5.41 (*CCL* 140.321.12ff.). Cf. Ep. 5.39 (*CCL* 140.315.32f.). On the dispute between Gregory and his Eastern colleagues over this title, see A. Tuilier, "Grégoire le Grand et le titre de patriarche oecuménique," J. Fontaine, R. Gillet and S. Pellistrandi eds., *Grégoire le Grand* (Congress, Chantilly 1982; Paris 1986), 69-81.

101. Ep. 5.39 (*CCL* 140.315.35f.).

102. On the development of the conception of a pope's power over local synods under Nicholas I in the ninth century, see Sieben, "Episcopal Conferences," 52-56.

attests, he was an active participant in a large number of provincial and African councils during his thirty-five-year ministry as bishop of Hippo.[103] He argues from synodal decrees in a number of controversial works,[104] but generally prefers to base his argument on Scripture or his own reasoning. Some of his caution is probably due to his opposition to Donatist ecclesiology. As an exclusive, fanatically nationalist church, the Donatists regarded the decisions of earlier gatherings of "faithful" African bishops as divinely inspired and permanently binding. Augustine, in contrast, argues that there is an essential difference between Scripture and any kind of conciliar document, in their normative value for faith. Only Scripture is infallible, and conciliar statements must be judged by its standard.[105] In keeping with his usual emphasis on the universal church, "the church that is spread throughout the world," as the true Body of Christ,[106] he stresses that the authority of particular councils--even Cyprian's--must always yield to the "unanimous authority of the whole church," as expressed in a universal council.[107]

In one famous passage in the *De Baptismo*, in fact, Augustine expresses quite clearly his sense of the hierarchy of norms determining Christian faith and practice, over against the Donatists' rigid clinging to the decisions of African synods of the past. The "sacred canon of Scripture," he writes, stands "absolutely over all later letters of bishops." All pronouncements of bishops must be tested against the truth, "either by the discourse of someone who happens to be wiser in the matter than themselves, or by the weightier

---

103. *Vita Augustini* 21 (*PL* 32.51).

104. See, e.g., his use of the letter of the Eastern bishops gathered at Philippopolis in 343, in the anti-Donatist work *Ctr. Cresconium* 3.34.38 [405/6] (ed. M. Petschenig: *CSEL* 52.445f.). For a full treatment of Augustine's knowledge and understanding of councils, see H. J. Sieben, *Die Konzilsidee der alten Kirche* (Schöningh: Paderborn 1979), 69-101.

105. On the notion that only Scripture is "canonical" and normative for faith, not the writings or councils of Cyprian, see *Ctr. Cresc.* 2.31.39-32.40 (*CSEL* 52.398ff.). Augustine here tersely summarizes his attitude towards the value of local traditions: "Primo esto in ecclesia, quam constat tenuisse ac praedicasse Cyprianum, et tunc aude velut auctorem sententiae tuae nominare Cyprianum. Primo imitare pietatem humilitatemque Cypriani, et tunc profer concilium Cypriani." (398.23-27)

106. See *Hom. on I John* 6.10 [407?] (*SC* 75.298); 10.8 (430): "Extende caritatem tuam per totum orbem, si vis Christum amare; quia membra Christi per orbem jacent. Si amas partem, divisus es; si divisus es, in corpore non es. . . ."

107. *De Baptismo* 2.4.5 (*CSEL* 51: 179.13-17); cf. 1.7.9 (*CSEL* 5.154.6-10).

authority and more informed experience of other bishops, or by the authority of councils." Local councils, in turn, "must yield, beyond all possibility of doubt, to the authority of universal councils which are formed for the whole Christian world; and even among these universal councils, the earlier are often corrected by those which follow them, when by some actual experience, things are brought to light which were before concealed."[108]

Conciliar statements form an important part, in Augustine's view, but still only a part, of the church's progressive historical witness to the saving truth revealed by God. Their role, like every instance of *auctoritas*, is to confirm and ratify what may previously have only been a matter of custom or surmise, and so to help the struggling human mind move from the hesitancy of faith to the confidence of knowledge.[109] As such, their value is material and heuristic, rather than formal. They are always revisable in the light of later statements by wiser or more universal gatherings, and they always stand under the overarching norm of truth itself, as it makes itself accessible to the individual and the community.

In the writings of Leo the Great, both local synods and imperial councils are spoken of as inspired by the Holy Spirit, who is actively at work in the church to guide it to the truth that saves.[110] Leo looks on local synods, however, mainly as means of regulating disciplinary matters and so of building the unity and peace of the church. If they are unable to reach agreement, they are to observe the pattern of subsidiarity evident in the church's hierarchical structure: bishops deferring to the judgment of their metropolitans and provincial synods, these in turn deferring to regional gatherings under the papal vicar, and these referring unresolved cases to the pope.[111]

---

108. *De Bapt.* 2.3.4 (*CSEL* 5.178.11-26).

109. See, for example, *De Bapt.* 1.7.9 (*CSEL* 5.154); 2.9.14 (*CSEL* 5.189f.). Cf. Sieben, *Konzilsidee*, 97-100, and further bibliography cited there.

110. See Ep. 166.1 (*PL* 54.1193 A3-12), on his experience of a Roman synod confirming what he had himself seen as the right choice; Ep. 144, alleging that at Chalcedon an understanding of the person of Christ was "defined, by the guidance of the Holy Spirit, for the salvation of the whole world" (*PL* 54.1113 A6f.; cf. 1112 B11ff.). On the inspiration of the Council of Chalcedon, see also Ep. 147.2 (*PL* 54.1116 C1ff.); Ep. 149.2 (*PL* 54.1120.A12ff.); Ep. 156.1 (*PL* 54.1128.B2-6); 157.3 (*PL* 54.1133 C11-14); Ep. 161.2 (*PL* 54.1142 C15-D2). On Leo's understanding of councils in general, see Sieben, *Konzilsidee*, 102-47.

111. See especially Ep. 14.11 (*PL* 54.676AB).

Leo speaks in different tones, however, about the great imperial councils of the Christian world. The canons of Nicaea, above all, are "laws destined to remain until the end of the world."[112] "All the rules of the church" would be dissolved, he writes to bishop Julian of Kos, if any of the canons of the "most holy decrees of our fathers" were to be violated.[113] Because it represents the teaching of the gospel and the apostles, and accords fully with the faith of Nicaea, Chalcedon's definition of faith also has "perennial validity," and rules out further discussion.[114]

Leo's charismatic understanding of the role of synods in the church parallels, to a great extent, his charismatic understanding of himself as the personification of Peter, still guiding his Roman flock.[115] Both are dynamic means for keeping alive the tradition that binds the church of his own day to the saving faith of the apostles. Yet there is an important difference: while it is the role of the great imperial councils, at least, to "define" and specify in binding form the truths of this tradition,[116] his role as bishop of Rome and representative of Peter is rather to *proclaim* that tradition ceaselessly to all the churches, "to make clear what you understand and to preach what you believe."[117] Leo never claims the right to *define* the content of the Christian faith himself. He sees his role, as Hermann Josef Sieben puts it, as the temporally "vertical" one of proclaiming the consensus of the church that reaches back to the time of the Apostles, while the role of councils includes also the "horizontal" dimension of defining or determining that consensus at

---

112. Ep. 106.4 (*PL* 54.1005 B6-10). Leo's main concern here is to convince Anatolius, bishop of Constantinople, that the privileges accorded him by canon 28 of Chalcedon were void in light of the canons of Nicaea.

113. Ep. 107.1 (*PL* 54.1009 B13-16).

114. Ep. 157.1 (*PL* 54.1132 C8-1133 A6); Ep. 146.2 (*PL* 54.1115 C4-9); Ep. 147.2 (*PL* 54.1116 B12-C3). Cf. Ep. 149.2 (*PL* 54.1120 B7): if the definition of Chalcedon is overturned, "the whole Christian religion will be in turmoil."

115. See, for example, Tract. 2.2 (*CCL* 138.32-39); Tract. 3.3 (*CCL* 138.12.58-13.71); Tract. 4.4 (*CCL* 138.20.105-21.118); 5.4 (*CCL* 138.24.76-83). On Leo's sense of himself as the personification of Peter, see McShane (above, n. 67), 140-47.

116. So, e.g., Ep. 144 (*PL* 54.1113 A6f.).

117. Ep. 165.1, to the Emperor Leo (*PL* 54.1155 A11f.). Cf. Ep. 89, to the Emperor Marcian (*PL* 54.930 B14-C1); Tract. 25.2 (Christmas, 444; *CCL* 138.118.28-31). Cf. Sieben, *Konzilsidee*, 123-28.

a particular point in history.[118] In reading his previous letters, he writes to a local synod meeting at Chalcedon in March of 453, "your holinesses can recognize that I am, with our God's help, the guardian both of the Catholic faith and of the legislation of our ancestors."[119] That legislation itself, and the binding articulation of the faith, are the work of the great councils.

Gregory the Great has less to say than either Augustine or Leo about the ecclesiological status of episcopal synods. He urged the Italian bishops to meet with the prescribed regularity, as we have seen, and seems to have considered synods the ordinary way to resolve special problems.[120] His understanding of his own role in the church as guardian of tradition and canonical order, and his sense of the collective and individual responsibilities of bishops, is close to that of Leo, but strikingly less self-assertive. Although he lived in a time of social and political decay, and showed, in consequence, a fairly constant sense of eschatological foreboding, Gregory was careful not to allow the prerogatives acquired by his predecessors to be eroded. For him as for Leo, the Roman See was the *caput omnium ecclesiarum* and the *caput fidei*, thanks to the special place of Peter among the Apostles.[121] So, as we have already seen, Gregory strenuously opposed the assumption of the title "ecumenical patriarch" by the bishops of Constantinople, at least partly because it seemed to claim a primacy rivalling that of Rome.[122] But Gregory, unusually sensitive to the corrosive effects of ambition in clerical life, scrupulously respected canonical precedent and required others to do the same. As a result, he continued to maintain that *no* bishop should style himself by such a magnificent title,[123] and chose to refer to himself rather as *servus servorum Dei*.

---

118. Sieben, *Konzilsidee*, 139; cf. 142, n.131.

119. Ep. 114.2 (*PL* 54.1031 A11ff.).

120. See, for example, Ep. 1.16 (*CCL* 140.16.13f.), inviting Severus, the schismatic bishop of Aquileia, to come to Rome "that a synod may be assembled, with God as its convener (*auctore Deo*)," and a decision reached on the possibility of reestablishing communion.

121. *Caput omnium ecclesiarum*: Ep. 13.49 (*CCL* 140A.1062.76f.); *caput fidei*: Ep. 13.38 (*CCL* 140A.1041.8); Peter: Ep. 2.39 (*CCL* 140. 125.8ff.); Ep. 5.37 (*CCL* 140.309.38-52); Ep. 7.37 (*CCL* 140.500.2-501.39). For a detailed survey of Gregory's style of governing, and especially of his relationships with other churches, see F. Homes Dudden, *Gregory the Great. His Place in History and Thought* (London: Longmans, Green, 1905) 1.361-476; 2.201-32.

122. See, e.g., Ep. 9.157 (*CCL* 140A.714ff.). On Gregory's dispute with the patriarchs of Constantinople over this title, see Tuilier, *op.cit.* (above, n. 100).

123. Neither Peter nor Leo had done so, he points out in Ep. 5.37!

Besides revealing his personal humility, Gregory's attitude to episcopal office had concrete effects on his way of dealing with local bishops and their synods. As guardian of canon law, he felt obliged to recognize the rights of each bishop, even if they limited his own exercise of power.[124] And his style of leadership led him towards even greater self-restraint. When two African bishops appealed to Rome in disputes with their colleagues, for instance, Gregory referred the cases back to local synods, even though the language of his communications implied he had the canonical right to decide the cases himself.[125] His own role, as he saw it, was principally to apply the church's legal and doctrinal tradition in cases where local bishops were deficient in doing so. When bishops anywhere in the world are at fault, he wrote, it is the duty of the Apostolic See to correct them, but when they are not at fault "all bishops, according to the principle of humility, are equal."[126] "I do myself an injury," Gregory commented in another letter, "if I disturb the rights of my brothers."[127] "Just as we defend our own rights," he wrote to Dominicus, bishop of Carthage, in 592, "so we preserve those of the several churches. I do not, through partiality, grant to any church more than it deserves, nor do I through ambition derogate from any what belongs to it by right. Rather I desire to honor my brethren in every way, and study that each may be advanced in dignity, so long as there can be no just opposition to it on the part of another."[128] This is the expression not only of a collegial spirit, but of an ecclesiology!

For Leo and Gregory, the purpose of local bishops' gatherings that is

---

124. See, e.g., Ep. 2.40 (*CCL* 140.128.52-129.58); Ep. 2.44 (*CCL* 140.136.103-10); Ep. 5.39 (*CCL* 140.315.35ff.); Ep. 11.24 (*CCL* 140A.895.12ff.).

125. See Homes Dudden, 1:424-28. These are the cases of Bishop Paul (Ep. 4.32 [*CCL* 140.251f.]; Ep. 4.35 [*CCL* 140.255f.]; Ep. 6.62 [*CCL* 140.436f.]; Ep. 6.64 [*CCL* 140.439f.]; Ep. 7.2 [*CCL* 140.444f.]; Ep. 8.13 [*CCL* 140A.531f.]; Ep. 8.15 [*CCL* 140A.533f.]) and Bishop Crementius (Ep. 9.24 [*CCL* 140A.584]; 9.27 [*CCL* 140A.588f.]).

126. Ep. 9.27 (*CCL* 140A.588.18-21). Cf. *Regula pastoralis* 2.6.

127. Ep. 2.44 (*CCL* 140.136.104ff.).

128. Ep. 2.40 (*CCL* 140.128.52-129.58). Gregory's famous remark to Patriarch Eulogius of Alexandria, on the subject of ecclesiastical titles, makes this same point with somewhat more pathos: "I consider something to be no honor, if I perceive my brothers losing honor by it. My honor is the honor of the universal church; my honor is the united strength of my brothers. Then and only then am I truly honored, when no one is denied the honor which is justly his." (Ep. 8.29: *CCL* 140A.552.62-66)

emphasized above all others is the furthering of mutual charity.[129] As post-Enlightenment Westerners, we must--as I have said before--resist the temptation to see this as simply a moral or affective ideal, the edifying personal by-product of an efficiently functioning institution. For the fathers of the church, both Eastern and Western, the church is above all a mystery of communion, and communion is best described in terms of unity, charity, fraternity, concord and peace. "Whoever breaks the peace and concord of the church, acts against Christ," Cyprian writes.[130] So he can assure four former schismatics who have recently been reunited to the church, "You are leading a life befitting your faith, and you are keeping the law of undivided charity and concord by sharing the Lord's peace."[131] In expressing their agreement with Cornelius, the bishop of Rome, and in affirming their communion with him, Cyprian and his fellow African bishops are realizing "the unity and, at the same time, the charity of the universal church."[132]

The reason for this constant emphasis on charity is that charity, like the sustaining and integrating life-force of a physical organism, makes the church a concrete reality. "The children of God," Augustine preaches, "are the members of God's Son; and anyone who loves them, by loving becomes himself a member: through love he becomes a part of the structure of Christ's Body. And thus the end will be the one Christ, loving himself; for the love of the members for one another is the love of the Body for itself."[133]

So when Leo speaks of the administrative effectiveness of local synods as

---

129. So Leo, Ep. 6.1 (*PL* 54.617 A13f.); Ep. 13.2 (*PL* 54.665 A4- 15); Ep. 13.4 (*PL* 54.666 B5-15); Ep. 14.11 (*PL* 54.675 B4 - 676 A6); Gregory, Ep. 1.1 (*CCL* 140.2.20), urging the bishops of Sicily to meet at least annually: "sacerdotes vos concordia, Deo placita, et caritas recognoscit."

130. *De unitate* 6 (Bévenot 66.11ff.). The whole argument of this work is that the saving, life-giving reality of the church is an *unitatis sacramentum* (ibid., 7).

131. Ep. 54.1 [251] (*CSEL* 3.2.621.16-19). His contemporary, Cornelius of Rome, writes to congratulate Cyprian on a similar reconciliation, observing that the returned schismatics are no longer "being tempted against the faith which is charity and unity": Cyprian, Ep. 51.1 (*CSEL* 3.2:615.3).

132. Ep. 48.3 (*CSEL* 3.2.607.17f.).

133. *Hom. in I Ep. Joan.* 10.3 (*SC* 75.414.15-19). Cf. Hom. 6.10 (*SC* 75.298ff.), 9.11 (402ff.), 10.8 (430); cf. also *De Doctrina Christiana* 1.16.15 (*CCL* 32.15): "Est enim ecclesia corpus eius. . . . Corpus ergo suum multis membris diversa officia gerentibus nodo unitatis et caritatis tamquam sanitatis adstringit."

the work both of the Holy Spirit and of the *caritatis studium* of a region's bishops,[134] or writes to the bishops about to gather at Chalcedon that he had hoped, "for the sake of the charity of our college (*pro nostri caritate collegii*), that all the Lord's priests would remain devoted to a single Catholic faith,"[135] or when Gregory later asserts that he and the bishop of Carthage must consider each other's pastoral concerns their own "through the structure of charity,"[136] they are not simply expressing a wish for brotherly good feelings among peers. They are talking about the purpose of their collegial ministry, the heart of episcopal office: preserving the unity of Christians. It is precisely this responsibility that makes the gathering of bishops to do the business of unity and peace a continuing necessity for the life of the church.

Some Conclusions

The purpose of these observations about bishops' meetings and the papacy in the early church has been, as I said at the start, to provide a context for our own reflections about bishops' meetings today. Clearly both doctrine and discipline are constantly developing in the Christian body, and it would be just as injurious to the church's life to cling rigidly to early institutions and practices, without regarding the context of the present world and its needs, as it would be crippling to faith to hold literally to ancient texts and terms with no attempt at interpretation. Still, if Christian faith is, at heart, the reception of the preached word about Jesus in a community of love, then the tradition which bears that word to us from apostolic times must also be relevant to the concrete shape of the love which still forms that community. We have to look at our origins, as we struggle to shape the church of the future.

So the look that we have taken here at early Christian synodal practice and theory makes possible at least a few general questions and observations,

---

134. Ep. 13.2 (*PL* 54.665.12ff.).

135. Ep. 93.1 (*PL* 54.937.1). The Greek translation of the letter, although it avoids the word "charity" (*agape*), brings out the ecclesiological import of the phrase more clearly still: "by the attitude that befits our organizational structure (*kata ten prosousan diathesin to hemetero systemati*)" (*ACO* 2:1.1.31.6f.). Cf. Tract 2.2 (*CCL* 138.8.37f.), where Leo sees in his fellow bishops, gathered to celebrate the anniversary of his election, "ordinatissimam totius Ecclesiae caritatem, quae in Petri sede Petrum suscipit."

136. Ep. 2.40 (*CCL* 140.128.49f.): "per caritatis compagem".

it seems to me, that are apt to our present discussion of episcopal conferences in the Western church.

1) A number of important assumptions in the recent *instrumentum laboris* are clearly not in accord with the early traditions that are said by *Christus Dominus* 36 to have inspired the reconstitution of episcopal conferences at Vatican II:

a) The distinction between national episcopal conferences, which meet on a regular basis, and occasional national particular councils with a somewhat larger membership and somewhat more restricted agenda, developed in *Codex Iuris Canonici* 439-59 and used as an axiom in section IV of the *instrumentum laboris*, has no parallel in the early church. It is a *novum*.

b) Likewise, the assertion that "episcopal conferences do not, properly speaking, as such enjoy [the] *munus magisterii*," but are "proposed, by their own nature, as operative, pastoral and social means" is a functional distinction without parallel in the first seven centuries of the church.

Bishops gathered in local, provincial, regional, and international synods in the early church, to deal cooperatively with all the problems that confronted them. Since the Council of Nicaea, they were officially obliged to meet twice a year in provincial or regional synods, and were repeatedly encouraged by the popes to live up to this obligation. Doctrine and discipline constantly merged with one another, since the church's pastoral practice offers no basis for their separation.

2) The conception of episcopal collegiality developed in the *instrumentum laboris* exhibits a degree of canonical formalism that stands in sharp contrast to the patristic origins of the idea. The document draws a sharp distinction, for instance, between actions "which involve the college as such with its head" and "those which gather the bishops in the name of their pastoral concern, but not in their universality."[137] Only an ecumenical council or "the collegial action of the bishops spread throughout the world" count as collegial activities in the strict sense; other kinds of episcopal cooperation represent an "*affectus collegialis*," perhaps, but not an "*actio collegialis*."[138] For Cyprian, Leo, or Gregory, as we have seen, all Christian bishops form a single *collegium* in virtue of the responsibility they share for the life and faith of the

---

137. "Draft Statement on Episcopal Conferences," *Origins* 17 (April 7, 1988): 733.
138. Ibid.

universal church. The actions of every episcopal gathering, insofar as they confirm the church's faith and reinforce its bond of charity, clearly realize this collegial *munus*. The charity that is realized in synods is not merely an *affectus*, but a structural and practical way of building the church.

3) Although the ecclesiological vision of the medieval canonists or of Vatican I is still part of the unknown future for the fathers of the church, there was clearly general agreement in the early centuries that active communion with the bishop of Rome is a touchstone for continuity in the tradition of apostolic faith and for membership in the catholic body. The requirements for this communion took different shapes at different periods, as we have seen, and the sense of universal pastoral responsibility shared by the bishops of Rome developed noticeably from the mid-fourth century onwards. Donatism, however, with all its insistence on the inspired self-sufficiency of national synods, was rejected by wider consensus from the time of its origin.

4) Even the strongest and most enterprising of popes in the fifth and sixth centuries carefully observed subsidiarity, reserving to their own jurisdiction only those *causae majores* from outside the metropolitan region of Rome which could not be resolved within local structures. Papal claims to a *sollicitudo omnium ecclesiarum*, based on the apostolic tradition of Peter and Paul, did not lead them to neglect the differences that historically existed between their relationship to the bishops of suburbican Italy, to those in the rest of the Latin West, and to the Eastern churches and patriarchates. Although the ecumenical reality in contemporary Christendom is obviously much more complicated, there clearly is a need in Roman Catholic ecclesiology and canon law today, supported by ancient precedent, for a better articulated realization of the subsidiarity principle.

5) With Augustine, we must continue to judge the importance of bishops' gatherings and collaborative projects by their international significance and their ability to represent Christian tradition--in other words, by their catholicity. And we must remind ourselves that the truth of revelation, as presented to us in the Scriptures and the tradition of faith, stands above any conciliar or synodal pronouncements. We must, in other words, relativize the importance of national episcopal conferences, and of all bureaucracies and councils, in terms of the fundamental faith of the church. And we should expect documents like the *instrumentum laboris* to do the same.

6) A look at the early church's synodal practice should remind us,

however, of how important regular gatherings of the Christian bishops in the various parts of the world have been through the centuries: as organs of ordinary Christian teaching and administration, as forums for pastoral planning and for the resolution of disputes, as instruments for the reception of the decisions of greater councils, and as practical means to realize the unity and peace that is the heart of the church. As we struggle today with the reception of the Second Vatican Council, and as we labor to rise to the perennial challenge of giving a concrete shape to Christian love, we could do worse than focus our attention on the *studium caritatis* displayed by the bishops of the early church when they gathered together.

Elizabeth K. McKeown

The "National Idea" in the History of the American Episcopal Conference

ELIZABETH MCKEOWN is associate professor of church history in the department of theology at Georgetown University.

The European war was over and Americans were beginning to cope with its aftermath when a meeting of the American hierarchy was called to order on September 24, 1919, in Caldwell Hall at Catholic University of America. In his first act as presiding officer, Cardinal James Gibbons of Baltimore appointed a press committee from among his fellow bishops. The gesture was rich in implications: These proceedings were considered to be of public importance, and information must therefore be properly managed. The reasons for this presumed interest lay in the proposal the bishops had come to consider. In annual meetings since 1884, the archbishops of the United States, a scant dozen in number, had met to review Catholic church matters in an informal and entirely private manner. Now nearly a hundred members of the hierarchy met in Caldwell Hall to respond to a plan to create an organization with the goal of achieving an effective Catholic voice in national affairs.

Dubbed "the national idea," the plan was ambitious. It called upon the bishops to adopt a new structure for mutual deliberation and to develop an agenda for public leadership. As a result of the war, the public was newly aware of the strength of the church in American political and social life. Catholic support of the mobilization effort had left a major impression on American civic leaders, and any sign that this Catholic show of strength would be extended into peacetime was cause for both interest and concern. But few Americans, Catholics included, had any idea of the delicate ecclesiastical issues raised by this proposal.

Supporters of the proposal knew very well that the plan constituted an innovation in ecclesiastical tradition. It called for an annual assembly of

American bishops to act as a consultative body on issues of common concern and social policy, and for a standing committee or "secretariat" in the nation's capital to execute the decisions of the assembly of bishops. The advocates of the plan recognized that the proposal could appear to threaten the traditional independence of each bishop in his own diocese and to intrude a potentially powerful decision-making body between the individual bishop and Rome. Nevertheless, they urged the bishops in Caldwell Hall to vote for the "national idea," describing it to both the hierarchy and the press as a necessary response to the times.

In the next order of business at the September meeting, the assembly elected Denis J. O'Connell, bishop of Richmond and former rector of the North American College in Rome, as secretary for the hierarchy. Although his duties were confined to taking the minutes of the meeting, Bishop O'Connell's election had a larger significance. His ecclesiastical colleagues were very aware of the role he played in the Americanist controversy of the 1890s. In that divisive period, members of the hierarchy broke into open dispute with one another over the issues surrounding the Americanization or "inculturation" of the church. Bishop O'Connell was an outspoken supporter of the Americanist view and had argued for the positive relationship between the American culture to Catholicism. Now, as the first officer to be elected by the American hierarchy in modern times, he would record the discussion of his fellow bishops as they considered the national plan.

Bishop O'Connell's minutes show that immediate concern and skepticism were voiced by bishops as they reviewed the proposal. Bishop Charles McDonnell of Brooklyn, for instance, felt that the proposed organization conflicted with canon law and threatened to interfere with the jurisdiction of bishops in their own dioceses. He also privately thought the new organization was the creation of certain "New York Catholics" interested in wresting dominance from the Knights of Columbus in the social and civic affairs of the church. And Cardinal William O'Connell of Boston brushed aside the arguments of supporters of the proposal, declaring that the church was already "divinely organized" and needed nothing more than perhaps "an annual meeting to discuss a few leading questions and pass on them." Bishop Michael Gallagher of Detroit noted that, after all, the proposed organization "would be only advisory [to the hierarchy] like a similar committee in Ireland."

But the minutes show that backers of the proposal had enough support and political deftness to win a sympathetic hearing for the proposal, and the

National Catholic Welfare Council (NCWC) was approved by a majority of the bishops.[1] The NCWC was announced to the press as the national organization of the American bishops, structured around an annual meeting of the hierarchy and an executive secretariat that would act as the agent of the hierarchy in the public interests of the church. In 1922 the name was changed from the National Catholic Welfare Council to the National Catholic Welfare Conference.

A number of organizational initiatives had prepared the way for the 1919 Caldwell Hall meeting. In 1900, several prominent lay Catholics, and a bishop or two, launched a movement to federate the large number of independent Catholic societies then in existence. The goal of the American Federation of Catholic Societies (AFCS) was to increase Catholic strength in American civic life by uniting the power of Catholic organizations. And in 1910, the National Conference of Catholic Charities (NCCC) was founded to encourage greater efficiency in Catholic social and civic work. When the United States entered World War I in 1917, leaders experienced in both of these earlier movements collaborated to form the immediate predecessor of the NCWC, the National Catholic War Council. A brief review of these three organizations will set the context for the 1919 meeting of the hierarchy.

The National Conference of Catholic Charities

The aims of the NCCC anticipated those of the NCWC, and many of the same Catholic leaders figured in both conferences. The NCCC was a voluntary forum for national consultation on questions pertaining to the reform of society and the delivery of social services by Catholics. It was created and sustained largely through the vision and energies of William Kerby, priest and sociologist at Catholic University of America. Kerby had for many years stressed the importance of organization for Catholics who wished to respond

---

1. "Minutes of the First Annual Meeting of the American Hierarchy," September 24-25, 1919. NCWC Papers, Archives of the Catholic University of America (ACUA). (The first day ended with a more mundane matter: "At this time there was a discussion, participated in by Archbishop Glennon and Bishop Curley, in regard to raising the offering for low masses to $2.00. Bishop Donahue moved, seconded by Bishop Schrembs, that the stipend be as it is at present, $1.00. Carried.")

to the "social question."[2] Eager to see Catholics develop organizational sophistication in support of their social welfare activities, he had promoted the creation of a national federation of Catholic women's organizations for social work in 1908. Called the St. Margaret's Union, its existence was brief, but its intentions were carried over in the organization of the NCCC.

The NCCC drew under its purview the whole range of social issues, from the problems of orphans and of single women working in the new industrial and service sectors of the cities, to the concern to stimulate social research and international contacts in support of Catholic charitable efforts. Modern charity is organized, Kerby argued, because modern conditions require it, and modern conditions make new requirements on the church as well. Meeting biannually until 1920, and then meeting once a year, the conference acted as national focus for the development of a Catholic social agenda, and pressed Catholics involved in charitable and social work to adopt the new methods of "scientific charity" and professional education. Conference meetings were attended by an ecumenical mix of clergy and laymen, particularly those involved in the activities of the Society of St. Vincent de Paul. There was also a notable presence of laywomen at the conference meetings. Both married and single, these women were eagerly seeking training in the new methods of social work and anxious to make a social contribution as volunteer and professional workers.

The American Federation of Catholic Societies

The other early organizational initiative that should be considered in reviewing the formation of the episcopal conference is the American

---

2. Details of Kerby's involvement in both the National Conference of Catholic Charities and the National Catholic Welfare Conference are available in Timothy Michael Dolan, "Prophet of a Better Hope: The Life and Work of Monsignor William Joseph Kerby" (Master's thesis, Catholic University of America, 1981).

Kerby's earlier articles in John Burke's *Catholic World* contained a careful analysis of what he called the "social reinforcements of the bonds of faith." He urged Catholic leaders to recognize the importance of social organization in the formation of identity and in the reinforcement of institutional loyalties. *Catholic World* 74 (January 1907): 508-522; (February 1907): 591-606.

Federation of Catholic Societies (AFCS). Initiated in 1900 as a means of developing a common social agenda among the large societies of lay Catholics in the country, the history of the federation bears witness to the strength of lay Catholicism in the years before World War I. It also offers evidence of the growing desire of some American bishops to exercise more direct influence on the activities and resources of these societies. The federation movement, led originally by lay Catholics from the large societies, sought to unite those ethnically identified societies in an effort to improve the position of Catholics in American public life.

In the years before the war, the inherent difficulties of the federation movement and growing concerns about the independence of lay organizations voiced by Cardinal William O'Connell of Boston and Bishop Joseph Schrembs of Toledo, led to the erosion of the civic basis of the organization and to the end of the organization itself. The National Catholic War Council took its place in 1917. Historian Alfred J. Ede has concluded that "the story of its [AFCS] inability to maintain sufficient lay autonomy provides an important link in the account of the centralization and bureaucratization of the American Church following World War One."[3]

The National Catholic War Council

When America entered World War I, the concerns and experience represented by the NCCC and the AFCS were borrowed and reworked to become the substance of a new organization, the National Catholic War Council. The architect of the new organization was William Kerby's friend, the Paulist editor of *Catholic World*, John J. Burke, C.S.P. Burke, who had long been interested in creating a national center for American Catholicism.

---

3. Alfred J. Ede, *The Lay Crusade for a Christian America: A Study of the American Federation of Catholic Societies, 1900-1919* (New York: Garland, 1988), 379. Ede also concludes that "The National Catholic Welfare Council would speak with greater authority. . . . The American Church would operate with greater efficiency through the new agency, but such centralization came at the cost of the kind of grass roots organization and lay leadership that the Federation had struggled to attain, but which in the end it was unable to adequately provide."

He moved quickly and with evident sophistication to take advantage of the opportunity offered by wartime conditions.[4]

As mobilization proceeded, several interested organizations of Catholics began to contribute to the American Catholic war effort. The Knights of Columbus entered war work with great enthusiasm, eager to best the efforts of the YMCA in providing social and religious support for the American troops. Catholic clergymen became involved in supplying chaplains for Catholic soldiers, and Catholic women's organizations were eager to outfit the chaplains and support the soldiers with home comforts. These women also provided housing, travellers' aid, and general support for the women and girls who began to move into industry and thus into new social circumstances during the war.

Good will and organizational self-interest grew apace as the months passed, and the combination provided an opportunity for the ambitions of John Burke. After consultation with William Kerby and Charles Neill, a former U.S. commissioner of labor and another of Kerby's long-time friends, Burke presented a plan for a national Catholic wartime organization to Cardinals James Gibbons of Baltimore, William O'Connell of Boston, and John Farley of New York. After these prelates approved his plans, Burke wrote all dioceses and national Catholic societies, asking them to send representatives to a meeting at Catholic University of America in August 1917. There, he urged the 115 delegates to form the National Catholic War Council.

---

4. John Burke's biographer John B. Sheerin, C.S.P., notes that many of Burke's associates were aware of his prior interests in national organization. His secretary Helen Lynch indicated that she had "often seen him working on a plan in his office years before [the war.]" And Loretta Lawlor, a graduate of the National Catholic School of Social Service, wrote that Burke had "occupied himself with a scheme of organization for some sort of ecclesiastical agency through which Catholic action might be provided. . . . The thinking behind it became part of himself." Burke himself later said that "the NCWC was not thought out by me: it was given to me. From the beginning it was like a self-evident proposition." John B. Sheerin, C.S.P., *Never Look Back: the Career and Concerns of John J. Burke* (New York: Paulist Press, 1975), 38-40.

The same observation appeared in the many memorial essays that appeared after his death in 1936. The following recollection was offered by Mary G. Hawks, "the prudent, militant and far-seeing president" of the National Council of Catholic Women: "Perhaps he was happiest in the seclusion of an editor's sanctum. But there he dreamed dreams in the manner of Hecker, of the extended organization and influence of the Church in America, dreams that were, inevitably, to draw him out into the larger arena of work for the Church." Mary G. Hawks, "Father Burke: Editor, Author, Critic," *Catholic Action* 18 (December 15, 1936): 27.

The record of the War Council indicates that Burke was notably successful in his effort to centralize Catholic war work under the control of his organization. He arranged in particular to place the Knights of Columbus in a subordinate relationship to the War Council, and he convinced the U.S. War Department to regard the council and its administrative Committee on Special War Activities as the official agency of the church for war work.[5]

His success in creating a single national organization for the direction of Catholic war work was complemented by his ability to raise funds for a war chest and to lobby for Catholic causes. He was able to arrange an increase in the supply of Catholic military chaplains, for instance, and to gain draft exemptions for divinity students. He also established a training school to prepare Catholic women for war work in the cantonments and in Europe. His attention to the energies and potential of Catholic women was well rewarded, for they provided him with the work force for his organization's war and reconstruction activities.

His talent is further apparent in the manner in which he took advantage of concerns about the moral atmosphere surrounding the training and deployment of troops to organize an interdenominational committee of prominent clergymen, which he called the Committee of Six. This committee was quickly granted advisory status by the War Department. As chairman of the committee, Burke was able to make it his vehicle for representing Catholic interests to the War Department. The chairmanship provided Burke the basis for cultivating important public contacts and for claiming the role of government insider in dealing with other Catholic leaders.[6]

---

5. Knights of Columbus historian Christopher J. Kauffman provides an account of the relationship between Burke's NCWC and the KC during the war. Kauffman stresses the role of the "Wall Street Catholics"--influential New York Catholic laymen who supported Burke's initiatives and opposed the claims of the Knights to a place of priority in war work. Kauffman suggests that the intervention of Bishop Muldoon as a member of the NCWC's Administrative Committee brought peace between "the Wall Street Catholics" and the Knights. Because Burke sought to create just this sort of episcopal oversight, Kauffman's conclusion underscores the sophistication with which Burke was able to pursue his goals. Christopher J. Kauffman, *Faith and Fraternalism: the History of the Knights of Columbus, 1882-1982* (New York: Harper & Row, 1982).

6. The other members of the committee were John R. Mott of the YMCA, Episcopal Bishop James DeWolf Perry, Robert E. Speer and William Adams Brown of the Federal Council of Churches, and Colonel Harry Cutler of the Jewish Welfare Board. The War

The picture of Burke's political and ecclesiastical finesse is rounded out by noting his ability to gain episcopal approval for his organizational initiatives. He wanted to be able to claim the sanction of the American hierarchy for his War Council, and he saw to it that sympathetic bishops were appointed as the Administrative Committee for the council. As there were no existing corporate procedures for arranging those appointments, Burke turned again to Cardinal Gibbons as the ranking member of the hierarchy. He urged Cardinal Gibbons to ask the American archbishops to assume formal control of the activities of the new War Council and to appoint four bishops to assume responsibility for the ongoing oversight of War Council activities. These included two bishops who had been prominently active in the AFCS, namely Peter Muldoon of Rockford and Joseph Schrembs of Toledo. The support of these two prelates for the goals of national organization and their efforts to preserve the gains made during the war are evident in the account of the transition to the National Catholic Welfare Council after the Armistice.[7]

From War to Welfare

Following the conclusion of hostilities in 1918, the leadership of the War Council endeavored to build support for the continuation of the national organization. Bishop Muldoon's postwar administrative report to the archbishops argued that "the general impression among both priests and people is that the National War Council should continue to care for the interests of the Church." And John Burke issued a strongly worded memorandum on the necessity of a permanent organization to protect Catholic interests. He rejected an alternate proposal for informal meetings of the hierarchy and argued that the welfare of the church would suffer "irreparable damage" unless some provision was made for "a national committee with headquarters in Washington constantly at work."[8]

Department's Commission on Training Camp Activities under the leadership of Raymond Fosdick quickly granted official advisory status to the Committee of Six.

7. For fuller treatment of these events see my account of the history of the War Council in Elizabeth McKeown, *War and Welfare: American Catholics and World War I* (New York: Garland Press, 1988).

8. John J. Burke, C.S.P., "Memorandum on the Necessity of a Permanent National Committee with Headquarters at Washington for the Study, Advancement, Protection and

Supporters of national organization recognized the opportunity presented by the celebration in February 1919, of the golden jubilee of Cardinal Gibbons. On that occasion, a committee of three archbishops and four bishops responded to a papal message calling on Catholics of the United States to "unite in their efforts for the spread of justice and charity among all the peoples of the world" by recommending both an annual meeting of the hierarchy and a committee of bishops to plan a further response. They asked Cardinal Gibbons to name that committee of bishops; and he complied, naming three of the bishops of the Administrative Committee of the War Council. These bishops carried through the spring and summer of 1919 as the Committee on General Catholic Interests and Affairs and set the agenda for the 1919 meeting of the hierarchy.

When the bishops assembled at Catholic University of America in September and approved plans for national organization, they also elected the same War Council bishops to act as their administrators with power to "pass in their name on all questions arising during the year between the meetings of the Hierarchy." Those administrator-bishops then named John Burke to be general secretary of the organization and "personal representative of the Chairman of the Administrative Committee." Burke and his staff eagerly returned to the Washington offices of the War Council at 1312 Massachusetts Avenue, which had been purchased and financed with funds collected during the New York Catholic War Work campaign, and completed the transition from War Council to Welfare Council.

The daily activities of the Washington office resembled those of other interest groups. The NCWC acted as an information clearing house, issued pamphlets on social and educational issues, attended congressional hearings, maintained a news service for its constituents, worked to increase the number of its lay affiliates, and formed associations with other national and international organizations. But to achieve its goals, the NCWC had to depend on more than Washington contacts and political sophistication. It also had to win the ongoing support of the hierarchy it existed to serve. The Washington leadership, therefore, spent a great deal of time trying to foster the "cordial association" of the diocesan ordinaries in the national concerns of the NCWC.

Promotion of Catholic Needs and Catholic Interests," July, 1919, NCWC Papers, Archives of the United States Catholic Conference, Washington, DC.

NCWC leaders could not afford to have voices of episcopal dissent raised against their organization. They needed financing from the dioceses and the cooperation of local ordinaries in efforts to organize diocesan affiliates of the national council.

Toward these ends and to quiet the suspicions of those who thought the "national idea" would interfere with local episcopal autonomy, the leadership of the council consistently and emphatically presented the NCWC as a voluntary organization. Attendance at the annual meetings of the hierarchy remained voluntary, and there was regular reiteration of the fact that the decisions of the bishops who did attend had no formal canonical status. The original choice of "council" rather than "conference" in the title of the NCWC reflected the desire of the leadership to avoid the appearance of creating a competitor to challenge existing Catholic diocesan and lay organizations. They wanted both the bishops and the laity to see the NCWC as an opportunity to "take council" with one another, and did not intend "council" to be understood in canonical terms.[9] Most bishops came to recognize the importance of establishing episcopal oversight in the development of "the national idea" and responded with some degree of active or tacit approval, as is evident from the fact that eighty percent of the bishops signed a statement to Rome supporting the council in 1922.[10]

---

9. Administrative Committee member Bishop Edmund Gibbons offered this 1920 account of that important distinction:

> I might remark in passing that the selection of that word "Council" was not haphazard. The Bishops regarded themselves not exactly as a new organization. They were already an organization. They were the representatives of the greatest organization in the world, an organization after which any merely human organization might well pattern; namely, the Catholic Church. There was no need of an organization, strictly so-called, but rather that the representatives of that organization and the members of that organization already existing should come together in common council, unite their efforts and forces for the general welfare. So they denominated this body a "Council," the National Catholic Welfare Council.

Edmund Gibbons, "How the Hierarchy Aids the Nation through the Welfare Council: Address to the Albany Diocesan Council of Catholic Men," *The National Catholic Welfare Council Bulletin* 2 (October 1920): 15.

10. Details of the threatened suppression of the NCWC in 1922 and an account of the defense made to the Vatican by council leaders are available in Elizabeth McKeown, "Apologia

The Washington leadership remained the primary agent in developing the agenda of the organization. Episcopal participation remained rather selective through the period until Vatican II, and, after the death of John Burke in 1936, effective control of the NCWC passed into the hands of only a few members of the hierarchy. The diocesan bishops of Toledo, Columbus, Cleveland, Detroit, and finally New York dominated the leadership positions throughout the thirty-year period from Burke's death to reorganization of the conference as the National Conference of Catholic Bishops (NCCB) in 1966.

Early Leadership

The early leadership of the council was an interesting group that included the episcopal champions of national organization and clergy trained in the new social sciences. Bishops Peter Muldoon and Joseph Schrembs had both been active in the American Federation of Catholic Societies. Priest-participants in the NCWC included sociologist William Kerby of the NCCC, anthropologist John Montgomery Cooper, and moral theologian John A. Ryan. All three were faculty members at Catholic University of America and were involved beyond the academy in a variety of social causes. The initiative also won initial support from laymen with business or professional backgrounds and War Council experience. These included Charles Neill, a former U.S. Commissioner of Labor, John Lapp, lawyer and civic organizer, and Michael Slattery, president of the Young Men's Catholic Union.

A great many laywomen with social service experience and reform concerns also supported the initiative to create a national organization after World War I, and they ultimately provided the work force for most of the activities of the NCWC, as they had for the War Council. Leaders among the women included: Agnes Regan, longtime school board member from San Francisco and executive secretary for twenty years of the women's affiliate of the council, the National Council of Catholic Women (NCCW); Gertrude Hill Gavin, daughter of railroad magnate James Hill and first president of the NCCW; educational psychologist Anne Nicholson, who served as field director of the National Catholic School of Social Service and field representative for the NCCW; and civic and labor organizers Linna Bressette and Rose

---

for an American Catholicism," *Church History* 43 (December 1974): 514-28.

McHugh, both of whom were active on behalf of the NCWC, working most often for the Department of Social Action.

These leaders, both male and female, cleric and lay, agreed that the social philosophy of the church and charitable activities of Catholics lacked efficiency and public impact. In addition, their wartime experience convinced them that it was necessary to exercise specific forms of political influence in order to make Catholic strength effectively present in the American public policy process. John Burke's description of the methods of interest-group politics expressed both his concerns about the potential damage such practices might do to the American political process, and his determination to adopt such of those practices as were ethical in order to improve the ability of the church to enter into that process. He described the techniques of lobbying, constituency-building, influence peddling, and manipulation of public opinion, and pointed out that the special interests had learned to solicit endorsements from well-known individuals who knew little of the real significance of the proposed legislation. These testimonials, he suggested, impressed senators and congressmen who were voting on the measures. The interests further magnified the volume of public opinion in support of their causes through the adroit manipulation of the press, concerted letter-writing campaigns, and personal appearances. "When the matter is actually presented in the halls of Congress they who are back of it have the big advantage of position, of initiative, of planned campaign."[11]

Burke argued that Catholics must be able to provide capable and ready representation in Washington to combat such efforts and "to preserve our own fundamental religious rights and contribute our preeminent share to the legislation that will shape and control the destiny of our country." Thus, for example, the charge to the NCWC's Department of Laws and Legislation included keeping current on proposed legislation, judging whether legislation was "favorable or inimical to [church] interests," funneling information on legislative proposals to Catholic organizations at the state and local level, and counseling those organizations in their efforts to support or oppose legislative initiatives.

The Washington leadership was quite aware that these practices would draw charges that the church was "in politics," and they took pains to draw a

---

11. John Burke, "With Our Readers," *Catholic World* 111 (May 1920): 279-87.

formal distinction between their activities and those of the other interests. They considered themselves to be pursing legitimate "policy" initiatives rather than narrowly self-interested "political" activities. Bishop Edmund Gibbons of Albany, an early member of the Administrative Committee of bishops, carefully insisted that the NCWC representatives were not "lobbyists" or "backroom politicians." They "come out openly and boldly into the light of day to invite an inspection of their motives and methods" and "clearly proclaim Catholic needs, Catholic principles, Catholic rights, and Catholic objections to measures that may be pending before the National Congress."[12] NCWC leaders continued to emphasize that difference even though they also yielded to the temptation to boast of their own political skills and to contrast them with those of the Federal Council of Churches and the YMCA.

Defending Catholic Interests

When the bishops assembled again at Catholic University of America in September 1920, to review the results of the first year's activities of the NCWC, their discussions relied heavily on the rhetoric of interest and defense. Archbishop Edward Hanna of San Francisco, in his report as chairman of the Administrative Committee, emphasized the role of the NCWC in defending Catholic interests, and argued that

> whatever our strength may be, if it is scattered, dissipated, unable to summon its entire self, it will be weak and helpless before the trained, organized, watchful enemy. It is not too much to say that the vigorous, progressive life of the Church depends upon our ability to meet and defeat such opposition with a united Catholic body, with representatives ever on the watch; a united Catholic body ready to act whenever necessary.[13]

The protection of "Catholic interests" quickly became a staple of NCWC self-understanding and was the key element in the successful defense of the

---

12. Gibbons, "How Hierarchy Aids the Nation," 16.
13. "Important Functions of the N.C.W.C. Executive Department," *The National Catholic Welfare Council Bulletin* 2 (October 1920): 10.

organization against a threat of Vatican suppression in 1922. When the bishops of the Administrative Committee sent the Vatican an apologia for their organization, they echoed Archbishop Hanna's remarks, recalling that

> the Welfare Council grew out of a great fear and a great hope: the fear that hostile forces or organizations would make a successful attack upon Catholic interests, particularly our schools: the hope that the bishops, by fraternal union, would be able not only to protect Catholic interests, but to advance them, for the sake of religion and of our country.[14]

In the early years of the council, however, the rhetoric of defense was always accompanied by a strong positive regard for America and a conviction that the best interests of the church and the culture went hand in hand. To communicate this positive regard, NCWC leaders relied on another kind of rhetoric with roots in the new theology of the Mystical Body. In this usage, the Catholic "body" would flourish in the American environment, drawing nourishment from its surroundings even as it defended itself against attack. By maintaining a distinctive and strong identity of its own, the Catholic body would also form the heart and sinews of the American "body," providing it with strength, discipline, and vision. Indeed, in emphasizing the intimacy of the connection, NCWC rhetoric often blurred the distinction between Catholic and American bodies. "No part of the body may say it is independent of the health of the body itself," according to a council statement in 1920, and "every part is necessarily affected for good or ill by the good or poor health of the body." The national interests of the church thus bore a strong positive correlation to the best interests of the nation in the minds of the original leadership.[15]

John Burke was particularly attracted to the theology of the Mystical Body and used it to express his understanding of the American church and to provide a rationale for the NCWC.[16] He presented the council as an organic

---

14. "Report to His Holiness Pope Pius XI on the Work of the Administrative Committee of the National Catholic Welfare Council," April 25, 1922, p. 8, NCWC Papers, Chairman's File, ACUA.

15. See, for example, "Bishops Bring United Counsel to Problems of National Importance," *The National Catholic Welfare Bulletin* 2 (October 1920): 1.

16. John Sheerin notes that "among Burke's literary and theological works were several

expression of the American church, aiding the church to grow and develop in its new environment. He also relied heavily on Mystical Body language to explain innovations within the organization itself, as for example, his decision to employ laywomen as the backbone of his organizational work force. In a memorable instance, when Burke needed a code for communicating with his agent William Montavon about diplomatic initiatives in Mexico, he made the following cryptic assignments: the Holy See was the "head," the American bishops the "hand," and Burke himself the "heart" of the body. More conventionally, however, he assigned the role of the head to "the hierarchy."

But the hierarchy's headship was exercised by the bishops' Administrative Committee and the Washington leadership.[17] The vision of a publicly active church with a positive contribution to make to the culture belonged particularly to Burke and his colleagues in Washington. They were proposing, in effect, a new American ecclesiology, using the figure of the Mystical Body to portray the church in the United States as a living organism, thriving on a blend of Roman and American nutrients, and being directed by the NCWC to make a positive contribution to American life.

These intentions can be highlighted by noting that NCWC leaders deliberately chose the term "welfare" in their organizational title to announce their concern for the health of both the church and the nation. "Welfare" was used to speak not only of church interests in political terms but to address the need for greater organization and rationalization of Catholic resources for public service. NCWC leaders intended to offer institutional support to the initiatives of the National Conference of Catholic Charities. They hoped to become instrumental in the efforts and to introduce the methods of "scientific charity" into Catholic charitable work and to develop a programmatic approach to issues of social justice and charity.[18] Therefore, they borrowed the

---

translations from the French, notably *The Doctrine of the Mystical Body of Christ* by J. Anger [New York: Benziger Books, 1931]. The doctrine of the Mystical Body runs like a golden thread through all his [Burke's] spiritual writings." Sheerin, *Never Look Back*, 34-35.

I am indebted to Anglyn Dries, O.F.M., for the suggestions contained in her "To Build Up the Body of Christ: Roman Catholic Ecclesiology in the United States: Baltimore II to 1918" (Berkeley, CA: Graduate Theological Union, 1987, Photocopy), in which she traces the development of the language of the Mystical Body in American ecclesiology.

17. Sheerin, *Never Look Back*, 28.

18. William Kerby's reflection on the NCWC amplifies these points:

term "welfare" from the emerging profession of social work and adapted it to embrace a broad range of public concerns, including child welfare and education, industrial relations, immigration, and housing, as well as the new interest in social case work.

The Role of the Family

Seeking a positive public role in American life, the NCWC framed its program in the terms provided by the developing tradition of Catholic social teaching. That tradition, and the NCWC expressions of it, depended on a particular understanding of the role of the family in social life. The substance of the idea in Catholic social teaching was clear and comprehensive. The family was viewed as the basic social unit, and it mediated between the individual and the state. In its ideal form, it behaved in response to a growing body of church teachings which defined the roles and responsibilities of family members and reinforced the obedience of parents to church directives. The ideal family also represented a bulwark against socialism and secularism, and, in its American version, was regarded as a means of improving the economic circumstances and encouraging upward mobility among members of the working class. NCWC leaders saw the family acting as the bridge between immigrants and other Americans, even while it provided common ground among the various groups of ethnic Catholics. They based their social program on this idea of the family, and consistently championed causes that promoted the family in American life.[19]

The present-day trend toward larger association, mutual discussion of methods and results, understanding among agencies that deal with like conditions could not have attained its present proportions without affecting the life and spirit of the Church. . . . [The NCWC] means the correction of a certain degree of provincialism, and helpful coordination of all of the geographical and institutional units of the Church's life. That this process holds forth promise of great stimulation and increased efficiency in our charities is beyond question.

William Kerby, *The Social Mission of Charity* (Washington, DC: NCWC, 1920), 165.

19. This view of the social program of the episcopal conference is developed at length in Elizabeth McKeown, "The Seamless Garment: The Bishops' Letter in the Light of the American Catholic Pastoral Tradition," in *The Deeper Meaning of the Economic Life: Critical Essays on the*

This view of family depended heavily on the role assigned to women, and it therefore included very explicit prescriptions for the behavior of women as wives, mothers, and church members. Any threat to this connection seemed to place the modern social teaching of the church and the program of the NCWC in jeopardy, and NCWC leaders therefore devoted a great deal of time to "the woman question." In their 1922 report to the Vatican, the bishops of the Administrative Committee voiced their concern that women were being malignly influenced by new ideologies and cultural practices. They drew Vatican attention to "the feminist movement" and to "women's societies [that] are in many cases the most active propagandists of evil." The Nineteenth Amendment was passed in 1919 and ratified in 1920, and the report suggested that "the granting of the franchise to women has made many of them aggressive, and their new power has excited many and led them to adopt the most radical ideas."[20]

The growing use of contraceptives by American women particularly worried the NCWC leadership, who saw it as a major challenge to their view of the family and thus to their social program. The 1922 report to Rome concluded that "if the effort of the Birth Control propagandists is successful, it will mean the degradation of the moral life of the entire social body." The bishops of the Administrative Committee portrayed the NCWC as a lonely defender of the society, insisting that "the power that has saved it [the social body] so far from such degradation is the National Catholic Welfare Council. That is the only strong organized power fighting this propaganda today."[21]

Reproductive issues have, of course, remained a key element in the identity and social program of the episcopal conference. The current efforts to pursue a "consistent ethic of life," in the social teaching and policy initiatives of the bishops' conference, originated in response to reproductive issues, although abortion has replaced contraception as the chief concern. It is noteworthy that already in the 1920s, Catholic leaders knew that the "propaganda of Birth Control" was reaching the Catholic population, and they began to voice private concerns about the use of contraceptives by Catholics,

---

U.S. Catholic Bishops' Pastoral Letter on the Economy, ed. Bruce Douglass (Washington, DC: Georgetown University Press, 1986).

20. "Report to His Holiness," 25.

21. "Report to His Holiness," 26-27.

even as they publicly stepped up their opposition to the practice. In a memorandum to the apostolic delegate in 1927, anthropologist John M. Cooper of The Catholic University of America acknowledged that "it is generally recognized by the Catholic clergy, and by Catholic and non-Catholic lay students of the problem, that contraceptive practices are very widespread among our Catholics in the United States." Cooper estimated that "perhaps up to 75% or at least 50% among the well-to-do and educated" used contraception, although the numbers decreased among the foreign-born Catholics and the working class. He informed the delegate that "we are destined almost inevitably to see a great increase in the prevalence of the practice among Catholics in this country within the next generation."[22]

The leadership of the council linked the social teaching on the family and the associated concerns about reproductive issues and women to a range of other NCWC agendas, including the promotion of Catholic parochial education, and the council's efforts to control and direct the new cultural forces of film and radio. Meanwhile, the ideal of the family, in which a woman worked at home raising children while the husband earned an adequate salary, was the basic premise of John A. Ryan's "living wage" proposals and of the NCWC's support of the proposed child labor amendment. John O'Hara's rural life program was developed around the rural family, and the National Council of Catholic Women devoted itself to promoting the NCWC's family-related programs. "Family" was the touchstone for the legislative activities of the NCWC and the basis of its efforts to enter the church into the formation of American public policy on behalf of justice and charity.

The NCWC continued to give programmatic attention to policy issues in the areas of housing, employment, co-operative ownership of industry, minimum wage, immigration, and peace, especially through the efforts of Raymond McGowan and Linna Bressette of the NCWC's Department of Social Action. But these initiatives were consistently overshadowed by the challenge to the family posed by birth control, the film industry, and the perceived threats to parochial schools. As a result of the demand made by these issues on NCWC attention and resources, and because of the ease with

---

22. John B. Cooper, "Memorandum on Prevalence of Contraception among Catholics of the United States," and cover letter to George Leech, secretary to the apostolic delegation, February 1, 1927, John B. Cooper Papers, Box #36, ACUA.

which these issues assumed priority in light of the family argument, the NCWC failed to sustain strong initiatives in other areas of social concern.[23]

The Response of Lay Catholics

John A. Ryan criticized the NCWC for its lack of success in shaping public policy on social justice issues as early as 1921, but he attributed much of the blame for the failure to the reactions of Catholic businessmen. "A few years ago, if someone had suggested to me that I should one day be in charge of a department on industrial relations [the NCWC's Department of Social Action] under the direction and with the support of the Hierarchy of the United States, I would have declared that it was an idle dream," he observed. "Now that I have been in that position for about a year and a half, I do not know that it is the beautiful situation that I had expected it to be." He judged many of the laity to be either ignorant or indifferent. "We reached up into the cloudland of Catholic social principles and pulled one down and set it going [in the open shop campaign]," he reported, only to find that "our social principles are not recognized by large sections of our own people, and when attempt is made to apply these principles to actual conditions, the expression of them is given the lie by the practice of powerful laymen."[24]

Many of those same "powerful laymen" who opposed the NCWC on economic and labor issues also repeatedly resisted calls to affiliate with the work of the council, and their absence left a vacuum that was largely filled by the clergy. The Catholic laity remained a missing or mismanaged ingredient

---

23. Joseph McShane has recently argued that the publication of John A. Ryan's "Program of Social Reconstruction" in 1919 marked the beginning of a new tradition of social liberalism on the part of the American bishops. The argument being developed in this paper suggests that the letter was issued in some haste by the post-war group of Washington leaders in an attempt to establish a social policy for the American church, and that the ideology of the family that provided the foundation of NCWC practice was not adequate to sustain a "progressive" social program in the NCWC. See Joseph McShane, *Sufficiently Radical: Catholicism, Progressivism, and the Bishops' Program of 1919* (Washington, DC: Catholic University Press, 1986.)

24. John A. Ryan, "Remarks to the National Council of Catholic Women," *Proceedings of the National Council of Catholic Women*, First Annual Convention, September 1920, NCCW Papers, ACUA.

in the development of the NCWC. John Burke warned explicitly against this outcome. In his 1919 memorandum urging the formation of the council, Burke insisted that the hierarchy "must not give the impression that it is assuming leadership in all activities nor inspiring all" and added that it would be "disastrous" to do so. "The laity must understand that they have both the pleasure and the responsibility of the heat of the day." And the 1922 report of the Administrative Committee to the Vatican argued that "in a democracy it is impossible to have power without the cordial cooperation of the laity," and suggested that Catholic lay societies "formed a channel through which Catholic influence could be brought to bear in the lobbying efforts of the Council."

NCWC leaders and field workers worked very hard in the early years of the council to win the support of the large societies of lay Catholics, urging them to accommodate themselves to the parish and diocesan organizational models prescribed by the NCWC. But this plan to make the powerful organizations of lay Catholics redistribute their influence through parish and diocesan channels reflected long-standing episcopal fears of lay independence. It clearly signaled the hierarchy's intention to exercise greater control over lay initiatives. The 1922 report to Rome noted that "there is a danger that ecclesiastical authority may not be duly regarded or consulted [by Catholic societies]. . . . Clerical control or direction is not always welcome. We have felt therefore, that there is need of the Hierarchy taking a more active interest in Catholic societies."[25]

Thus, in spite of the efforts of Washington and the support of many of the bishops, the lay organizations of men continued to resist "the national idea" under NCWC leadership. The Knights of Columbus, to cite only the most prominent example, had been at odds with War Council leadership during the war and continued to refuse to affiliate its large membership with the NCWC. The continued weakness of the men's affiliate, the National Council of Catholic Men, deprived the council of the financial and professional support of active laity, and is an example of the passivity that developed

---

25. Bishop Schrembs made it clear to Anthony Matre, the national secretary of the declining American Federation of Catholic Societies, that the new national organization would change the role of the independent lay Catholic societies: "It is true that the present arrangement has made quite a change in the status of lay activities and societies, placing them absolutely under our present committee. . ." Reported by Anthony Matre to C. Steeger of Belgium, October 10, 1919, NCWC Papers, Overseas, Box 8, Folder 24, ACUA.

toward the NCWC after the initial period of independent leadership and enthusiasm.[26]

Besides being unsuccessful in attracting the support of organizations of Catholic laymen, the NCWC was unable to overcome the racism of its own constituency in order to incorporate the energies and good will of black Catholics into its program. The most obvious example of that failure is available in the account of a group of black Catholics led by Thomas Wyatt Turner. Turner organized his group for the express purposes of opposing racism in American Catholicism and furthering the participation of black Catholics in the church. Initially calling themselves the "Committee against the Extension of Race Prejudice in the Church" (1917) and then the "Committee for the Advancement of Colored Catholics" (1919), Turner and his supporters eventually formed the Federated Colored Catholics in the United States (1924) and met annually until 1932. These Catholics consistently sought to establish some connection with the NCWC in order to advance its causes and strengthen its own organization, but the NCWC was completely unresponsive, and the black leadership was given to understand that the time was inopportune.[27]

---

26. In 1956, C. Joseph Nuesse, then dean of the School of Social Sciences at The Catholic University of America observed that:

> European visitors, after first visit to the N.C.W.C., have been heard to remark that priests are over-represented on the staff. The organization is, of course, the instrument of the bishops. Moreover, for fairly evident historical reasons, laymen have seldom been appointed in the United States to certain types of positions in ecclesiastical structures which are open to them in Europe. . . . It can only be said that, whatever view is taken of an alleged tendency to "clericalism" in American Catholicism, the N.C.W.C. can hardly be represented as a principle instrument of such a tendency.

C. Joseph Nuesse, "N.C.W.C.," in Louis Putz, *The Catholic Church in the United States* (Chicago: Fides Publishers, 1956).

27. See Marilyn Wenzke Nickels, *Black Catholic Protest and the Federated Colored Catholics, 1917-1933* (New York: Garland, 1988). NCWC organizers had not been unaware of, nor free from, the racism of the American Catholic church. In his first annual report, Archbishop Hanna noted that the bishops of the administrative committee saw the NCWC as "one of the most effective means of settling racial difficulties. . . . For example, we have planned for an auxiliary colored division of the Men's and Women's Council that will both show our interest in and our solicitude for their people, and encourage and help them to work among and for their own."

The Women of the NCWC

In the case of white Catholic women, however, the record is distinctly different. The NCWC sought the support of women and received a dedicated response from both individuals and organizations. Incorporated as the National Council of Catholic Women (NCCW), they successfully organized diocesan councils, created an international network of Catholic women, and enlisted thousands of women in support of council initiatives. NCCW members also acted as the paid field organizers of the Social Action Department (SAD) and travelled extensively on behalf of its initiatives and causes.

The major commitment of the NCCW was to finance and conduct their own school of social work, the National Catholic School of Social Service. This initiative endured in the face of great financial and organizational difficulties, sustained by the conviction of women like Agnes Regan, who acted in leadership capacities in both the NCCW and the NCSSS until her death in 1943. The women who attended the school located on 19th Street in Washington studied the new social sciences, received instruction in social work methods, and listened to lectures on Catholic social thought and moral theology from priest-activists like John A. Ryan, William Kerby, and Raymond McGowan. They completed a two-year graduate program and went on to employment with diocesan Catholic charities and to secular social work positions. Their schooling and professional contributions figured prominently in the larger agenda of the "national idea."

The NCWC also intended to open a school for men. But the tepid response from the male lay societies made such an initiative impossible. Eventually, John O'Grady, who was Kerby's student and his successor as secretary of the NCCC, opened a school of social work for men at Catholic University. His primary goal in that initiative was not to train lay Catholic men in social work, but to train priests to become directors of diocesan Catholic charities. O'Grady acted as the first dean of the school, but did not survive long in the office. The school was not solidly established until it absorbed the students and resources of the women's school after the death of Regan.[28]

Such auxiliaries were never formed, and blacks were not invited into the lay councils until after World War II.

28. See accounts of this episode in the O'Grady Papers (ACUA) and in the following

In the meantime, the NCWC continued to form the agenda for the women being trained at the NCSSS. The 1922 report of the bishops of the Administrative Committee to Rome emphasized the importance of social work and social workers and underlined the NCWC's role in founding the school for women. The bishops noted that the American Catholic church was not "nearly as well equipped for this work as our non-Catholic fellow-workers," and then using the rhetoric of defense, they went on to explain to the Vatican that they sought to obtain workers from the NCSSS "to counteract the influence of social centres which have become centres of radical propaganda or of Protestant proselytism, and thus have seduced many from the Faith."[29] The bishops drew a close connection between the work of these professional women and the interests of the American church, and although their assignment was couched in very defensive terms, women workers were clearly becoming an important part of the program of the NCWC. Through its school of social work, the NCCW was providing a new professional woman for the American church.

Perhaps because of the importance of the women's council to the goals of the NCWC, the parent organization persistently cautioned against NCCW independence and urged the subordination of women to episcopal authority. The desire to retain control of the NCCW was evident in the initial insistence of the bishops of the Administrative Committee that NCCW must organize itself along diocesan lines rather than by affiliation with independent national societies of Catholic women, such as the Daughters of Isabella or the Christ Child Society. There was a good deal of reaction to this plan, and the reaction eventually forced the bishops to compromise and permit affiliation through the societies as well as through the diocese. But the episcopal fears of NCCW independence persisted. An admonition of Bishop Joseph Schrembs provides an example of the episcopal style.

Bishop Schrembs was the bishop administrator of the NCWC's Department of Lay Organizations and had oversight of the NCCW in the 1920s. He addressed the yearly conventions of the NCCW and stressed on

---

institutional records in ACUA: Meetings of the Faculty, School of Social Work (CUA); Minutes of the Advisory Committee of the Diocesan Directors of Catholic Charities to the School of Social Work, 1933-39 (CUA); and Papers of the National Catholic School of Social Service.

29. "Report to His Holiness," 25.

each occasion the importance of obedience. "Don't imagine for one minute," he told 800 delegates in 1921, "that you can pull away and go out on your own personal responsibility, loose from the leaders of the church." That action, he added, would constitute "one of the most damnable heresies of the present day."[30] The bishop then went on to urge the women to commit their organization in opposition to the Equal Rights Amendment and to the campaign for birth control, and they did so. The subsequent record of the National Council of Catholic Women demonstrates that the contributions of women were central to the goals of the NCWC. Women had come out to work for the church and for the "national idea" after World War I. As the vision of the public work of national Catholic organization was translated into specific programs, the presence of women was clearly welcomed, and their energies and talents were carefully controlled and channeled to support the family foundation of that public work.[31]

Conclusion

Although their original leaders saw them as necessary partners in "the national idea," the National Conference of Catholic Charities remained quite distant from the NCWC and, under the leadership of John O'Grady, the national charities organization seemed committed to maintaining a separate organizational identity. But the diocesan charities that formed the NCCC

---

30. Joseph Schrembs, "Remarks to the National Council of Catholic Women," *Proceedings of the National Council of Catholic Women*, First Annual Convention, September 1920, NCWC Papers, ACUA. The stenographer's report of the convention proceedings carefully noted that women greeted Schrembs' remarks with "laughter and applause."

31. Printed sources bearing on the history of the National Council of Catholic Women include the *National Catholic Welfare Conference Bulletin* and its successor *Catholic Action*, and Loretto Lawlor's history of the National Catholic School of Social Service, *Full Circle* (Washington, DC: Catholic University of America Press, 1951). There are two master's theses on the subject, including Dorothea Doane Keplinger, "A Study of the Conventions of the National Council of Catholic Women of the National Catholic Welfare Conference, 1920-1939" (Washington, DC: Master's thesis, National Catholic School of Social Service, 1940) and Mary Martinita Mackey, "The Formal Structure of the National Council of Catholic Women: Patterns of Formal Organization in a Federated Group" (Master's thesis, Catholic University of America, 1949). There is also quite a rich oral resource in the women who were schooled by the NCSSS or who worked for the NCWC/NCCW.

experienced a development parallel to that of the NCWC, and became committed to a similar "family" approach to modern social questions and to public policy issues. Under the impact of the development of co-operative fund-raising for charities in the 1920s, state welfare in the 1930s, and the evolution of the profession of social work away from social reform and toward casework and psychiatric models, Catholic charities became increasingly devoted to the practice of family casework and eager to incorporate the family argument of modern Catholic social teaching. They also became centralized under diocesan control and developed a characteristic organizational structure in which professionally trained women constituted the vast majority of case workers and supervisors, while clergy acted as executive officers of the increasingly powerful diocesan charity organizations. The NCCC did not join the NCWC's efforts to shape national policy, nor did it succeed in establishing a substantial position on its own in public policy decisions, in spite of several efforts by John O'Grady to represent social justice issues in Congress.[32]

In the meantime, "the national idea" remained alive in the NCWC, but in a much transformed manner. The organization survived an attempt on the part of its opponents in 1922 to have it suppressed by the Vatican, but it seemed to lose the original vision of an organization in which the church-- laity, clergy, and bishops--could together make a positive contribution to American public life. The change of the title of the organization at the behest of the Vatican in the 1922 from "Council" to "Conference" seems in retrospect to have marked the eclipse of that original animating spirit and to announce instead the mood of defensiveness that became characteristic of the work of the conference.

The leadership of the conference did become Washington insiders. And the NCWC did come to be perceived by politicians and other national interest groups as the "voice" of American Catholicism, as it continued to act as the liaison between the church and the White House and Capitol Hill. But the conference leadership grew increasingly suspicious of modern America, and lost its desire to mobilize a positive Catholic contribution to the public life. Instead, the NCWC spent its dollars and time defending Catholic interests,

---

32. For an extended account of O'Grady's activities in this regard see Thomas W. Tifft, "Toward A More Humane Social Policy: The Work and Influence of Msgr. John O'Grady," (Ph.D. dissertation, Catholic University of America, 1979).

urging Catholics to keep a distance from culture, and concentrating on the management of its own internal organization. Neither Burke's public theology of the Mystical Body nor the later Catholic Action initiatives of the bishops were able to overcome this growing sense of cultural suspicion and internal preoccupation.

In spite of the loss of the original vision, however, "the national idea" did provide the necessary inducement to persuade a majority of the members of the American hierarchy to accept a national episcopal organization and to acknowledge a public role for the church. The history of that conference since its reorganization in 1966 suggests, furthermore, that the goal of making the church a positive presence in American public life in support of justice and charity has been reanimated. These reflections on the NCWC are therefore intended as a context for the current discussions of Catholic social teaching and the public policy role of the church. The focal issues which have emerged from these discussions have important parallels in the history of the NCWC. These issues include: the exercise of joint episcopal authority; the relationship of the teaching of principles to the practice of policy formation; the developing roles of professionals and citizens, men and women, in the public work of the church; the relationship of justice to charity and of politics to spirituality in Catholic tradition; and the role of family and of reproductive issues in Catholic social teaching and practice.

In light of the parallels thus suggested between the NCWC and the NCCB, and with a large sense of the scholarly work yet to be done to develop those parallels, a preliminary conclusion might be stated as follows: Just as efforts to develop the "national idea" led to the creation of the episcopal conference in the United States and encouraged Catholic concern for the public good, so the current activities of the conference may serve both to refine the process of decision making in the American church and to enhance the ability of Catholic Christians to make a positive contribution to American public life. If so, the lessons gained from the history of the NCWC should prove to be very useful.

Gerald P. Fogarty, S.J.

The Authority of the National Catholic Welfare Conference

GERALD FOGARTY is professor of church history at the University of Virginia, Charlottesville

The National Catholic Welfare Council was formed in 1919--the subheading on its stationery was "The Hierarchy of the United States of America." It came into being at a time of increased centralization of legislative authority. The Code of Canon Law of 1917, for example, removed the right of primates to preside over plenary or national councils and gave it to papal legates or delegates[1]--a dead issue for the church in the United States,, which did not have a primatial see. The only provision in the code for episcopal "conferences" was the quinquennial gathering of bishops of each province who were to draw up the agenda for provincial councils to be held every twenty years.[2] This left the presidency over national meetings or "conferences" of bishops vague, but seemed to place it in the hands of whoever was senior cardinal.[3] The new code and other legislation from Rome stood in sharp contrast with the earlier canonical tradition of the church in the United States.

Collegiality in the Nineteenth Century

In the nineteenth century, the American bishops had developed a strong sense of collegiality. They held provincial councils on a regular basis from 1829 to 1849, when new metropolitan provinces were established. They petitioned, unsuccessfully, that Baltimore be declared the primatial see of the United

---

1. *Codex Iuris Canonici*, c. 281.
2. Ibid., c. 292.
3. Ibid., c. 239, §1, no. 21.

States--a distinction that would have empowered the archbishop of the nation's oldest see to preside over plenary councils. In the three plenary councils that were held in 1852, 1866, and 1884, the archbishop of Baltimore was delegated by the Holy See to preside over the assemblies.

The American bishops, however, not only acted collegially; they also consciously expressed their concept of acting as a college under the presidency of the pope. At their first provincial council in 1829, they touched upon the notion of collegiality in their treatment of the relationship of Scripture to authority in their pastoral letter.

> We know not that it is the word of God, except by the testimony of that cloud of holy witnesses which the Saviour vouchsafed to establish as our guide through this desert over which we journey towards our permanent abode. Together with the book they gave to us the testimony of its meaning. . . . Thus the recorded testimony of those ancient and venerable witnesses, who in every nation and every age, proclaimed in the name of the Catholic church, and with its approbation, the interpretation of the Holy Bible, whether they were assembled in their councils or dispersed over the surface of the Christian world, is an harmonious collection of pure light, which sheds upon the inspired page the mild lustre which renders it pleasing to the eye, grateful to the understanding, and consoling to the heart.[4]

The bishops were, of course, only stating that the bishops of the early church testified not only to what was the word of God but also to its meaning. But Francis P. Kenrick, a theologian at that first council, and later bishop of Philadelphia and archbishop of Baltimore, saw that charism continuing in the bishops of his own age. In his *Theologia Dogmatica*, he wrote that the church of the Apostles, of the fathers, and of his own age continued to be under divine guidance in such a manner that one or even many bishops could fall into error, but "infallibility" or "the privilege of inerrancy" continued to reside "in the body of the bishops, under the presidency of the Roman Pontiff."[5]

---

4. Hugh J. Nolan, ed., *Pastoral Letters of the American Hierarchy, 1792-1970* (Huntington, Ind.: Our Sunday Visitor, 1971), 51-52.

5. Francis P. Kenrick, *Theologia Dogmatica*, vol. 1 (Baltimore: J. Murphy, 1858), 227-28.

At the Second Plenary Council in 1866, only three years before Vatican I, the American bishops were yet more explicit in stating their sense of participating in the magisterium. Among the conciliar decrees was the following:

> Bishops, therefore, who are the successors of the Apostles, and whom the Holy Spirit has placed to rule the church of God, which He acquired with His own blood, agreeing and judging together with its head on earth, the Roman Pontiff, whether they are gathered in general councils, or dispersed throughout the world, are inspired from on high with the gift of inerrancy, so that their body or college can never fail in faith nor define anything against doctrine revealed by God.[6]

By the Third Plenary Council in 1884, however, the American bishops had begun to lose the theology that underlay their practice of collegiality. First of all, the council was the only one convoked at Roman and not American initiative. In preparation for the council, the archbishops were summoned to Rome for preliminary meetings in 1883 with officials of the Congregation of Propaganda to draft the schemata for the council--the only time the American metropolitans were summoned to Rome until 1989. But that council did occasion the emergence of a new form of collegiality. As a result of certain conciliar legislation and the right of archbishops to be consulted on the candidates for vacant metropolitan sees, the archbishops began to hold annual meetings in 1890. These meetings were strictly consultative, and the prelates received a strong rebuke when they sought at their first meeting to assume the right to reject the canonical lists for a metropolitan see of Milwaukee and substitute one of their own.[7] These meetings did, however, provide a basis for a more formal consultation of the American episcopacy on national affairs.

There were other changes in American canon law on the eve of the 1917 code, however, that diminished the earlier sense of collegiality. Since the

---

6. *Concilii Plenarii Baltimorensis II. In Ecclesia Metropolitana Baltimorensi a die VII. ad diem XXI., Octobris A.D. MDCCCLXVI. Habiti et a Sede Apostolica Recogniti Acta et Decreta*, 2nd. ed. (Baltimore: John Murphy, 1894), no. 50, p. 41.

7. See Gerald P. Fogarty, *Vatican and the American Hierarchy from 1870 to 1965* (Wilmington, Del.: Michael Glazier, Inc., 1985), 49-53.

Second Plenary Council of 1833, bishops of each province had drawn up a
terna of candidates for any vacant or newly established see. In 1884, under
pressure of the Congregation of Propaganda, the bishops decreed that certain
"quasi-parishes" were to enjoy irremovability. The "quasi-pastors" of these
churches, together with the diocesan consultors, were now to draw up a *terna*
when their diocese was vacant, and this *terna* was to be submitted to the
bishops of the province. In 1916, the Consistorial Congregation rescinded this
decree. Henceforth, the bishops of each province were secretly to gather
names of potential episcopal candidates and submit them to the metropolitan.
Every two years, the metropolitan and his suffragans were to meet and
determine on a list of priests who were deemed worthy of the episcopacy. This
list was then sent to the apostolic delegate for forwarding to Rome. Significantly, the bishops of American provinces no longer actually made
nominations for a particular see, and the apostolic delegate now received a
greater official role in shaping the American episcopate.[8] This new legislation
on the appointing of bishops, together with the Code of Canon Law a year
later, provided the immediate context for the formation of the National
Catholic Welfare Council.

National Catholic War Council

World War I was the occasion for the American hierarchy to take the
first steps toward forming a national organization to coordinate Catholic
efforts on the national level. First, the American archbishops, at their annual
meeting in 1918, formed the National Catholic War Council, a committee
under their auspices to coordinate Catholic activity during World War I. Then,
in 1919, the War Council found a new lease on life. On February 20, the
hierarchy gathered for the golden jubilee of Cardinal James Gibbons,
archbishop of Baltimore, a celebration postponed from the previous year.
Gibbons was the last survivor of the First Vatican Council and of the Third
Plenary Council of Baltimore. He was, in fact, the senior bishop in the entire
hierarchy of the universal church.

Pope Benedict XV sent as his representative Archbishop Bonaventura
Cerretti, secretary of the Congregation of the Extraordinary Affairs of the

---

8. Ibid., 33, 129, 203, 208-209.

Church. Now that the world war was over, Cerretti, in the name of the pope, called for the American bishops to unite their efforts in working for peace, especially in the areas of education and social justice. Gibbons immediately appointed a committee to devise a proposal complying with the pope's wishes. The committee consisted of three archbishops and four bishops, including Bishops William Russell of Charleston, Joseph Schrembs of Toledo, and Peter Muldoon of Rockford, each of whom had been members of the War Council. The next day, the committee submitted a proposal calling for annual meetings of the hierarchy and for a standing committee appointed by the hierarchy to coordinate Catholic activities between the annual meetings. On April 10, Benedict XV gave his approval to what became known as the National Catholic Welfare Council.[9]

The NCW Council depended, to a great extent, on the benign neglect of Cardinal Gibbons, the senior cardinal in the American church--in 1919, William H. O'Connell of Boston was the only other American cardinal. But to listen to Archbishop Giovanni Bonzano, the apostolic delegate, Gibbons's influence was baneful. When Gibbons died in 1921, Bonzano reported on the state of the archdiocese of Baltimore. First, he reminded the cardinals of the Consistorial Congregation that the Congregation of Propaganda, with Pius IX's approval, had refused to name the archbishop of Baltimore the primate of the American church, but, instead, had designated that the see was to enjoy "prerogative of place." Second, he reported that many archbishops had complained that their annual meetings had been a waste of time and money, for they arrived without any agenda and Gibbons permitted little discussion. Bonzano concluded that "never should any archbishop of Baltimore or cardinal acquire the preponderance that in all affairs, by right or manipulation, Cardinal Gibbons assumed, not only in the meetings concerning the [Catholic] University but also in those of the archbishops and bishops."[10]

Bonzano made sure that no archbishop of Baltimore ever acquired dominance of the hierarchy by recommending only Michael J. Curley of St.

---

9. Elizabeth McKeown, "The National Bishops' Conference: An Analysis of Its Origins," *Catholic Historical Review* 66 (1980): 575-76; John Tracy Ellis, *Life of James Cardinal Gibbons: Archbishop of Baltimore, 1834-1921*, vol. 2 (Milwaukee: Bruce Publishing Co., 1952), 293-97.

10. Archivo Segreto Vaticano (Vatican City), DAUS, Liste Episcopali, 215, Bonzano to De Lai, n.p., May 12, 1921 (copy).

Augustine to be the new archbishop of Baltimore. Curley would never assume the dominance in national affairs of his predecessor. But there was another cardinal waiting in the wings to assume a role of domination. In 1921, Dennis Dougherty, archbishop of Philadelphia, had been named a cardinal. But O'Connell was the senior cardinal, a position that, according his reading of the Code of Canon Law--and the interpretation of Bonzano--gave him the right to preside over meetings of the American bishops. O'Connell, however, was not so much interested in sharing authority collegially with the other bishops as in exercising superiority over them.

Reeling from scandal in his own archdiocese that led to the dismissal of his nephew from the priesthood--he had been secretly married for over eight years--O'Connell received a sharp reprimand from the Holy See in the spring of 1921. Only a few months later, however, he was still pouring out his soul to his friend, Cardinal Raffaele Merry del Val, secretary of state under Pius X and then secretary of the Holy Office. "All around about," he said, there was "an intangible something which would seem to emanate from too much politics, diplomacy and intrigue--too much meddling with affairs which don't concern us. But thank God it does not exist around me." He longed for "the wonderful days of Pio X when the chief concern was God and when cheap politics and free-masons were kept in their place." He cherished the "memory of those days," for "conditions then were as near ideal as they ever can be," but he questioned: "Will they ever return?" For himself, he declared that "I shall live in the spirit of that holy time and rate intrigue at its true value--just zero."[11] Merry del Val, too, regretted "the prevalence of too much politics, worldly diplomacy and intrigue that are hardly in keeping with the lofty ideals of our mission, nor profitable to the best interests of God and of his Church. Here alas! we come up against it at every step, all day and every day."[12]

NCWC Attacked

It soon appeared that O'Connell and Merry del Val would have the opportunity to return the church to the ideal days of Pius X. On January 22,

---

11. Archives of the Archdiocese of Boston (hereafter AABo), O'Connell to Merry del Val, sometime after October 24, 1921 (copy).

12. AABo, Merry del Val to O'Connell, November 24, 1921.

1922, Benedict XV died. O'Connell and Dougherty arrived in Rome on February 6, only to learn that a new pope had been elected only a half hour before. O'Connell most probably would have voted for Merry del Val, though it is doubtful if a majority of the other cardinals would have wanted to return to the old order they had rejected in electing Benedict in 1914. But O'Connell was not done with his efforts to achieve dominance in the American church. As Dougherty was leaving Rome, he was handed a decree of the Consistorial Congregation, signed by Cardinal Gaetano De Lai, another of O'Connell's friends, and dated February 25. It ordered the immediate disbanding of the NCWC.

The members of the administrative committee of the NCWC took immediate action. First, they cabled Pius XI not to publish the decree until they could make a representation in Rome. With the permission of Cardinal Pietro Gasparri, the secretary of state, they then delegated Bishop Joseph Schrembs of Cleveland to take the case personally to Rome. Next, they circularized the trustees of the Catholic University of America and then the entire hierarchy to support a petition to save the NCWC. Finally, they arranged to have all the documents translated into Italian by Filippo Bernardini, professor of canon law at the Catholic University and a consultant to the apostolic delegation--it did not hurt that Bernardini was also Gasparri's nephew. They then entrusted this documentation to Archbishop Henry Moeller of Cincinnati, who was joining Schrembs in Rome.[13]

Bishop Louis Walsh of Portland, Maine, a member of the administrative board, saw in the Consistorial Congregation's action "a dangerous underhand blow from Boston, aided by Philadelphia, who both realized at our last meeting that they could not control the Bishops of this country and they secured the two chief powers of the Consistorial, Cardinals De Lai and Del Val [sic] to suppress all common action." Walsh hoped to enlist the support of Archbishops Curley of Baltimore and Patrick J. Hayes of New York in the effort to ward off the condemnation. To Hayes he added the comment that O'Connell had managed in Rome to mitigate some of the charges made

---

13. Archives of the NCWC, Administrative Board, April 6, April 25, April 26, pp. 32-36. For the text of the petition, see Elizabeth McKeown, "Apologia for an American Catholicism: The Petition and Report of the National Catholic Welfare Council to Pius XI, April 25, 1922," *Church History* 43 (1974): 514-28.

against his nephew and was now trying to take out his vengeance on the hierarchy.[14]

As O'Connell told Cardinal De Lai, he regarded this circularizing of the bishops as a "plebiscite" designed "to annul the force of the decree. The customary maneuver demonstrates again more evidently the wisdom of the decree. Today we are in full 'Democracy, Presybterianism, and Congregationalism.'" But, as O'Connell continued his fulminations, he revealed his ecclesiology:

> And now it seems more than ever that this N.C.W.C. shows more clearly that not only does it tend little by little to weaken hierarchical authority and dignity, but also wishes to put into operation the same tactics against the Consistorial.
>
> It is incredible that Rome does not see the danger of conceding today in order to have to concede *much more tomorrow*.[15]

Reading between the lines, O'Connell seemed to imply that hierarchical authority could not be exercised collegially, but that each individual bishop was dependent on the Holy See and even on one of the congregations. Of course, it helped if the individual bishop was the senior cardinal in the hierarchy with connections with the Consistorial. It mattered not to him that his "plebiscite" was signed by ninety percent of the American hierarchy.

In Rome, the American delegation found that the Consistorial readily believed O'Connell and Dougherty's protests against the NCWC because of the old specter of Americanism and the congregation's fear of such a large hierarchy meeting on an annual basis. The Consistorial's decree, moreover, reflected tension between Gasparri, who was supporting the Americans, and those cardinals who wanted a return to the policies of Pius X--so great was the tension that Pius XI sent Gasparri a public letter of support in the summer of 1922, which Gasparri faithfully forwarded to O'Connell. Ultimately, the American representation was successful. On July 4, 1922, the Consistorial

---

14. Archives of the Archdiocese of New York (hereafter AANY), Walsh to Hayes, Portland, April 9, 1922.

15. AABo, O'Connell to De Lai, Boston, May 10, 1922 (copy). O'Connell wrote a similar letter to Merry del Val.

issued a new instruction. The NCWC was to remain, but the congregation recommended, among other things, that perhaps the meetings of the hierarchy not take place every year, that attendance at them be voluntary, that decisions of the meetings not be binding or construed in any way as emanating from a plenary council, and that the name "council" in the title be changed to something like "committee."[16]

Council to Conference

The administrative board of the NCWC voted to change the name from "council" to "conference." This, too, evoked a charge of disloyalty to the Holy See from O'Connell, but the name remained until 1966. Though his ecclesiology was flawed, however, he did have a point. The National Catholic Welfare Conference was used interchangeably for three entities: the administrative board (the term "committee" was also used), the standing secretariat with its departments, and the annual meetings of the hierarchy.[17] This organization resulted in ambiguity. On the one hand, it was merely consultative in regard to individual bishops and the Holy See. On the other, it was perceived by the government and the public at large as the official voice of the American bishops. This ambiguity caused confusion about the organization's function within American society and within the hierarchy. Several examples will here suffice.

Dougherty and O'Connell distinguished between the standing secretariat and the annual meetings of the hierarchy. Dougherty made a point of not contributing to the NCWC fund,[18] but he attended the annual meetings of the hierarchy gathered as a conference. O'Connell told Dougherty in 1923 that the administrative committee of the NCWC was "a condensed form of Sulpicianism *contra mundum* but especially *contra nos*."[19] He also protested vehemently

---

16. See Fogarty, *Vatican*, 223-24.

17. This ambiguity appeared in the petition to Pius XI of the administrative board of the Welfare Council. In explaining the organization, the petition stated that "the National Catholic Welfare Council is the whole body of the episcopate organized for purposes of defense and welfare." AANY, "Petition," April 25, 1922.

18. Archives of the Archdiocese of Philadelphia, List of Allotments and Payments to the NCWC Fund for 1920-1925.

19. Archives of the Archdiocese of Philadelphia, O'Connell to Dougherty, Boston, October

against the support given to an amendment to the Constitution prohibiting child labor by Father John A. Ryan, director of the Social Action Department of the NCWC. The proposed amendment, the cardinal wrote Curley, was "soviet legislation," as anyone could see who did not have "the special privilege of J. A. Ryan, Jane Adams [*sic*] and a few more socialistic teachers and writers."[20]

Fulminations aside, O'Connell not only attended the annual meetings but also demanded to issue the official summons to them and preside over them, at least in the early years. Later, American cardinals alternated the presidency over the meetings. At the annual meeting in 1934, for example, O'Connell presided in the morning and Cardinal George Mundelein of Chicago presided in the afternoon. O'Connell's auxiliary bishop, Francis Spellman, incidentally, recorded that "I met him for the first time in months & kissed his ring before everybody." This was Spellman's first experience of an annual meeting, but he was "not greatly impressed."[21]

The chairman of the administrative board or committee, elected by the bishops, was largely a figurehead in the early days of the conference. He was always an archbishop, but never a cardinal. Archbishop Edward J. Hanna of San Francisco was elected chairman every year from 1919 to 1935, when he was forced to resign his see. For 1936, the bishops elected a new chairman, Edward J. Mooney. Mooney had been the apostolic delegate to India and later Japan, until his appointment in 1933 as bishop of Rochester with the personal title of archbishop. Named first archbishop of Detroit in 1937, Mooney held the chairmanship until 1939. In 1940, he was replaced by Archbishop Samuel Stritch of Milwaukee. In 1941, he was again elected and held the post through 1945, when Stritch was again elected. When both he and Stritch, who had been transferred to Chicago in 1939, were named cardinals in 1946, Archbishop John T. McNicholas, O.P., of Cincinnati was elected chairman and served until his death in 1950.

Beginning with Mooney, the chairman assumed a greater role at least in the liaison between the church and government. This would become particularly important during World War II. Noticeably absent from the list

2, 1923, given in Fogarty, *Vatican*, 227.

20. AABo, O'Connell to Curley, Boston, November 2, 1924.

21. AANY, Spellman Diary, November 13-14, 1934.

of chairmen was Francis Spellman, who became archbishop of New York in 1939. He was, however, elected to the administrative board as secretary from 1941 to 1946. In May 1941, he announced to Pius XII his election "to the administrative Board of the Bishops," and added that "when I do not agree with the proceedings I am frank to state my viewpoint & thus far in every single case the other Bishops have accepted my viewpoint."[22] About the issues on which he disagreed Spellman did not elaborate. In 1941, the year for which Spellman was elected to the board, there was also a change in its composition. While the chairman had always been an archbishop, the vice-chairman had usually been a bishop. An archbishop was now elected to that position and to most of the other key positions.[23] The administrative board was becoming restricted to the metropolitans.

In the meantime, by 1924, Pius XI was encouraging the formation of episcopal conferences in other nations, but wished to keep their functions separate from those of councils, provided for in the 1917 Code of Canon Law. In 1926, the Consistorial Congregation and the Congregation for the Extraordinary Affairs of the Church issued guidelines for these conferences, but they took a variety of forms. In France, for example, the conference consisted only of the archbishops and cardinals, while in Belgium and Germany all the bishops met.[24]

Back in the United States, the administrative board had long sought to prove to the Holy See the usefulness of the NCWC for influencing public opinion on Catholic issues. In late 1925 or early 1926, Schrembs wrote Giuseppe Pizzardo, then in the secretariat of state, that "the best vindication of the National Catholic Welfare Conference" was its legal department's work in having the United States Supreme Court declare unconstitutional an Oregon law prohibiting parochial schools.[25] The Holy See, for its part, also saw the advantage of using the NCWC to influence American opinion. In the late 1920s, Archbishop Pietro Fumasoni-Biondi, the apostolic delegate to the

---

22. AANY, Spellman to Pius XII, n.p., May 3, 1941 (draft).

23. Raphael M. Huber, O.F.M., *Our Bishops Speak* (Milwaukee: Bruce Publishing Company, 1952), 383-94.

24. Andrea Riccardi, "Pio XI e l'episcopato italiano," paper delivered at Colloquium on "Achille Ratti Pape Pie XI," École français de Rome, March 17, 1989, p. 1.

25. Archives of the Diocese of Cleveland, Schrembs to Pizzardo, n.d. (copy).

United States hierarchy, was also named delegate for Mexico, then torn by anticlerical revolution. Fumasoni-Biondi, in turn, appointed Father John Burke, C.S.P., general secretary of the NCWC, as his liaison with both the Mexican bishops and the State Department. Burke's negotiations ultimately resulted in the *modus vivendi* between the Mexican church and government in 1929.[26] But both the Oregon school case and the persecution in Mexico were issues where the NCWC proved to be useful in influencing the United States government. Neither case pertained to legislative authority within the American church.

Charles Coughlin

In terms of binding bishops to a particular course of action, the NCWC had no authority. During the 1930s, for example, several bishops sought in vain for a means of showing that Father Charles Coughlin, the popular radio priest, did not speak for the church at the same time that they did appear to be open to the charge of restricting his freedom of speech. Cardinal O'Connell handled the situation simply enough by stating that Coughlin had no authority whatsoever. This provoked Archbishop McNicholas to comment that

> His Eminence is eminently clever. He is speaking, he says, as a Catholic citizen. He objects to a parish priest speaking beyond the limits of the parish. It is just a bit strange to have him speak as a citizen to all the Bishops and people of the United States on a matter which belongs strictly to episcopal supervision. His words, of course, are those of a Bishop, and he transgresses the very rules he lays down of speaking to other Bishops and dioceses.[27]

McNicholas realized that the American people did not understand the hierarchical structure of the Catholic church well enough to know that a cardinal did not have jurisdiction in some way over Coughlin's ordinary, who continued until his death to support his priest.

---

26. See Fogarty, *Vatican*, 230-36.
27. Archives of the Archdiocese of Cincinnati, McNicholas to Noll, Cinn. April 21, 1932 (copy).

Early in 1936, Archbishop Amleto Cicognani, the apostolic delegate, approached McNicholas, widely regarded as the leading theologian among the bishops, about having the administrative board of the NCWC issue some sort of statement on Coughlin. McNicholas drew up and forwarded to Mooney, then the chairman, a general statement recognizing Coughlin's right as a citizen to air his opinion, but stating that he spoke neither "for the Catholic Church of the United States, nor for the American Hierarchy."

Mooney immediately saw the canonical problems of any such statement and the limitations of the authority of the administrative board. As he told McNicholas:

> It is unwise, perhaps, for me to start with this thought (or "hunch"), but I am wondering whether, when all concerned, including the Delegate, see the only kind of statement which they feel can be made, they will not all conclude that it is not worth making. After all, there are just two authorities who can, with clear right, step into this affair, his own Bishop and the Holy See. His own Bishop has spoken--and how! Evidently the Holy See does not care to speak--and in this, as in so many other things, it is probably very wise. Where then do we come in and how? Of course, if there is any transgression of faith or morals, then, as you say, anyone of us can step to the front, but, short of that, what can we say that will not result in greater confusion? If supreme authority wishes to exercise some indirect control, could that not better be done by bringing pressure to bear on the Ordinary than through the medium of a necessarily vague statement of a group whose competence is not clear enough to defy a challenge--perhaps on the part of the proper Ordinary who is something of a challenger? I very much fear that any statement which stops short of condemnation--and it must do that--will almost inevitably be taken as some sort of approbation.[28]

Mooney's evaluation of the situation was accurate, and, as the archbishop of Detroit, he would inherit the Coughlin problem. The administrative board of the NCWC simply lacked competence effectively to address such an issue. What is of more interest was that Cicognani, a trained canonist, even thought

---

28. Quoted in Fogarty, *Vatican*, 244-45.

of asking the administrative board to issue a statement, when Roman authorities seemed unwilling. But this was a period of transition when Cicognani and certain American bishops saw the need for a united authoritative voice. This became all the more necessary as the United States entered World War II.

When the United States declared war on the Axis powers in December 1941, Archbishop Mooney, after consultation with the administrative board, issued a statement to President Franklin D. Roosevelt that said in part: "We, the Catholic bishops of the United States, spiritual leaders of more than twenty million Americans, wish to assure you, Mr. President, that we are keenly conscious of our responsibilities in the hour of our nation's testing." Mooney went on to affirm the pastoral letter of the Third Plenary Council attesting to American Catholics' patriotic duty and to give the president "the pledge of our wholehearted cooperation in the difficult days that lie ahead." Mooney concluded by stating that, as chairman of the administrative board, he was "authorized to forward this letter in the name of the bishops of the United States."[29]

Not all the bishops, however, agreed that Mooney and the administrative board spoke for "the bishops of the United States." Archbishop Francis Beckman of Dubuque, an outspoken opponent of intervention and supporter of Coughlin, threatened to dissent from Mooney's statement. Cicognani won his silence by reminding him that the Vatican secretariat of state had issued a statement the previous September opposing public dissent among the bishops. The delegate also reminded the archbishop of the consequences of acting contrary to the unanimous opinion of the episcopate.[30] Mooney's consultation of the administrative board hardly qualified as gathering the opinions of all the bishops, but, in the exigency of war, the Vatican was thus demanding conformity, though not collegiality, among the bishops. For the moment, the administrative board was seen as the official voice of the American hierarchy.

---

29. Hugh J. Nolan, ed., *Pastoral Letters of the United States Catholic Bishops*, vol. 2 (Washington, DC: National Conference of Catholic Bishops and United States Catholic Conference, 1983), 36-37.

30. Cicognani to Maglione, January 5, 1942, in Pierre Blet, S.J., Angelo Martini, S.J., Robert Graham, S.J., and Burkhart Schneider, S.J., eds., *Actes et documents du Saint Siège relatifs à La Seconde Guerre Mondiale*, vol. 5 (Vatican City: Typis Polyglottis Vaticanis, 1965-1980), 361-62.

CCD New Testament

During the war, Cicognani also assisted the American bishops in asserting their authority against Roman intervention, but, again, this was not properly an exercise of collegiality. For some time, Father Charles Callan, O.P., had opposed the translation of the New Testament done under the auspices of the episcopal committee of the Confraternity of Christian Doctrine. As a consultor to the Pontifical Biblical Commission, he won the support of Cardinal Eugene Tisserant, president of the commission. The new translation had been published in the spring of 1941, with a letter in the frontispiece commending the work. A year later, however, Tisserant wrote Bishop Edwin Vincent O'Hara, chairman of the CCD committee. Callan's influence on the letter was patent. The Pontifical Biblical Commission had compared the Confraternity New Testament and the Challoner version, said the cardinal,

> and certain stylistic divergencies have been revealed which seemed less favorable to the new text. In view of the high esteem and authority in which Challoner's Version has always been held in all English-speaking countries by reason of the excellency of its classical style and theological accuracy, the new version should not depart from the primitive text except for very serious reasons and for definitely justified corrections.
>
> Therefore, as the intervention of the Pontifical Biblical Commission in this matter has been formally requested by the Confraternity of Christian doctrine--an intervention accepted most willingly in the interests of your praiseworthy and splendid enterprise--, I esteem it my duty, for the benefit of the new Catholic Version, as well as for the name of the Biblical Commission, to recommend a serious revision, which should be entrusted to the representative of the Pontifical Biblical Commission in America, the Very Reverend Father Charles J. Callan, O.P.[31]

Tisserant went on to say that his letter, printed in the frontispiece of the translation, was intended merely as an encouragement but not as a recommendation. The letter could not have been more of an affront to the American hierarchy. O'Hara lost no time in mobilizing opposition.

---

31. Ibid., Tisserant to O'Hara, Rome April 17, 1942.

He consulted the other members of the episcopal committee, notably Archbishop McNicholas, who composed a blistering rebuttal to the proposal of having Callan direct further revisions of the translation. Next, he enlisted the aid of Cicognani, who wrote a letter in support of the action of the episcopal committee and particularly of the letter drafted by McNicholas. The Dominican archbishop had said in part that "to put Father Callan . . . in a position where all the Scripture scholars of the United States will have to accept the 'serious revision' made by him will shock our Bishops and priests; it will belittle the work of the Commission of Scripture scholars representing the Bishops of the United States, and it will be interpreted as a withdrawal of the confidence of Rome in the work of this committee."[32] The letter was strong, and it certainly did not hurt the cause of the American bishops that such opposition to Callan came from a fellow Dominican.

With mail during wartime slowed down, Tisserant did not reply until October 14. The committee was "correct," he said, in stating that the Biblical Commission did "not wish to be associated officially with the work of revision," for "it is the unquestioned privilege of the Episcopal Hierarchy to procure for the faithful committed to their care suitable translations in the vernacular of the Sacred Scriptures." In regard to "the recommendation . . . of Father Callan," continued the cardinal, this "was intended simply as a suggestion submitted to the Episcopal Committee, which we cordially thank for the frankness of its statement in his regard." He concluded by stating that "it is enough for me to know that the Members of the Episcopal Committee are personally supervising the preparation of the revised English Translation of the Sacred Scriptures; I had never doubted their capacity and zeal."[33] Tisserant's response, couched in curial rhetoric, was, of course, a complete retraction of his earlier letter.

Callan was neither the first nor last cleric to try to present himself as representative of Roman authority in the American church. What was significant was Cicognani's recognition of the legitimate claim of the episcopal committee of the CCD, elected by the hierarchy, to supervise and approve a translation of the Scripture. Cicognani continued to defer to the administrative board of the NCWC in other matters that arose after the war. In 1947, for

---

32. Ibid., Episcopal Committee of the CCD to Tisserant, n.d., n.p. (draft).
33. Ibid., Tisserant to O'Hara, Rome, October 14, 1942 (copy).

example, he received a query from the Holy Office about priests in certain American dioceses taking part in baccalaureate exercises and Thanksgiving Day services. Cicognani forwarded the question to McNicholas, then the chairman of the administrative board. McNicholas, in turn, sought the advice of Stritch and Mooney, who, as cardinals, were not members of the board. He then put together a report that Cicognani thought "will be very valuable to the Holy See in forming a proper appreciation of the problem as it exists in this country."[34]

Cicognani was deft in dealing with the administrative board and one reason may have been his occasionally strained relations with Cardinal Spellman. As delegate, he did not attend the annual meetings of the hierarchy, except by invitation. This would not be the case with his successor, Archbishop Egidio Vagnozzi, who not only tried to intrude into the legitimate spheres of activity of the American bishops, but also demanded to address their annual meeting. Spellman, as the senior cardinal, invited Vagnozzi to address the bishops during their luncheon, not an official part of the meeting, and then politely informed the bishops that they could resume their meeting after the delegate had departed.[35] The general practice of not having the delegate attend the annual meetings, however, was more appropriate in the situation where the conference existed only as a means of fraternal consultation among the bishops on issues of common concern. Vatican II, however, dramatically altered the role of episcopal conferences.

Episcopal Conferences at Vatican II

The first mention of episcopal conferences in a conciliar document was in the constitution on the liturgy, which assigned to them the regulation of certain aspects of the liturgy. Joseph Ratzinger, a theologian at the council, noted at the time that previously episcopal conferences "did not exist, from the standpoint of canon law," but were of "a merely deliberative character." It was ecclesiologically significant, he concluded, that

---

34. Archives of the Archdiocese of Cincinnati, Cicognani to McNicholas, Washington, May 14, 1947.

35. Interview with Archbishop Karl J. Alter, Cincinnati, May 26, 1974.

now that they possess as a right a definite legislative function, they appear as a new element in the ecclesiastical body politic, and form a link of a quasi-synodal kind between the individual bishops and the pope. A synodal element has thus been inserted into the structure of the Church as a permanent factor and a new function has thereby accrued to the body of the bishops.[36]

The council's subsequent provision for the establishment of episcopal conferences in every nation gave approval to a strengthened expression of collegiality that had merely been tolerated in the United States in 1922. The American hierarchy restructured the NCWC. The bishops now formed the National Conference of Catholic Bishops (NCCB), a canonical entity consisting of all the bishops of the nation to enable them to exchange views and jointly exercise their pastoral ministry. The United States Catholic Conference (USCC) is a civil entity whereby the bishops join with others in fostering voluntary collective action on the interdiocesan level in areas such as educational and social concerns of the church.

At the present time, the *instrumentum laboris* on the "Theological and Juridical Status of Episcopal Conferences" challenges the competence of conferences in a number of areas. The draft document makes it clear that conferences do not have the same "legislative competence" as "particular councils"[37] and that they "are not organs of magisterium in the strict sense."[38] In this, the document accurately reflects the distinction drawn by Vatican II itself between particular councils and episcopal conferences.[39] By implication, therefore, the last uniquely American expression of the magisterium was the Third Plenary Council in 1884. The argument is that particular councils participate in the magisterium because they receive papal review, whereas pastoral letters do not. Yet, there remains the question of the process the American bishops used in issuing the last two pastorals "The Challenge of

---

36. Joseph Ratzinger, "The First Session," *Worship* 37 (1963): 534.

37. "Theological and Juridical Status of Episcopal Conferences" (Vatican City: Congregation for Bishops, July 1, 1987, photocopy), 19. Also printed as "Draft Statement on Episcopal Conferences," *Origins* 17 (April 7, 1988): 731-37.

38. Ibid., 24.

39. *Christus Dominus* 36-38, in Austin Flannery, O.P., ed., *Vatican Council II: The Conciliar and Post Conciliar Documents* (Collegeville, Minn.: The Liturgical Press, 1975), 586-88.

Peace" and "Economic Justice for All." Earlier pastoral letters of the hierarchy were pretty much the work of a small group or even of an individual. Those issued by councils in the nineteenth century were theoretically not part of the conciliar legislation itself--they were issued at the close of the councils before the decrees received Roman approval. The process used in the last two pastorals, however, more closely approximated that of a council. The bishops issued a draft for discussion, held hearings, and then voted on the letters. In light of the history of the church in the United States, it might be appropriate to reexamine the propriety of holding national councils from time to time, as Vatican II itself suggested.

The history of the NCWC surveyed in this paper indicates that it was never more than a strictly consultative organization. The confusion in the name meant that frequently bishops freely dissented from statements emanating from the standing departments--yet, this dissent was usually expressed in private. Cicognani's role in attempting to have the NCWC administrative board issue a statement on Coughlin is interesting, but not indicative that he actually thought it had the juridical competence to address the issue--the point that Mooney made so clearly. The Holy See did insist that every bishop adhere in public to the administrative board's support of the declaration of war in 1941, but this has to be seen in the context of its recognition that the United States would hold the balance of power in the war and that it was imperative for the bishops to support the government. What was present in the NCWC in an attenuated form was an expression of collegial action, but without the theology of collegiality that had been lost by the end of the nineteenth century.

Part II:

Analytical

Studies

Thomas J. Reese, S.J.

Conflict and Consensus in the NCCB/USCC

THOMAS REESE is a fellow of the Woodstock Theological Center at Georgetown University

Introduction

Much of the theological and canonical writing on episcopal conferences urges bishops to make decisions by consensus rather than by a majority vote. Whereas a decision by a simple majority may alienate a sizeable minority within the conference, decision by consensus, it is hoped, reflects and furthers unity within the faith community. Imposing a decision opposed by 49 percent of the bishops could be harmful to unity.

The *instrumentum laboris* on the theological and juridical status of episcopal conferences, for example, urges the conferences to have "in possible cases, the indication of the goal of pursuing a morally unanimous consensus, without making this a juridical norm, which would seem too paralyzing."[1]

Canon law does not normally require unanimity before a juridic body can act. Although the Code of Canon Law, quoting Justinian, states that "what

---

1. Translation by Joseph Komonchak. See his article in this volume for an analysis of the Vatican working paper. The Vatican translation reads: "possibly, the indication of an aim to pursue a morally unanimous consensus, without however making this a juridical norm, which would be too paralyzing. . . ." See "Theological and Juridical Status of Episcopal Conferences" (Congregation for Bishops, Vatican City, July 1, 1987, photocopy), 20. Also see Congregation for Bishops, "Draft Statement on Episcopal Conferences," *Origins* 17 (April 7, 1988): 736.

touches all as individuals must be approved by all,"[2] the code rarely indicates where this rule applies. Furthermore, the meaning of the terms "touches" and "approved" is much debated by canonists.[3]

Normally, what is required of juridic bodies is less demanding than consensus: "that action will have the force of law which, when a majority of those who must be convoked are present, receives the approval of an absolute majority of those who are present. . . ."[4] In other words, as long as a majority of the body is present, a majority of those present may make legally binding decisions.

For episcopal conferences, however, more than a majority is required for legally binding decisions. According to canon law, decisions that are binding on the bishops must be approved by at least a two-thirds majority of the conference membership and must be reviewed (*recognita*) by the Holy See.[5] Strictly speaking, this canonical requirement applies only to "decrees,"[6] not to statements or pastoral letters.

In 1968, however, the American bishops decided to require a two-thirds majority vote of their membership for approval of "joint pastorals" and "statements" by the National Conference of Catholic Bishops (NCCB) or the United States Catholic Conference (USCC).[7] This is a self-imposed restriction

---

2. *The Code of Canon Law: Latin-English Edition* (Washington, DC: Canon Law Society of America, 1983), Canon 119, 3º.

3. Ellsworth Kneal, "Title VI: Physical and Juridic Persons," in James A. Coriden, Thomas J. Green, and Donald E. Heintschel, eds., *The Code of Canon Law: A Text and Commentary* (New York: Paulist Press, 1985), 84.

4. Canon 119, 2º.

5. Canon 455, §2. What is required is a two-thirds vote of the de jure members, which in the NCCB includes active diocesan bishops and auxiliaries but does not include retired bishops.

6. Decrees are laws properly speaking (general decrees) or determinations of how to observe laws (general executory decrees). See canons 29 and 31. Also see the article by Thomas Green in this volume.

7. In 1968, the regulations said a joint pastoral letter or statement "shall be adopted only by a two-thirds vote." See *Minutes of the Fourth General Meeting of the National Conference of Catholic Bishops* (April 23-25, 1968), 50- 56. Revised versions of these regulations were approved in November 1971 and November 1981. The 1971 version reads: joint pastorals and formal statements "must be approved by two-thirds of the Conference membership. If this becomes impractical owing to limited attendance at the general meeting, the Conference President may rule that two-thirds approval of all de jure members is sufficient." See *Minutes of the Eleventh General Meeting of the National Conference of Catholic Bishops* (November 15-19, 1971), 81.

which is not required by canon law. "These rules were proposed," according to Walter J. Woods, "in order to deal more effectively with problems related to the number of statements being considered, the priority among them, the need to assure sufficient consideration of a text before voting on it, and the very process of amendment and approval."[8] The "rules facilitate the formation of a consensus among the bishops and insure that they will have control over the actual text to be adopted or rejected."[9]

In the regulations, the bishops' conference distinguishes among "joint pastorals," "formal statements," "special messages," and "resolutions and other brief statements."[10] The difference between a joint pastoral and a formal statement is procedural, not substantive. "They seemed to be almost interchangeable," admitted Archbishop John Roach, then NCCB president, except that a joint pastoral may only be issued by the NCCB assembly while a formal statement may be approved by either the NCCB or the USCC assembly.[11]

The bishops have tended to use joint pastorals for more important pronouncements. But formal statements also carry great weight. "A formal statement is one with an official character which commits the conference to a particular position."[12] Formal statements by the NCCB require a two-thirds

---

Because the Holy See objected to the American custom of allowing retired bishops to vote, the statutes and bylaws were revised. The 1981 version of the regulations read: joint pastorals and formal statements of the NCCB "require the approval of two-thirds of the membership," but formal statements of the USCC "require the votes of two-thirds of the members present and voting for approval." *Handbook: National Conference of Catholic Bishops, United States Catholic Conference* (Washington, DC: USCC, March 1982), 57-58.

8. Walter J. Woods, "Pastoral Care, Moral Issues, Basic Approaches: The National Pastoral Texts of the American Bishops from the Perspective of Fundamental Moral Theology" (S.T.D. diss., Gregorian University, 1979), 222 n. 24.

9. Ibid., 225.

10. "Revised Regulations Regarding NCCB/USCC Statements," in *Minutes of the Eleventh General Meeting of the National Conference of Catholic Bishops* (November 15-19, 1971), 80-85. Also see "Appendix: Revised Regulations Regarding NCCB/USCC Statements" in *National Conference of Catholic Bishops: Statutes and Bylaws* (Washington, DC: USCC, July 1976), 41-48.

11. "National Conference of Catholic Bishops, Monday, November 16 [1981], Morning Session, First Part" (USCC Press Release, Washington, DC, November 16, 1981, photocopy), 6.

12. "Revised Regulations Regarding NCCB/USCC Statements," in *Minutes of the Eleventh General Meeting of the National Conference of Catholic Bishops* (November 15-19, 1971), 81. Also

vote of the membership, but formal statements by the USCC can be approved by two-thirds of those present and voting at a meeting. Special messages, resolutions and other brief statements can be approved by two-thirds of the bishops "present and attending the general meeting."[13] In addition, less notice to the membership and less review by committees is required of these latter documents before their consideration by the assembly.

All these regulations apply to both the NCCB and the USCC. Cardinal Lawrence Shehan of Baltimore, who drafted the 1968 regulations, attempted to distinguish the kinds of statements that would be issued by each:

> The body of U.S. Bishops may speak collectively through either of its two agencies, the NCCB and the USCC. Which agency is used depends upon the determination of the Bishops and the subject matter involved. No hard and fast rule can be set for the choice of one agency as opposed to another. As a practical matter, however, the language of the Booz, Allen & Hamilton report provides a general guideline.
>
> NCCB shall address itself to "matters pertaining to the canonical rights and responsibilities and pastoral role of the United States hierarchy functioning as a national episcopal conference."
>
> USCC shall address itself to "matters in which the Bishops collaborate with others in social, economic, civic and educational affairs."[14]

Sometimes the bishops, when dealing with "social, economic, civic and educational affairs," have wanted to issue pastoral letters and not simply "formal statements," exposing a weakness in Shehan's distinction. Since the USCC cannot issue pastoral letters, these matters have been dealt with by the NCCB. The result has been a gradual absorption of USCC responsibilities by the NCCB.

---

see "Appendix: Revised Regulations Regarding NCCB/USCC Statements," in *National Conference of Catholic Bishops: Statutes and Bylaws* (Washington, DC: USCC, July 1976), 43.

13. Ibid.

14. *Minutes of the Fourth General Meeting of the National Conference of Catholic Bishops* (April 23-25, 1968), 51.

The Record

What in fact has been the record of consensus and conflict within the NCCB/USCC assembly? Have decisions been made by consensus or have a small majority been able to impose their will on the rest of the bishops? What issues have divided the bishops and on what issues has there been consensus?

To answer these questions, I will examine the NCCB/USCC as a legislative assembly using social science methods that have been applied to political legislatures for many years. No denial of the spiritual nature of the church or of the NCCB/USCC is intended. Social science cannot measure the activity of the Holy Spirit. It can, however, be used to measure and evaluate empirical data, and explain how the conference actually operates.

From the perspective of a social scientist, the National Conference of Catholic Bishops is a legislative assembly that meets periodically, follows parliamentary procedures, elects officers, and decides matters by votes. Since the teaching role of episcopal conferences is especially under challenge, I will limit my analysis to the formulation of major statements issued by the conference. Major statements are here defined as those printed by the conference itself in *Pastoral Letters of the United States Bishops*.[15] I will not look at conference elections, staff, lobbying efforts, budgets, or liturgical and canonical policies.

Consensus Statements

If the only evidence examined is the final vote on documents, the NCCB/USCC seems to have a high degree of internal consensus. Of the ninety-four NCCB/USCC assembly statements printed in *Pastoral Letters of the United States Bishops* for 1966-1983,[16] the minutes[17] indicate that at least

---

15. Hugh J. Nolan, ed., *Pastoral Letters of the United States Bishops*, vols. 3-4 (Washington, DC: U.S. Catholic Conference, 1983). Volumes 1 and 2 contain statements of the American bishops prior to the creation of the NCCB/USCC in 1966.

16. Ibid. Volumes 3 and 4 contain 131 NCCB/USCC statements since 1966, but only ninety-four were passed by the full assembly. The others were by NCCB/USCC officers or committees.

Of the ninety-four approved by the full assembly, we do not know the final vote on five: "The Church in Our Day" (November 1967), "Declaration on Conscientious Objection and Selective Conscientious Objection" (1971), "Basic Teachings for Catholic Religious Education"

thirty-one (a third) passed unanimously (see table on pages 132-35). These include resolutions on political-ethical issues such as birth control (1966), race relations and poverty (1966), welfare (1967), aid to parents of Catholic school students (1971), the environment (1971), population programs (1972 and 1973), pro-life constitutional amendment (1973), the Middle East (1973), farm labor (1973, 1974, and 1975), pro-life activities (1975), the economy (1975), housing (1975), Human Life Foundation (1975), migrants (1976), Cuban and Haitian refugees (1980), hostages in Iran (1980), and health care (1981).

Total consensus was also shown on church issues like the *Dutch Catechism* (1967), "Christians in Our Time" (1970), the Campaign for Human Development (1970), the foreign missions (1971), Eucharist and hunger (1975), the movie *Jesus of Nazareth* (1977), church arbitration procedures (1978), the papal visit (1979), the laity (1980), and the mission of the conference (1981).

Eighteen other statements received nearly unanimous approval with ten or fewer negative votes: three statements on Vietnam (1966, 1971, and 1972), "Human Life in Our Day" (1968), abortion (1970), directives for health facilities (1971), housing (1972), Catholic-Jewish relations (1975), society and the aged (1976), political responsibility (1976), American Indians (1977), religious liberty in Eastern Europe (1977), the bicentennial consultations (1977), justice (1978), the handicapped (1978), the Middle East (1978), Central America (1981), and peace (1983).

(1973), "Behold Your Mother" (1973), and "Catholic Higher Education and the Pastoral Mission of the Church" (1980). The 1973 statements were approved on a mail ballot and received at least two-thirds vote.

Nolan indicates that the 1971 "Declaration on Conscientious Objection and Selective Conscientious Objection" was issued by the USCC Division of World Justice and Peace (Nolan, *Pastoral Letters*, vol. 3, pp. 61 and 228). Woods, who examined the minutes of the Administrative Committee and Administrative Board, indicates that the declaration was approved by a two-thirds vote in a mail ballot. See Woods, "Pastoral Care," 291. I therefore count it as an assembly statement. Of the nineteen statements Nolan is considering for inclusion in the next volume (1983-87), thirteen were passed by the full assembly of bishops. Of the thirteen, eight were approved unanimously. The rest were approved by a voice vote or had less than ten negative votes. (Nolan correspondence to me, May 19, 1988).

17. The official minutes of the NCCB/USCC assemblies from November 1966 to June 1988 were examined, except for those held in executive (closed) session beginning in 1972 when most meetings became open to the press. Also examined were the press releases issued by the USCC press office which summarized the meetings.

Another twenty-six statements passed on voice votes with no one concerned enough to ask for a written ballot (only six bishops are needed to require a written ballot): peace (1967, 1968), clerical celibacy (1967 and April 1969), Catholic schools (1967), the race crisis (1968), due process in church (1968), farm labor (1968), abortion (1969), poverty (1969), prisoners of war (1969), ecumenism (1970 and 1974), welfare reform (1970), the Catholic press (1970), the United Nations (1970), birth control laws (1970), the declaration of human rights (1973), prisons (1973), the world food crisis (1974), ecclesiastical archives (1974), guidelines for fund raising (1977), family ministry (1978), Cambodia (1979), and Iran (1979 and 1980).

Thus of the ninety-four NCCB/USCC statements published in *Pastoral Letters*, all but nineteen were passed by voice vote or with ten or fewer bishops in opposition. On five of the nineteen statements we do not know the vote results except that they received at least a two-thirds vote.[18] These seventy-five statements cover issues that have divided American society and the church, but the bishops were able to find consensus on them. Before examining the statements that had some opposition, it is important to emphasize how extraordinary this level of consensus is. It is empirical evidence supporting the view that consensus formation is a highly prized operation norm of the NCCB/USCC.

Conflict: Capital Punishment 1974 and 1980

No statement of the NCCB/USCC has ever been adopted by a slight majority. Only one statement was approved by less than two-thirds of those voting: the 1974, one-sentence USCC "Resolution Against Capital Punishment" passed 108-63.[19] The bishops broke their own regulations in approving this resolution with less than a two-thirds vote.[20] But no one made a point of order

---

18. See footnote 16 above.

19. "That the USCC goes on record in opposition to capital punishment." See "Thursday - P.M. Session, NCCB/USCC Annual Meeting, November 21, 1974" (USCC Press Release, Washington, DC, November 21, 1974, Mimeographed), 1 and 4.

20. In fact, the resolution may not have even received a majority vote of those "present" since at one point at least 236 bishops were attending the meeting. On November 19, 1974, 236 bishops voted on whether there should be province consultations on the issue of general absolution. The capital punishment motion was approved on November 21, 1974, the second to

when Cardinal John Krol, the NCCB/USCC president, declared the resolution passed with a majority vote.

The one-sentence resolution was drafted by Bishop John L. May, then of Mobile, after a seven-page statement on capital punishment, written by the Committee on Social Development and World Peace, was defeated in the assembly on a close vote (103-119). This committee statement has the distinction of being the only statement ever formally voted down by the assembly. After the statement's defeat, Bishop May immediately offered his one-sentence resolution, but debate on it was postponed for two days. After the resolution was debated, Cardinal Krol ended discussion and called for a vote, commenting that "this matter had been debated more than any other four or five topics."[21]

Six years later, the 1980 "Statement on Capital Punishment" passed 145 to 31 with 41 abstentions, the highest number of abstentions ever recorded.[22] The bishops once again broke their own regulations in adopting this statement. Before 1981, "formal statements" needed a two-thirds approval of the entire membership, not a two-thirds approval of those casting votes.[23] But since no

---

the last day of the meeting with only 108 yes votes, less than half of 236.

21. "Thursday - P.M. Session, NCCB/USCC Annual Meeting, November 21, 1974" (USCC Press Release, Washington, DC, November 21, 1974, Photocopy), 1.

22. The general secretary, Bishop Thomas Kelly, O.P., announced for the chair that in computations "we don't count abstentions, and so the document has a 2/3 vote and is accepted as a conference statement." See "NCCB/USCC General Meeting, A.M. Session, Thursday, November 13 [1980]" (USCC Press Release, Washington, DC, November 13, 1980), 7.

Bishop Kelly appears to have miscalculated and believed that the motion did not receive a two-thirds vote of those handing in ballots. In fact, the statement just barely received two-thirds approval from those voting or abstaining: 145/217 = 66.8 percent. As will be seen below, his interpretation of the rules (or the advice he received from the parliamentarian) appears to have also been inaccurate.

23. "Revised Regulations Regarding NCCB/USCC Statements," in *Minutes of the 11th General Meeting of the National Conference of Catholic Bishops* (November 15-19, 1971), 81. Also see "Appendix: Revised Regulations Regarding NCCB/USCC Statements," in *National Conference of Catholic Bishops: Statutes and Bylaws* (Washington, DC: USCC, July 1976), 43. The regulations were changed in November 1981 so that a formal statement by the USCC could be approved by a two-thirds vote of those present and voting.

The statement on capital punishment was voted on the last day of the meeting, November 13, 1980. If this 3,000-word document is considered a "formal statement," it required a two-thirds approval of the entire membership, not a two-thirds of those casting votes.

If the document is simply a "resolution or brief statement," then it only required a two-bishop rose to make a point of order, the statement became conference policy.

The closeness of the votes indicates that the two capital punishment statements were the most controversial statements ever issued by the conference. Many bishops were concerned that a rejection of capital punishment might appear to be a rejection of church tradition, which long had acknowledged a state's right to capital punishment. On the other hand, many other bishops wanted to show that the hierarchy held a fully consistent ethic of life and was opposed not only to abortion but also to capital punishment. Approving such controversial statements necessitated the breaking or bending of their own self-imposed regulations requiring a two-thirds vote on statements.

More Conflict

Five other statements approved by the NCCB/USCC had more than thirty negative votes on final passage: the 1966 "Pastoral Statement on Penance and Abstinence" (156-32), the November 1969 "Statement on Celibacy" (145-68), the April 1970 "Statement on Abortion" (114-52), the 1976 statement "U.S.-Panama Relations" (170-61), and the "conclusion" of the 1970 "Statement on the Implementation of the Apostolic Letter on Mixed Marriages" (172-49).

Penance 1966

The 1966 minutes are not very helpful in describing the conflict over the "Pastoral Statement on Penance and Abstinence" at the first meeting of the

---

thirds approval of those "present and attending the general meeting." If only those voting or casting abstentions are considered "present," then as a "brief statement" the document squeaked by.

If there were others "present" who did not cast ballots, the motion would have required more yes votes. In fact, on an earlier vote (November 12, 1980), thirty-seven more bishops (254) voted on the "Pastoral Letter on Marxist Communism." If even one of them was still "present and attending the general meeting" but did not hand in a ballot, then the statement did not receive a two-thirds vote of those "present."

It is difficult to believe that the "Statement on Capital Punishment" can be considered a "brief statement." Woods notes that "resolutions and other brief statements . . . are generally regarded as less momentous than the other three categories [joint pastorals, formal statements, and special messages]." Woods, "Pastoral Care," 224.

NCCB. Archbishop John Cody of Chicago introduced the revised text which had taken into consideration "insofar as possible" the *modi* (amendments) submitted by thirty bishops. The statement, which Bishop John J. Wright helped write, announced the reduction in the number of days of fast and abstinence. At the same time, the bishops wanted to avoid the impression that they were downgrading penance or that all laws could change.

After the statement was approved, the bishops added an additional paragraph saying that Catholics should understand "that fast and abstinence regulations admit change, unlike the commandments and precepts of that unchanging divine moral law which the church must today and always defend as immutable."[24] This final addition may have been an attempt to placate those who originally voted no.

Celibacy 1969

The handling of the November 1969 "Statement on Celibacy" is interesting if ambiguous. At one point sixty-eight bishops voted against issuing the paper, which strongly defended clerical celibacy, as a conference document. Can it be inferred from the vote that sixty-eight bishops favored optional celibacy?[25] Probably not.

Actually, there were three votes on the celibacy statement. First, the document's content was approved in substance, subject to *modi*, with only one negative vote. Second, the bishops voted 145-68 to issue the document as a conference statement, rather than merely to make it available to the bishops. Third, a series of *modi* were unanimously accepted.

The different results for the first and second votes are interesting. While only one bishop voted against the document in substance, moments later sixty-eight voted against issuing it as a conference statement. Why did these sixty-seven additional bishops suddenly turn against the document?

---

24. *Minutes of the Annual Meeting, National Conference of Catholic Bishops* (November 14-18, 1966), 208.

25. Only one archbishop during the debate said that one should not rule out the possibility of change or the ordination of mature, stable married men. The chairman of the drafting committee answered that in his opinion the statement did not preclude such a possibility. See *Minutes of the Seventh General Meeting of the National Conference of Catholic Bishops* (November 10-14, 1969), 53.

Some bishops felt the statement was too defensive and apologetic in tone. They observed it did not relate celibacy to ministry, and they feared that priests would believe the bishops were not really aware of the problems confronting their clergy. But all of these points had been made during the debate prior to the first vote. Those who changed their votes may have felt that the document was good enough for private distribution to the bishops but not good enough for publication.

Another influence may have been the manner of voting. The first vote was public (by voice or a show of hands) while the second was secret (by ballot). Some have argued that public votes coerce the minority into going along with the majority. Others argue that public votes discourage bishops from voting against Vatican policy. Both factors could have been at work here if some of the sixty-seven favored optional celibacy but were afraid to say so publicly. The *periti*, nonepiscopal experts who had helped prepare the statement, were less reticent: they indicated before the meeting that they did not want to be associated with the statement as it was drafted.

Abortion 1970

Issuing the April 1970 "Statement on Abortion" was opposed by fifty-two bishops. Does this mean that fifty-two bishops favored abortion? Not likely. The bishops appear to have been objecting to procedure, not substance.

The conference had already issued "Human Life in Our Day" (1968), a pastoral letter that included four paragraphs on abortion. As more states liberalized their laws, the NCCB Administrative Committee decided that more needed to be said. The NCCB approved on a voice vote a short statement on abortion in 1969.

The 1970 statement was presented by the Rev. James T. McHugh, then director of the USCC Family Life Division. A revised version was prepared by an ad hoc committee headed by Bishop Raymond J. Gallagher in light of the *modi* they received during the meeting. More *modi* were suggested when the revised version was presented. The president, Cardinal John Dearden, asked that the committee again revise the draft and bring it back to the assembly.

Some felt, however, that this procedure would delay the document. Archbishop Philip Hannan moved that the ad hoc committee be authorized to revise the document in light of the observations made on the floor and then proceed immediately to the release of the document in the name of the conference. Most of those who voted in the negative probably agreed with Cardinal Dearden that the committee should come back to the assembly for final approval of the revised text. Seven months later, in November 1970, a "Declaration on Abortion" passed with only eight negative votes. This was the last statement of the bishops prior to the Supreme Court decision in Roe v. Wade (January 22, 1973).

U.S.-Panama Relations 1976

In 1976 the NCCB issued a statement supporting the Panama Canal Treaty. Considering how divided American society at large was over returning the Panama Canal Zone to Panama, it is surprising that the American bishops were not more divided than the final vote of 170-61 implies. The lobbying efforts of the Panamanian hierarchy led by Archbishop Marcos McGrath of Panama City played a pivotal role in overcoming the bishops' reluctance to touch this political controversy. Despite the "heated debate"[26] and the sixty-one negative votes, the statement had a profound political impact. The Carter Administration identified the conference as its most important supporter in the Senate ratification of the Panama Canal Treaty.

Mixed Marriages 1970

Finally, there is the 1970 "Statement on the Implementation of the Apostolic Letter on Mixed Marriages." This was the third draft of the statement; the second draft failed to receive a two-thirds vote in a mail ballot. Each section of the third draft was discussed and amended on the floor in accordance with the discussions. Each section was voted on separately. The conclusion received the most negative votes (172-49), and there was no vote on the whole document.

The minutes give no details about the debate or amendments, and the USCC press releases give very little information. A reading of the text does not reveal anything very controversial in the conclusion. Perhaps some bishops

---

26. Nolan, *Pastoral Letters*, vol. 4, p. 26.

objected to the idea of the USCC Family Life Division being instructed to "develop basic pre-marriage and marriage education programs incorporating the norms and spirit of this document." The NCCB committee on ecumenism was also asked "to explore the possibility of an ecumenical form for mixed marriage." Or perhaps the bishops voting in the negative did so because they wanted something in the conclusion that was not there.

Mostly Consensus

Another six statements received twenty to thirty negative votes: the 1969 "Statement in Protest of U.S. Government Programs against the Right to Life" (143-20), the 1972 pastoral "To Teach as Jesus Did" (197-29), the 1976 statement "Teach Them" (153-30), the 1976 statement "Let the Little Children Come to Me" (201-23), the 1976 statement "To Live in Christ Jesus" (172-25), and the 1979 pastoral letter "Brothers and Sisters to Us" (215-30).

Thus from 1966 through 1983, only thirteen of the ninety-four NCCB/USCC statements published in *Pastoral Letters of the United States Bishops* had more than nineteen negative votes. The rest were approved by voice vote or received less than twenty negative votes. As a result, 85 percent[27] of the NCCB/USCC statements were supported by at least 90 percent of the bishops voting (if one presumes that on voice votes fewer than 11 percent of the bishops voted in the negative, a fairly safe presumption since it only takes six bishops to require a written ballot).

Judging from the final votes on documents in *Pastoral Letters*, the NCCB/USCC is clearly an assembly that operates by consensus. Although this is a fair judgment, it is not a complete picture. Judging the NCCB/USCC only by the final votes on documents in *Pastoral Letters* would be like judging a restaurant by the food brought to your table. It would be an accurate judgment, but it would miss all the excitement that goes on in the kitchen. Thus while the 1983 peace pastoral and the 1986 economic pastoral were both approved with only nine negative votes, hundreds of amendments were offered and voted on prior to the final ballots.

---

27. On five of the ninety-four statements we do not have a record of the votes (see footnote 16 above). Of the eighty-nine statements for which we have a record, seventy-six passed with fewer than twenty negative votes: 76/89 = 85 percent.

Legislative Procedures

Despite what their critics may think, the statements of the American bishops are not approved with little or no consideration. This may have been true in a few instances when sessions were closed to the public, but since the press has been admitted in 1972, the bishops have given statements due consideration before approval.

The conference's 1971 regulations require that joint pastorals and formal statements "be formally initiated only by the general membership or the Administrative Committee in consultation with the appropriate committees." In 1981, this was made more explicit so that a committee had to get the assembly's approval before drafting a major statement. The regulations indicate that time constraints may not always permit this ideal, but the assembly must be given the opportunity to say whether or not it wishes to consider a particular issue before a draft is formally presented.

Before an item (especially a joint pastoral or formal statement) is dealt with by the assembly, it is normally considered by a NCCB or USCC committee. On each issue, the committee and its staff may hold hearings, consult widely, and/or prepare a series of drafts. A final draft must be circulated to all the bishops with requests for suggestions at least one month before it is considered at a conference meeting. Often a committee will distribute preliminary drafts for comment.

A series of questions and answers, presented by Cardinal Krol and adopted by the assembly in 1973, describes the process employed in preparing a conference document:

> A statement can be drafted in many different ways. It can be written by one author. It can be divided into sections and each section can be written by a different person. It can be written from the start by a bishop or bishops. It can be drafted by a consultant or consultants and submitted for review to a committee of bishops.
>
> It can be prepared through a process of extremely wide consultation at the national and local levels; consultation can be restricted to a small number of specialists in the field being treated; or there can be no consultation at all. Circumstances will dictate the process--including the time available, the purpose or purposes of the document, the preexistence

(or nonexistence) of widespread consensus in the Catholic community regarding the subject matter, etc. In so far as possible, a process should be devised and implemented which is suited to the exigencies of this particular document.

Also, in future it may prove increasingly desirable to provide interested individuals and organizations outside the bishops' conference with drafts of major documents and invite them to submit their criticisms and suggestions for revision--without, of course, guaranteeing that their views will prevail. Among other things, such a procedure is likely to increase the acceptance of bishops' statements among concerned parties.[28]

When a committee wishes to submit an item to the full assembly, it must first go through the NCCB Administrative Committee or the USCC Administrative Board which set the agenda for their respective bodies. The membership of the Administrative Committee and the Administrative Board is identical. Once presented to the assembly, the item is normally subject to amendment from the floor. Amendments can be approved by a majority vote, but a two-thirds vote is necessary for final passage.

I do not have the time or space here to deal with the pre-assembly process involving staff, committees, and consultation. These are, of course, critical to consensus formation, but it is more difficult to get information on them. The focus in this paper will be on the process by which NCCB/USCC statements· are amended on the floor by the bishops. Here consensus and conflict can be measured in votes and in both victories and defeats.

Conciliar Procedures

When the legislative histories of the seventy-three statements published in *Pastoral Letters* are examined, one discovers that some of the statements

---

28. "Appendix II: Questions to be Considered in Drafting NCCB/USCC Statements," in *Minutes of the Thirteenth General Meeting of the National Conference of Catholic Bishops* (November 12-16, 1973), 100. Also in *National Conference of Catholic Bishops: Statutes and Bylaws* (Washington, DC: USCC, July 1976), 50. To improve readability, this quote was broken into three paragraphs.

achieved consensus almost immediately, while others achieved it only after much debate and many revisions.[29]

How statements were discussed and revised changed over time in the conference. The procedures followed in the assembly in its early years were modeled on those of the Second Vatican Council rather than *Robert's Rules of Order.*[30] The move from conciliar rules to *Robert's Rules of Order* began during Cardinal Krol's presidency (1972-74) and was formalized under NCCB President Joseph Bernardin (1975-77). Although either set of rules can be used to develop consensus, conciliar rules give more influence to conference leadership and the drafting committees, while parliamentary procedures strengthen the assembly vis-à-vis the drafting committees and the conference leadership.

When operating under conciliar rules in the past, the assembly would discuss a draft and suggest *modi*, but the amendments were rarely voted on. The drafting committee was allowed to use its judgment in determining which *modi* to accept or refuse. The committee was supposed to accept those that would increase consensus, but without a vote to show the mood of the assembly, the decision could be subjective.

For example, thirty bishops offered *modi* to the 1966 "Statement on Penance and Abstinence," but these were not voted on. Instead the drafting committee itself, chaired by Archbishop Cody, would either accept the *modi*, in which case they were included, or reject them, in which case they were forgotten. Likewise, a draft of "The Church in Our Day" was mailed to the bishops a month before their November 1967 meeting. The bishops discussed a revised version that was circulated at the meeting. *Modi* on both versions were submitted to the drafting committee headed by Bishop John J. Wright, but it does not appear that any amendments were actually voted on. Bishop

---

29. Other than the official minutes and the USCC press releases, there are few sources of information on the legislative history of the statements issued by the NCCB/USCC. Nolan has an introduction to each collection of statements in *Pastoral Letters*. Another excellent source is Walter J. Woods, "Pastoral Care, Moral Issues, Basic Approaches: The National Pastoral Texts of the American Bishops from the Perspective of Fundamental Moral Theology" (S.T.D. diss., Gregorian University, 1979). Finally, there are the news stories by the NC News Service.

30. For an excellent analysis of conciliar procedures and consensus building, see Richard T. Lawrence, "The Building of Consensus: The Conciliar Rules of Procedure and the Evolution of *Dei Verbum*," *Jurist* 46 (1986): 474-510.

Wright also made changes, "generally stylistic in nature," after the document was approved.[31]

If the leadership of the conference is not happy with a draft or its revision, it can also expand the number of bishops working on the document. Expanding the committee has usually been a strategy for developing consensus. For example, in 1967, the "Statement on Celibacy" was first drafted by the Committee on Doctrine chaired by Bishop Alexander Zaleski. A second draft was presented by Cardinal Krol, the NCCB/USCC vice president. The final draft, revised in light of the floor discussions, was presented by Bishop Wright, who was helped by a drafting committee including Cardinal Krol, Archbishop John Carberry, Archbishop Paul Hallinan, Bishop Loras Lane, and Bishop Zaleski.

A less complicated procedure was used on the 1967 "Statement on Peace." Cardinal James F. McIntyre simply moved that the statement be accepted with any changes or additions the drafting committee might wish to make in view of the comments given on the floor. This motion passed, indicating a high degree of confidence in, or deference to, the committee.

The process of approving the 1968 pastoral "Human Life in Our Day" proved to be much more complicated. It is the first statement on which there were a number of amendments and votes. Prior to the November meeting, Bishop Wright surveyed the membership to see what kind of pastoral 'they wanted. The responses indicated that most bishops wanted to do more than simply quote from Vatican II and *Humanae Vitae*. They wanted to discuss abortion and birth control (194-19), to give pastoral guidance to the faithful (161-17), and to deal with the morality of war (153-44), including the Vietnam War (121-67). But just over a third of the bishops opposed applying the principles of Vatican II to the Vietnam War.

The issues of "guiltless" contraception and dissent were considered so delicate that the bishops voted to have the results of their ballots on these issues kept confidential even from themselves. A third vote occurred on whether the bishops wished to indicate that those who are subjectively guiltless

---

31. Woods, "Pastoral Care," 338. The official minutes are almost totally silent about the 1967 pastoral letter "Church in Our Day" which Cardinal Krol and Father Nolan refer to as the bishops' "first purely doctrinal pastoral." Nolan, *Pastoral Letters*, vol. 3, pp. 1 and 54. "Behold Your Mother" (1973) is also referred to by Nolan as "one of their rare completely doctrinal statements." Nolan, *Pastoral Letters*, vol. 3, p. 243.

in practicing contraception have nonetheless done something which is objectively evil. Also, regarding the morality of contraception, several terms were suggested: "sin," "objective disorder," "objective evil," "disorder." A written ballot determined that "objective evil" would be used. It appears that the vote counts in these instances were never revealed to the bishops. As a result, it is impossible to measure the degree of conflict and consensus on the motions, but the final document had the support of all but eight bishops.

Likewise at the same meeting, the bishops voted 145 to 65 to omit any reference to the grape boycott in their 1968 "Statement on Farm Labor," apparently because they did not want to upset small farmers in the Midwest.[32] Within five years, in a 1973 statement that passed unanimously, the bishops supported the boycott until the workers were allowed to choose a union through a secret ballot.

In 1970, the conference tried a new procedure and had separate votes on each of the eight sections of the "Statement on the Implementation of the Apostolic Letter on Mixed Marriages." Each section received more than a two-thirds vote, with the "conclusion" receiving the most negative votes, as described above. Later in the meeting, after many of the bishops had left, the assembly declared the existence of a quorum (despite visual evidence to the contrary) and then approved their statement on population control.

In 1971, the push toward consensus is seen when the bishops worked on their "Resolution on Southeast Asia." After Cardinal McIntyre had failed to have the resolution tabled, it passed 158-36. But the bishops appeared to be upset that so many voted in the negative. One sentence of the text was changed, and the resolution re-passed with just two no's. The original sentence read: "It is our firm conviction, therefore, that further prosecution of the war cannot be justified by traditional moral norms." This was changed to read: "It is our firm conviction, therefore, that the speedy ending of this war is a moral imperative of the highest priority." By weakening the statement, the bishops increased consensus.

---

32. From the minutes it is unclear what was the position of the Farm Labor Committee, which drafted the statement, on this amendment. It appears that the committee supported the boycott and was overturned by the assembly. If so, this is the first indication of a committee being overruled by an assembly vote.

Open Sessions

With the opening of NCCB/USCC meetings to the press in 1972, the actions of the conference became more public and the offering of amendments became more frequent. That year the pastoral letter on education, "To Teach as Jesus Did," received only a few minor amendments. The major challenges to the document were beaten back, in one case by the smallest of margins. Bishop Romeo Blanchette, who prided himself as a defender of orthodoxy, offered an amendment adding the words "which cannot essentially change" to a section on church teaching. Archbishop John Whealon, chairman of the Committee on Doctrine, and Bishop John Quinn argued that Bishop Blanchette's concerns were dealt with elsewhere in the document. A voice vote was inconclusive, and when the ballots were counted, the amendment lost 102-103. Another motion by Bishop George Lynch "that any teachings contrary to the Catholic faith should not be permitted under the guise of academic freedom or for other alleged reasons . . ." lost on a voice vote when it was opposed by the Committee on Education.

During the same meeting, the 1972 "Resolution on the Imperative of Peace" was amended by Archbishop Patrick O'Boyle, over the objections of the drafters, to include a reassertion of the right of self-defense (138-60). This is one of the first instances of a document being amended in a way that was opposed by the committee that drafted the statement.

Robert's Rules of Order

With the election of Archbishop Joseph Bernardin as NCCB/USCC president, the conference completed the move to *Robert's Rules of Order* and in 1975 even hired as parliamentarian, Mr. Henry Robert, the grandson of the author. For the most part though, amendments were few and fairly noncontroversial until May 1977, when the bishops offered fifty-five amendments to the pastoral letter on moral values, "To Live in Christ Jesus." Another sixty-one amendments were offered in 1977 to "The Bicentennial Consultation: A Response to the Call to Action." Clearly by 1977, the NCCB/USCC assembly procedures allowed individual bishops to challenge and change documents presented in final draft form by conference committees.

"To Live in Christ Jesus" was drafted by an ad hoc committee chaired by

Bishop John McDowell. Before any amendments were even offered, Bishop Francis Mugavero tried to send the letter back to committee because he felt it was too harsh in tone. He lost 65-162. As far as can be determined by the minutes and press releases, the bishops supported the committee's preferences most of the time in accepting or rejecting amendments.[33] Of the fifty-five amendments offered, forty-three were approved. One was close enough to require a standing vote, the rest were decided by voice votes.

Often the amendments reflect a tension in the conference between those bishops who want to insist on the obligation to follow church teaching and those who want to show pastoral concern for people. The assembly has tended both to accept amendments that strengthened the presentation of church teaching, and to reject amendments that toned down the pastoral concern. Thus an amendment changing "ask them" to "urge them" in the section dealing with birth control and the faithful passed, but another amendment to drop "understanding" as a modifier to "pastoral" was defeated. The assembly refuses to choose between being sensitive pastors and emphatic teachers. The bishops want to be both.

The 1977 response to the bicentennial consultation gave the bishops' reply to the Detroit Call to Action conference which had representatives from dioceses all over the United States. Here again, the assembly almost always followed the recommendations of the drafting committee in dealing with amendments.[34] A little over half the amendments were approved. Again the conflict was often between those who wanted to clearly articulate the hierarchy's positions on issues and those who wanted to show sensitivity to the people who participated in the Detroit meeting. Rather than being confrontational, the bishops tended to treat the Detroit participants with respect, accepting what they could, while reaffirming the bishops' and Vatican's position on controversial issues like women priests, celibacy, and birth control.

---

33. The committee's position on amendments was unclear in the minutes for more than half the amendments. When the minutes and press releases are silent, it can probably be presumed that the committee did not object to the amendment.

34. Of the sixty-one amendments offered, the minutes indicated the position of the task force on thirty-seven. In every case but one, the assembly followed the task force's recommendation in approving or rejecting the amendments. Archbishop Peter L. Gerety's amendment to have an ad hoc committee to respond to the recommendations passed over the objections of the task force.

Sometimes the bishops use parliamentary procedure to dispose discreetly of controversial but perhaps ancillary issues. For example, several recommendations from the Detroit conference were simply referred to a NCCB or USCC committee with little comment and never heard of again. A similar procedure was used on an amendment from twenty-seven bishops calling for more dialogue with the pope after his 1979 visit. Although many bishops felt there should have been more opportunities for dialogue between the pope and various groups, including themselves, few wanted to make a public issue of it in the resolution they passed following the pope's visit. The amendment was referred to the ad hoc committee on the papal visit. Although the amendment never reappeared, structured dialogues as well as papal speeches were scheduled in his 1987 visit. In March 1989, the dialogue continued with the American archbishops meeting with the pope and curial officials in Rome for twelve hours of discussions.[35]

Group Amendments

At their November 1977 meeting, the NCCB became clogged with amendments as it considered the "National Catechetical Directory." Over three-hundred amendments were proposed, although about half were withdrawn by their authors prior to a vote. In a few instances, the assembly approved as many as twelve amendments to the directory at once, but most amendments were voted on individually. This experience convinced the bishops that some other way had to be devised for handling minor amendments.

After the "National Catechetical Directory," the assembly considered more and more nonsubstantive and stylistic amendments in groups. Thus when the 1978 "Statement on the Middle East" was considered, the assembly voted at one time on thirteen amendments that were found acceptable to the drafting committee. A similar procedure dealt with thirty-two amendments to the 1978 "Pastoral Statement on the Handicapped."[36] Both motions were approved unanimously by the bishops. Likewise, sixty-four amendments were

---

35. Thomas J. Reese, "Archbishops Go to Rome," *America* 160 (March 4, 1989): 187-88, and "Discussions in Rome," *America* 160 (March 25, 1989): 260-61.

36. While the "Statement on the Handicapped" was noncontroversial, whether to spend money to have a national office for the handicapped divided the bishops.

accepted in one vote to the 1979 pastoral letter on racism, "Brothers and Sisters to Us."

This grouping of noncontroversial amendments speeded up the assembly process. Often by accepting these amendments the committee also expanded the support for its document among the bishops. One staff person reported that he was instructed by his committee to accept any amendment sent in by a bishop that did not contradict the text.

The committees also continued to turn down amendments that they thought were detrimental. In 1980, the Committee on Social Development and World Peace opposed an amendment exempting terrorists from the ban on capital punishment in its document, and the assembly followed the committee. Likewise, when amendments infringing on academic freedom were offered to the 1980 document on higher education, the Committee on Education succeeded in getting the assembly to reject them.

In 1981, on the other hand, when the Committee on Social Development and World Peace accepted an amendment to delete reference to U.S. arms shipments to El Salvador from their "Statement on Central America," Archbishop James Hickey objected. He feared that the deletion would look like a retreat from the conference's long-standing opposition to U.S. military aid to El Salvador. The assembly agreed and preserved the committee's original text. Likewise when the same committee agreed to strike a section dealing with drugs and smoking from "Health and Health Care," the assembly balked. In both cases, the assembly felt the committee had gone too far in accommodating individual bishops and their amendments.

The final document in volume 4 of *Pastoral Letters* is "The Challenge of Peace," completed in May 1983. For two solid days the bishops considered amendments and for the most part supported the committee's position.[37] About 140 votes were taken, and only in about thirteen cases did the assembly go against the drafting committee. One 115 amendments (Group IV), approved by the committee, were accepted in one vote. And, for the first time, another vote rejected 111 amendments (Group III) at once.

The votes going against the committee indicate that the assembly was often more "liberal" than the committee, which had tried to maintain

---

37. See Thomas J. Reese, "The Bishops' 'Challenge of Peace'," *America* 148 (May 21, 1983): 392-95, and Jim Castelli, *The Bishops and the Bomb* (Garden City, NY: Doubleday, 1983).

consensus by pleasing "conservatives." In three amendments by Archbishop John Quinn the assembly strengthened the document's position against first use of nuclear weapons. The assembly also supported the idea of a global body that would have authority to settle international disputes and impose peace. The assembly, with the approval of the drafting committee, also went back to an earlier draft calling for a "halt" to nuclear weapons rather than simply a "curb."

But the most interesting vote placed the assembly on record against any use of nuclear weapons, a position Cardinal Bernardin, chairman of the drafting committee, was later able to get the assembly to reverse. He explained that it was difficult to defend the possession of nuclear weapons for deterrence if any use of them was immoral. Since the bishops were going to accept deterrence conditionally, they would have to leave the question on use open, Bernardin argued. It also was hinted that the Vatican did not want this amendment.

The bishops also wanted to add to the letter the strong statements against nuclear weapons from the 1976 "To Live in Christ Jesus" and from the congressional testimony of Cardinal Krol on SALT II. Again Cardinal Bernardin was able to stop them from going beyond what the drafting committee and the Vatican felt was defensible.

Conclusion

In this analysis I have concentrated on assembly floor votes as a means of measuring conflict and consensus in the NCCB/USCC. I have purposely avoided basing the study on quotations from the floor debate because, regardless of the rhetoric of any given individual speaker, it is difficult to measure whether he speaks only for himself or for a large number of bishops. For example, the impassioned attacks on the peace pastoral by Archbishop Hannan had minimal support in the assembly.

An examination of the NCCB/USCC floor votes leads to the following conclusions:

1. USCC/NCCB statements are issued with great consensus. Final votes on major statements have reflected overwhelming support among the American bishops. Eighty-seven percent of the statements were supported by at least 90 percent of the bishops. These are clearly consensus statements. The

only statement not having at least a two-thirds majority was the 1974 "Resolution against Capital Punishment."

2. The amendment process encourages the building of consensus behind the major statements. Not only do the statements pass with the overwhelming support of the bishops, amendments are normally decided by voice votes and large majorities. The outstanding exception is the 1972 Blanchette amendment to the letter on education that lost by one vote.

3. In most cases, the assembly follows the drafting committee's recommendation on amendments. This could indicate: a) a high degree of congruence in thought between the members of committees and the members of the assembly; b) a high level of trust in the committees by the assembly membership; c) a conflict avoidance strategy whereby the committees anticipate the desires of the assembly when drafting documents or accepting amendments (this raises the question of who is following whom); and/or d) a willingness of most bishops to compromise rather than fight in public.

4. The assembly is not a rubber stamp for the drafting committees. The adoption of *Robert's Rules of Order* in place of conciliar procedures has strengthened the power of the assembly vis-à-vis the conference committees and the conference leadership. Any bishop can offer an amendment, and if he is supported by the assembly, the drafting committee is overruled. In face of hundreds of amendments the assembly sometimes limits debate, but this is a self-imposed rule which requires a two-thirds approval.

5. Sometimes the committees are more willing to compromise than the assembly. Committees have agreed to changes in their texts which the assembly later repudiates. This occurred in the 1981 "Statement on Central America" and in "Health and Health Care." Likewise in the peace pastoral "halt" was changed to "curb" and back to "halt" because the majority of bishops felt the committee had gone too far in compromising with a small minority of bishops.

6. The bishops are reluctant to back away from positions that they have taken in the past. Thus they supported including objections to military aid to El Salvador in their 1981 "Statement on Central America" and the inclusions of quotes from their 1976 "To Live in Christ Jesus" in the 1983 peace pastoral.

7. The possibility of seeming to retreat from traditional church teaching makes the assembly very nervous. The relaxing of the fast and abstinence laws in 1966 caused concern. The 1972 Blanchette amendment wanted to emphasize the unchanging nature of church doctrine. Also, the 1972 O'Boyle amendment,

reasserting the traditional right of self-defense, was inserted in the "Resolution on the Imperative of Peace." Objections to capital punishment encountered similar concerns in 1974 and 1980.

This concern for tradition made the bishops supportive of *Humanae Vitae* in 1976 and nervous about some of the recommendations of the Detroit Call to Action conference. The assembly also had difficulty understanding how any use of nuclear weapons could be justified under the traditional just war theory. At the same time, they did not want to be branded as consequentialists because of their arguments in conditionally approving deterrence.

All of this would indicate that a clearer understanding of the development of dogma would be most helpful to the bishops in their role as teachers in the NCCB/USCC. How do they distinguish whether a new teaching is a legitimate development or an abandonment of the traditional teaching of the church? A greater sophistication and consensus in this area would certainly ease decision making.

8. Finally, this analysis raises theological questions: Should *Robert's Rules of Order* or conciliar procedures be the paradigm for episcopal conference procedures? How should we think theologically about statements constructed through compromise? Is the authority of a document lessened if it is supported by a majority but not a two-thirds majority? What is the authority of statements approved while breaking NCCB/USCC rules and regulations? Does the Spirit work only on the mind of a bishop so that he understands the argument in a document, or is the Spirit also working when the bishop trusts the judgment of the drafters? Can episcopal conferences take a leadership role in the development of dogma or must they be followers?

Social science cannot answer these questions. But an examination of the history and procedures of the NCCB/USCC shows that they are important.

Table 1: Major NCCB/USCC Statements[1]

Statement	Vote[2]
Statement on the Government and Birth Control (1966)	Vu
Peace and Vietnam (1966)	B 169-5
Statement on Penance and Abstinence (1966)	B 156-32
Statement on Race Relations & Poverty (1966)	B 172-0
Resolution on Antipoverty Legislation (1967)	Vu
Resolution on Peace (1967)	V
Statement on Clerical Celibacy (1967)	V
Statement on Catholic Schools (1967)	V
The Church in Our Day (1967)	u[3]
On the Dutch Catechism (1967)	Vu
Statement on National Race Crisis (1968)	V
Resolution on Peace (1968)	V
Statement on Due Process (1968)	V
Human Life in Our Day (1968)	B 180-8
Statement on Farm Labor (1968)	V
Statement on Abortion (1969)	V
Resolution on Celibacy (April 1969)	V
Statement on Celibacy (Nov. 1969)	B 145-68
Statement in Protest of U.S. Government Programs against the Right to Life (1969)	B 143-20

1. Based on those printed in Hugh J. Nolan, ed., *Pastoral Letters of the United States Bishops* (Washington, DC: USCC, 1983), vols. 3-4.

2. "Vote" indicates how the motion passed: "V" indicates a voice vote, "B" a written ballot (followed by the number for, against, and abstaining), "H" a show of hands, "M" a mailed ballot, "S" indicates a standing vote. A "u" following any of these indicates the vote was unanimous. When the minutes do not indicate the method of voting, it is presumed to be a voice vote.

3. There is no record in the minutes of a vote on this document. Wright said no one voted against it. A. E. P. Wall, "Pastoral Meets Today's Faith Problems: Wright," *National Catholic Reporter* 4 (January 24, 1968): 2.

Resolution on Crusade against Poverty (1969)	V
Statement on Prisoners of War (1969)	V
Ecumenism (1970)	V
Christians in Our Time (1970)	Vu
Statement on Abortion (1970)	B 114-52
Resolution on Welfare Reform Legislation (1970)	V
Catholic Press (1970)	V
Statement on 25th Anniversary of the U.N. (1970)	V
Statement on the Implementation of Apostolic Letter on Mixed Marriages (1970)	B^4
Declaration on Abortion (1970)	B 224-8
Birth Control Laws (1970)	V
Resolution on the Campaign for Human Development (1970)	Vu
Resolution on Conscientious Objection and Selective Conscientious Objection (1971)	M 2/3^5
Ethical and Religious Directives for Catholic Health Facilities (1971)	B 232-7-2
Statement on Parental Rights and the Free Exercise of Religion (1971)	Vu
Resolution on Southeast Asia (1971)	V ???-2
Christian Concern for the Environment (1971)	Vu
Statement on the Missions (1971)	Vu
Population and the American Future: A Response (1972)	Vu
Where Shall the People Live? (1972)	B 206-9-1
To Teach as Jesus Did (1972)	B 197-29-4
Resolution on Imperatives of Peace (1972)	B 186-4

---

4. Separate votes on eight sections, from 214-9 to 172-49 (conclusion).

5. Nolan indicates that this was a statement by the USCC Division of World Justice and Peace (*Pastoral Letters*, vol. 3, pp. 61 and 228). Woods, who examined the minutes of the Administrative Committee and Administrative Board, indicates that the declaration was approved by a two-thirds vote in a mail ballot ("Pastoral Care," 291).

Basic Teachings for Catholic Religious Education (1973)	M 2/3
Statement on Population (1973)	Vu
Resolution on the Pro-life Constitutional Amendment (1973)	Vu
Resolution on the 25th Anniversary of the Universal Declaration of Human Rights (1973)	V[6]
Resolution towards Peace in the Middle East (1973)	Vu
The Reform of Correctional Institutions (1973)	V
Resolution on Farm Labor (1973)	Vu
Behold Your Mother: Woman of Faith (1973)	M
Resolution Against Capital Punishment (1974)	B 108-63
Resolution on Farm Labor Legislation (1974)	Hu
Statement on World Food Crisis (1974)	V
Statement on Ecclesiastical Archives (1974)	V
Resolution concerning the 10th Anniversary of the Decree on Ecumenism (1974)	V
The Eucharist and the Hungers of the Human Family (1975)	B 177-0
Pastoral Plan for Pro-life Activities (1975)	Vu
The Economy: Human Dimensions (1975)	Vu
The Right to a Decent Home (1975)	Vu
Statement on Catholic-Jewish Relations (1975)	B 190-6
Resolution on Farm Labor (1975)	Vu
Resolution on Human Life Foundation (1975)	Vu
Society and the Aged (1976)	B 211-8
Political Responsibility (1976)	B 176-5
Teach Them (1976)	B 153-30
Let the Little Children Come to Me (1976)	B 201-23
U.S.-Panama Relations (1976)	B 170-61
Resolution on the Pastoral Concern of the Church for People on the Move (1976)	Su

---

6. Passed easily, according to press release.

To Live in Christ Jesus (1976)	B 172-25
Resolution in Honor of Cardinal Krol (1976)	Vu
Statement on American Indians (1977)	B 254-8-3
Religious Liberty in Eastern Europe (1977)	B 252-2-1
The Bicentennial Consultation:	B 179-7-1
A Response to the Call to Action (1977)	
Resolution on *Jesus of Nazareth* (1977)	Vu
Principles and Guidelines for Fund Raising (1977)	V
To Do the Work of Justice (1978)	B 236-6
The Plan of Pastoral Action for	V
Family Ministry (1978)	
Statement on Handicapped People (1978)	B 216-2
Statement on the Middle East (1978)	B 213-8
Procedures on Conciliation and Arbitration (1979)	Vu
Brothers and Sisters to Us (1979)	B 215-30-2
Resolution on Cambodia (1979)	V
Resolution on Iran (1979)	V
Resolution on the Papal Visit (1979)	Vu
Resolution on the Iranian Crisis (1980)	V
Resolution on Cuban and Haitian Refugees (1980)	Vu
Pastoral Letter on Marxist Communism (1980)	B 236-17
Catholic Higher Education (1980)	B ???
Called and Gifted (1980)	Vu
Statement on Capital Punishment (1980)	B 145-31-41
Resolution on the Hostages in Iran (1980)	Vu
Statement on Central America (1981)	S ???-10
Health and Health Care (1981)	Vu
NCCB/USCC Mission Statement (1981)	Vu
The Challenge of Peace (1983)	B 238-9

Thomas J. Green

The Normative Role of Episcopal Conferences in the 1983 Code

THOMAS GREEN is professor of canon law at
The Catholic University of America

Numerous theological, canonical, and historical questions have been raised by the existence of episcopal conferences in the postconciliar church.[1] In 1985, the extraordinary synod called for a study of their theological status and doctrinal authority.[2] This prompted an international colloquium on episcopal conferences held in Salamanca in January 1988.[3] Meanwhile, the Vatican drafted a working paper on the theological and juridical status of episcopal conferences that was not released by the Congregation for Bishops until after the Salamanca meeting.[4] Some responses to the Vatican instrumentum laboris from theologians, canonists, and episcopal conferences,

---

1. For a listing of some issues for potential scholarly inquiry in this area see "Toward the Future: Perspectives and Proposals for Academic Research on Episcopal Conferences," *Jurist* 48 (1988): 397-401.

2. Synod of Bishops, "Final Report," *Origins* 15 (December 19, 1985): 444-50, especially II, C, 8.

3. For an English text of the papers resulting from this colloquium see *Jurist* 48 (1988): 1-412. Also H. Legrand, J. Manzanares, and A. García y García, eds., *The Nature and Future of Episcopal Conferences* (Washington, DC: Catholic University of America Press, 1988).

4. "Draft Statement on Episcopal Conferences," *Origins* 17 (April 7, 1988): 731-37. For some critical reflections on the draft see the articles by Avery Dulles, James Provost, Ladislas Orsy, and Joseph Komonchak in *America* 158 (March 19, 1988): 293-304. Also Herman Pottmeyer, "Was ist eine Bischofskonferenz?" *Stimmen der Zeit* 206/7 (July 1988): 435-46. For an overview of various issues on episcopal conferences prompted by the issuance of the *instrumentum laboris* see Felix Wilfred, "Episcopal Conferences--Their Theological Status," *Vidajyoti* 52/10 (October 1988): 470-94. See also H. Müller and H. Pottmeyer, eds., *Die Bischofskonferenz Theologischer und juridischer Status* (Dusseldorf: Verlag Patmos, 1989). Some of the articles are German versions of the papers presented at Salamanca whereas others are new works prompted by the issuance of the *instrumentum*. One article is particularly relevant to our current discussion: P. Leisching, "Die Bischofskonferenz in der kirchlichen Kodifikation von 1983" (158-177).

including that of the National Conference of Catholic Bishops, were quite critical.[5]

The normative[6] authority of episcopal conferences is an important canonical issue which has been treated in various sources.[7] Although the conference's ecclesial significance transcends its normative prerogatives, for many these prerogatives symbolize the strength or weakness, acceptance or rejection of this institution.

The conference's normative competence must be situated within the broader context of the decentralized governmental processes in the 1983 Code of Canon Law, which enhanced the normative discretion of diocesan bishops in governing their particular churches. Such expanded episcopal discretion is an example of the law's implementation of the principle of subsidiarity.[8]

---

5. For a detailed critical analysis of the *instrumentum laboris* see the Komonchak article in this volume. For the text of the NCCB response see "Response to Vatican Working Paper on Bishops' Conferences," *Origins* 18 (December 1, 1988): 397, 399-402.

6. I speak generically of the conference's "normative" function rather than more narrowly of its "legislative" function. Most of the sources consulted did not limit their analysis to the strictly legislative arena because differentiating between strict laws and general executory decrees in the code is occasionally rather difficult (as will be indicated later). In addition, a discussion of the normative function will give a more accurate understanding of the conference's legal status.

7. See especially W. Aymans, "Wesensverständnis und Zuständigkeiten der Bischofskonferenz im Çodex Iuris Canonici von 1983," *Archiv fur Katholisches Kirchenrecht* 152 (1983): 46-61; J. Calvo, "Las competencias de las conferencias episcopales y del obispo diocesano en relación con el munus sanctificandi," *Ius Canonicum* 24/47 (1984): 645-73; C. de Diego Lora, "Competencias normativas de las conferencias episcopales: primer decreto general en España," *Ius Canonicum* 24/47 (1984): 527-70; B. de Lanversin, "De la Loi générale à la Loi complémentaire dans l'Église Latine depuis le nouveau Code," in *Liberté et Loi dans l'Église Les Quatres Fleuves* 18 (Paris: Éditions Beauchesne, 1983), 121-34; P. Leisching, "Die Grenzen der heiligen Gewalt. Erwägungen über die Bischofskonferenz als hierarchische Zwischenstruktur," *Oesterreichisches Archiv fur Kirchenrecht* 36/3 (1986): 203-222; G. Melguizo et al., "Las conferencias episcopales en el nuevo Código de Derecho Canónico," *Universitas Canonica* 3/7 (1983): 41-61; F. Morrisey, "Decisions of the Episcopal Conferences in Implementing the New Law," *Studia Canonica* 20 (1986): 105-122; D. Murray, "The Legislative Authority of the Episcopal Conference," *Studia Canonica* 20 (1986): 33-48; J. Provost, "Title II: Groupings of Particular Churches," in *The Code of Canon Law: a Text and Commentary*, ed. J. Coriden, T. Green and D. Heintschel (New York: Paulist, 1985), 368-73; F. Uccella, "Le conferenze episcopali nel nuovo codice di diritto canonico: prime riflessioni," *Il Diritto Ecclesiastico* (1986): I, 95-154.

8. See Thomas Green, "Subsidiarity during the Code Revision Process: Some Initial

An area of tension during the code revision process was the interrelationship between the episcopal conference, the Holy See, and the diocesan bishop. During the revision process, the normative competency of the conference was gradually reduced,[9] partly because of fears that the conference jeopardized church unity by exaggerating nationalism and impairing the legitimate autonomy of individual bishops.[10] Interestingly, comparable fears of excessive centralization did not seem to be expressed in connection with the dicasteries of the Holy See.

Although *Christus Dominus* 36 called for the revitalization of other intermediary level governmental authorities such as particular councils (canons 439-446), this has not actually happened. On the contrary, there has been a noteworthy, if not always steady, postconciliar enhancement of the normative competence of episcopal conferences.[11] Whatever be the pre-1983 code history

---

Reflections," *Jurist* 48 (1988): 771-99. For an overview of various examples of particular law in the revised code see F. Campo del Pozo, "El derecho particular de la Iglesia según el Código de 1983," *Estudio Augustiniano* (1985): 473-528. For some helpful reflections on this issue not long before the promulgation of the code see F. Morrisey, "The Significance of Particular Law in the Proposed New Code of Canon Law," *Proceedings of the Canon Law Society of America* (1981): 1-17 (hereafter cited *CLSA Proceedings*).

9. The conference's gradually diminished normative competency during the revision process is a complex issue requiring a separate study. However, the second part of this article contains some brief references to different areas in the code exemplifying that diminished status.

10. For concerns about the possible impairment of the exercise of the episcopal office especially through an expanding conference bureaucracy see P. Gouyon, "Les rélations entre le diocèse et la conférence épiscopale," *L'Année Canonique* 22 (1978): 1-23. For some other thoughtful reflections on episcopal conference-diocesan bishop relationships see H. Muller, "The Relationship between the Episcopal Conference and the Diocesan Bishop," *Jurist* 48 (1988): 111-29.

11. For a thoughtful consideration of such enhanced conference competence in the early postconciliar period see G. Feliciani, *Le conferenze episcopali* (Bologna: Società Editrice Il Mulino, 1974), 529-45. In light of this development, section IV, 1 of the theological part of the *instrumentum laboris* observes somewhat questionably that canon law makes more attributions to particular councils than to conferences ("Draft Statement," 734). While the meaning of such "attributions" is not entirely clear, there is simply no comparison between the two institutes in terms of the attention the code devotes to them. The councils are dealt with almost exclusively in canons 439-446, which describe their main features. On the contrary, numerous references to conference functions are made throughout the code although some canonists sought even broader provisions, especially in the normative area. The *instrumentum* seems unwilling to broaden the conference's normative competency because doing so would presumably attribute to it the same dignity and authoritative power as particular councils and Oriental synods. Yet

of episcopal conferences,[12] this article focuses on their current legal status, especially in canons 447-459 of the 1983 code, which clarify their basic nature, structure, and functioning.[13] Other canons that specify the conference's normative competency regarding the church's teaching, sanctifying, and pastoral governance mission will also be examined. Despite certain differences among the commentators, the author attempts to express the scholarly consensus on those issues.

This presentation is divided into two general sections. The first section considers the place of conferences in the code: their essential nature and varied functions, their normative competency, and their relationship to diocesan bishops and the Holy See. The second section indicates specific examples of conference normative competency in the code with occasional references to restrictions on that competency that developed during the process of revising the code.

---

the *instrumentum* does not explain why this is unacceptable in principle.

12. For a couple of particularly useful canonical discussions of episcopal conferences at Vatican II shortly after the council see F. McManus, "The Scope of Authority of Episcopal Conferences," in *The Once and Future Church*, ed. J. Coriden (New York: Alba House, 1971), 129-78 and K. Moersdorf, "Commentary on *Christus Dominus*, c. III: concerning the Cooperation of Bishops for the Common Good of Many Churches," in *Commentary on the Documents of Vatican II*, ed. H. Vorgrimler, vol. 2 (New York: Herder & Herder, 1968), 280-300. For a detailed listing of conciliar references to episcopal conferences see W. Leahy, "References to Episcopal Conferences in Conciliar and Other Related Documents," in *Once and Future Church*, ed. J. Coriden, 277-99. For a detailed discussion of the conciliar treatment of the conferences see Feliciani, *Le conferenze episcopali*, 353-443. For the most thorough recent analysis of the conciliar debates on episcopal conferences see R. Sobanski, "The Theology and Juridic Status of Episcopal Conferences at the Second Vatican Council," *Jurist* 48 (1988): 68-106. For some brief but useful remarks on the canonical history of conferences through Vatican II see B. Franck, "La conférence épiscopale et les autres institutions de collégialité intermédiaires," *L'Année Canonique* 27 (1983): 69-80.

13. For commentaries on these canons see the following: J. I. Arrieta, "De las conferencias episcopales," in *Código de Derecho Canónico*, ed. P. Lombardia and J. I. Arrieta (Pamplona: Ediciones Universidad de Navarra, SA, 1983), 319-27; G. Damizia, "Le conferenze dei vescovi," in *Commento al Codice di Diritto Canonico*, ed. P. V. Pinto (Rome: Urbaniana University Press, 1985), 262-69; J. Listl, "Die Bischofskonferenzen," in *Handbuch des Katholischen Kirchenrechts*, ed. J. Listl, H. Müller, and H. Schmitz (Regensburg: Verlag Friedrich Pustet, 1983), 308-20; Provost, "Title II," 350-77; J. Sanchez y Sanchez, "De las conferencias episcopales," in *Código de Derecho Canónico*, ed. L. de Echeverría et al. (Madrid: Biblioteca de Autores Cristianos, 1983), 245-52.

SOME GENERAL REFLECTIONS

The place of episcopal conferences in the revised code[14]

Vatican II affirmed that the church is a communion of churches--a reality partly expressed through the groupings of such churches generally within a territory (*LG* 23). The council called for a revitalization of such groupings for greater pastoral effectiveness and a more unified approach to the church's teaching, sanctifying, and pastoral governance mission (*CD* 36 and 40). The council formalized the preexisting practice of bishops gathering in conferences to exchange ideas, discuss common concerns, and provide mutual support.[15]

The present code, reflecting such conciliar concerns, situates the primary canons on episcopal conferences (cc. 447-459) within the broader context of the law on the diocese, between the canons on bishops (cc. 368-430) and those on other diocesan and parish institutes (460-572).[16] In the 1917 code, conferences did not enjoy their own proper status but were treated briefly as pastoral consultative organs within the larger context of particular councils.[17] Such councils were viewed not as exercising distinctly episcopal authority but

---

14. For some brief but helpful reflections in this area see Provost, "Title II," 350-351; 363-64.

15. Feliciani expresses the significance of Vatican II for episcopal conferences rather succinctly: "*Christus Dominus* transformed conferences from unofficial meetings into instances framed by the Church's constitutional law, from voluntary assemblies into *coetus* which were now obligatory in terms of both establishment and participation, from meetings which were heterogeneous in form and composition into essentially homogeneous *conventus*, from organisms of merely moral authority into institutions capable of juridically binding deliberations, even if these were limited to specific matters and under rather rigorous conditions." G. Feliciani, "Episcopal Conferences from Vatican II to the 1983 Code," *Jurist* 48 (1988): 12.

16. For some comments on the code commission discussion of intermediary level governance figures see T. Green, "Critical Reflections on the People of God Schema," *Studia Canonica* 14 (1980): 294-303; T. Green, "Persons and Structures in the Church: Reflections on Selected Issues in Book II," *Jurist* 45 (1985): 78-83.

17. See CIC-17 (1917 Code of Canon Law), cc. 281-292 on plenary and provincial councils. Canon 292 called for meetings of the provincial bishops every five years to see what was to be done in their dioceses, to promote the good of religion, and to prepare for future provincial councils, which were technically to be held every twenty years (CIC-17, c. 283).

as sharing in supreme church authority, comparable to the college of cardinals (CIC-17, cc. 230-241), the Roman curia (CIC-17, cc. 242-264), and papal legates (CIC-17, cc. 265-270). On the contrary, the 1983 code treats both particular councils and episcopal conferences separately from the aforementioned institutes and views the former as exercising distinctly episcopal power, reflecting the pastoral solicitude of individual bishops for the good of all the churches. The basic canons on episcopal conferences (cc. 447-459) deal with various issues; however, this article examines only their nature and purpose, their functions, and their issuing of binding decisions.[18]

The Nature and Purpose of Episcopal Conferences

Unlike particular councils, which are primarily legislative entities (c. 445: ". . . *potestate gaudet regiminis, praesertim legislativa* . . . "), episcopal conferences are viewed primarily as instruments of pastoral communication and coordination among the bishops of an area (c. 447).[19] The conference is an obligatory institutionalization of the collegial responsibility of the bishops for the welfare of the church and the larger society. The conference is a significant expression of that mystery of ecclesial unity in diversity referred to in *Lumen Gentium* 23.

Among the pastoral benefits of conferences are the sharing of information and the possibility for collaboration on issues transcending diocesan and even regional boundaries. If the church's threefold mission is to be realized effectively, its pastoral approach must be adapted to diverse circumstances of time and place. Numerous pastoral issues require serious and sustained

---

18. Besides the commentaries mentioned in n. 13 on the canons on episcopal conferences see A. Acerbi, "The Development of the Canons on Conferences and the Apostolic See," *Jurist* 48 (1988): 146-52.

19. Instead of a general reference to competency in matters of faith and discipline not already determined by universal law--the competence of particular councils--the conferences can make binding decisions only on issues enumerated in the code or in virtue of a special Holy See mandate granted on its own initiative or upon conference request (*Christus Dominus* 38, 4; cc. 455, §1-2). Such restrictive provisions for conference competency contrast with the broad provisions for conference decisional activity envisioned in the 1963 conciliar schema on bishops and governance of dioceses. In this connection see Sobanski, "The Theology and Juridic Status of Episcopal Conferences at the Second Vatican Council," 84-85.

corporate study, discussion, and action if they are to be addressed knowledgeably.

Secondarily, but still rather significantly, the episcopal conference may exercise governmental authority in various areas, especially by the issuance of general decrees. The exercise of conference power, however, must respect the pastoral governance prerogatives of the Roman pontiff and the diocesan bishops. Such conference decisions have a corporate character, for the conference is an entity distinct from the individual bishops who compose it (c. 448, §1 and 450). Its authority is more than the sum of their individual powers in their respective dioceses.[20]

The episcopal conference is a collegial subject of ordinary proper power (c. 131), whose implications are explicitated throughout the code. Such power is to be exercised by the conference as a whole and not by subordinate organs such as the permanent council (e.g., NCCB Administrative Committee) (c. 457) or any individual committees (e.g., NCCB Committee on Doctrine).[21]

The conference can exercise delegated power if it is authorized by the Holy See to issue a general decree in an area not specified in the law. Such a mandate might result either from the initiative of the Holy See or at the conference's request (c. 455, §1). Unlike particular councils, which function only for a time, the conference is a permanent institute exercising the functions specified generically in canon 447 and more specifically throughout the code.

The conference's power is derived not from supreme church authority (as in the 1917 code) but from the bishops themselves exercising distinctly episcopal authority in the particular churches. That the Holy See regulates the functioning of the conference does not make it any less an exercise of episcopal power than that exercised by the diocesan bishop, who is also regulated in his governmental activity by the Holy See in view of the unity and advantage of the universal church (*Christus Dominus* 8a; c. 381, §1).[22]

---

20. See J. Manzanares, "Las conferencias episcopales a la luz del derecho canónico," in *Las conferencias episcopales hoy* (Salamanca: Universidad Pontificia, 1975), 49-53.

21. See June 10, 1966, response of Central Commission for the Coordination of Post-conciliar Work and the Interpretation of Conciliar Decrees in *Canon Law Digest* 7: 131.

22. In this connection one might note the tensions involved in a papal visitation of the archdiocese of Seattle several years ago and the appointment of an auxiliary with special faculties. The CLSA is currently conducting an interdisciplinary study of the history and present

The Functions of Episcopal Conferences

Canon 447 speaks of the bishops' jointly exercising certain pastoral functions (*munera quaedam pastoralia*) for the good of the church and society at large. The precise meaning of such functions can be discerned only after a thorough examination of the code. The conference's normative activity is only one aspect of a much broader range of functions articulated in the code. Furthermore, the full significance of the conference's legal status can be clarified only by reviewing not only the 1983 code but also extra-code documents identifying other conference functions.[23]

It is not always easy to differentiate precisely the various conference functions, partly due to the code's lack of terminological consistency in specifying them. For example, the code has no standard vocabulary to indicate when the conference may pass a new law for its territory (general decree as in c. 29) as distinct from its issuing a general executory decree (c. 31) when a code provision needs to be implemented.[24]

In a general overview of the conference in the code, Joseph Listl helpfully articulates both some general rubrics and some specific examples of conference functions.[25] He differentiates conference functions in terms of five general rubrics: 1) general decrees (c. 29); 2) general executory decrees (c. 30); 3) administrative competency; 4) a right of collaboration or consultation regarding Holy See decision-making; and 5) certain communication and information rights and duties in conference-Holy See, conference-diocesan bishop, and inter-episcopal conference relationships.[26] Listl then specifies

---

canonical legislation and practice regarding the human and canonical rights of diocesan bishops on the occasion of such a visitation. See *CLSA Proceedings* (1986): 325-26; *CLSA Proceedings* (1987): 272.

24. For example, see no. 7 of the June 1, 1988, directory of the Congregation for Divine Worship on Sunday celebrations in the absence of a priest. The conferences may regulate such celebrations in greater detail in view of differing cultures and the conditions of their people. Such decisions in turn are to be reviewed by the Holy See. Congregation for Divine Worship, "Directory for Sunday Celebrations in the Absence of a Priest," in *Origins* 18 (October 20, 1988): 301, 303-307.

24. See Provost, in "Title II," *The Code of Canon Law: A Text and Commentary*, ed. Coriden et al., 369-70.

25. See Listl, "Die Bischofskonferenzen," 313-20.

26. For a comparable analytical approach see Aymans, "Wesensverständnis," 51-54. He

areas of conference concern following the order of the code: decisions on clerical formation, altar service and priestly life (six instances); rights relative to church associations (three instances); determinations regarding relationships, communications, and mutual information pertinent to episcopal conference-Holy See relationships (six instances); conference competency regarding the particular churches (seven instances); cooperation between episcopal conferences and religious communities (one instance); conference competencies regarding the church's teaching mission (fifteen instances); conference competencies regarding the church's sanctifying mission (twenty-five instances); conference competencies regarding temporalities (eight instances); and finally, conference competencies regarding procedures (eight instances).[27]

Other authors approach the issue differently. Both de Lanversin[28] and Morrisey[29] use an Italian episcopal conference schema on conference activities

---

differentiates between 1) the conference's competency to issue general decrees (e.g., c. 230, §1 on criteria of eligibility for lectors and acolytes and c. 242 on the preparation of a *Ratio institutionis sacerdotalis*), 2) the conference's administrative powers in certain instances (e.g., c. 312 on establishing a national association of the faithful or c. 320 on suppressing such an association for due cause), and 3) the conference's collaboration rights regarding the activity of other canonical entities (e.g., c. 372 on its being consulted by the Holy See before the establishment of a personal rather than a territorial particular church and c. 467 on its receiving the declarations and decrees from diocesan synods). Subsequently, Aymans lists forty-eight examples of conference competency in the area of general decrees (pp. 54-58), twenty-nine examples of administrative competencies (pp. 58-60) and thirteen examples of collaboration rights (pp. 60-61). Provost, in "Title II," 368-72, differentiates between general decrees (c. 29) and general executory decrees (c. 30) and then lists various areas of conference functioning based on a two-fold division, i.e., the conference's competence to issue general decrees (twenty-nine instances) and other instances of conferences' being mentioned in the code (fifty-three cases).

27. For a comparable effort to clarify similar types of conference functions see Melguizo et al., "Las conferencias." This examination of episcopal conferences in the code contains a relatively brief section on the general status of the conference (cc. 447-459) and its juridic authority (pp. 42-46) and a more detailed section on conference functions throughout the code (pp. 46-58). Two concluding appendices indicate areas where the conference's normative role is not envisioned (pp. 58-59) and where such a function is called for (pp. 59-60). See also Uccella, "Le conferenze episcopali," 137-40. For some detailed reflections on diverse conference functions in the early postconciliar period that help to contextualize comparable conference functions in the current law see Feliciani, *Le conferenze episcopali*, 529-61.

28. See de Lanversin, "De la Loi Générale," 129-33.

29. See Morrisey, "Decisions of Episcopal Conferences," 108-120.

although each articulates its implications somewhat differently. First, as de Lanversin notes, a series of so-called 'informative canons' derives from the conference's function of fostering collaboration, planning, and communion among the particular churches. Second, another set of canons calls for in-depth studies by the conference of certain problems affecting the life and mission of the particular churches and church-state relationships. A third set of canons provides for the conference's exercising normative power under certain conditions.

There are other ways of understanding the conference's manifold functions.[30] Further reflection on the code, on the law in extra-code sources and on the experience of conferences in implementing the code[31] will surely lead to more satisfactory classifications of such functions. However, with the aforementioned functions in mind, we can examine the conference's normative role more thoroughly.

The Normative Role of the Episcopal Conference

A proper understanding of the conference's normative role presupposes

---

30. For example, see Uccella, "Le conferenze episcopali," 142-43:

> Di vero, ci sono canoni, in cui si explicitano le prerogative esclusive, concorrenti o addirittura surrogatorie rispetto alla potestà dei singoli vescovi diocesani e loro equiparati; oppure ove la competenza e attribuita *ex iure* che le raffigura come fonti di diritto oggettivo, certamente da non sottovalutare; o nei quali si evidenzia la loro attività latamente amministrativa anche a natura consultiva o di carattere coordinatorio con le singole diocesi; o nei quali l'esercizio della potestà legislativa è facoltativo. Infine, dalle norme si ricava anche la possibilità, per esse, di svolgere una notevole mole di lavoro informativo per il Popolo di Dio (cann. 825, par. 1 e 2, 838, par. 3, 775, par. 2, 3), perche si assicurino l'unità della fede e la disciplina dei costumi (can. 823, par. 2), nonchè di coordinare ed attuare una determinata politica ecclesiale (cann. 459, 708, 961, par. 3, 1316).

31. I will not examine the activities of individual conferences such as the NCCB. For a brief discussion of the NCCB implementation of the revised code see Daniel Hoye, "NCCB Implementation of the 1983 Code of Canon Law on the National Level: Progress and Problems," *CLSA Proceedings* (1984): 1-11. Donald Heintschel, "NCCB Implementation of the Code of Canon Law," *CLSA Proceedings* (1987): 61-66. No clear pattern seems to have emerged regarding the promulgation of conference decrees. For a useful discussion of this problematic see Morrisey, "Decisions of Episcopal Conferences," *passim*.

an examination of canon 455, which specifies the conditions under which conferences may issue general decrees.[32] This canon raises various questions regarding the relationship between the conference, the Holy See, and the diocesan bishop which need to be considered in clarifying the conference's legal status.[33]

The key source of canon 455 seems to be *Christus Dominus* 38, 4, whose formulation occasioned sharp conciliar debate over the binding force of conference decrees. Both the conciliar text and the canon reflect a compromise position that attempts to integrate various values and ensure proper respect for the universal oversight role of the Holy See and the decisional preeminence of the diocesan bishop in his particular church. Canon 455 modifies the conciliar text by indicating that the conditions specified in the canon are applicable to 'general decrees' (*decreta generalia*), a somewhat more narrow term than the term 'decisions' (*decisiones*) used in *Christus Dominus*.

What does canon 455 state? Provost summarizes the matter precisely:

> General decrees issued by a conference of bishops in accord with canon 455 have the force of particular law for the territory represented in the conference (c. 29). The authority of the

---

32. Canon 451 requires the conference to formulate its statutes on various key issues such as membership/voting rights, plenary sessions, permanent council, and the general secretariat. The conference is largely free to shape its structure in accord with its own legal-pastoral needs since the code specifies very little about such statutes, though they must be reviewed by the Holy See. The importance of conference discretion in formulating its statutes is particularly highlighted by Müller, "The Relationship between the Episcopal Conference and the Diocesan Bishop," 124-29. For a very useful presentation and analysis of the statutes of European episcopal conferences see R. Astorri, *Gli statuti delle conferenze episcopali I Europa* (Padua: CEDAM, 1987). Unfortunately, the *instrumentum* gives insufficient attention to this significant aspect of conference normative competency. Due to limitations of space the author will not consider this canon or canon 456 requiring the conference to forward the acts and decrees of its plenary sessions to the Holy See, the former for information purposes and the latter for *recognitio* purposes. This text further explicitates the rather cryptic reference to Holy See *recognitio* of conference decrees in canon 455, §2.

33. The author is particularly indebted to Provost for his analysis of canon 455, yet other relevant insights will be integrated into the following observations. Another especially helpful source has been an unpublished manuscript of F. McManus entitled "Local, Regional, and Universal Church Law" (Washington, DC: Catholic University of America, Canon Law Dept., photocopy).

conference to issue general decrees extends to those matters specified in general law or for which special authorization has been given by the Apostolic See. Two-thirds of the voting members, whether present for the vote or not, must adopt such a general decree, and their action must be reviewed by the Apostolic See before it can be promulgated and have binding effect for the area. In all other matters, a conference can act in the name of all the bishops only if all the members agree unanimously.[34]

Three important issues should be treated briefly in this connection. First, the notion of the 'decrees' treated in the canon bears examination along with the kind of authority exercised by the conference. Second, some general comments will be made on the conference's relationship to the diocesan bishop. Finally, the relationship between the episcopal conference and Holy See will be briefly addressed, particularly regarding the required *recognitio* of conference decrees.[35]

---

34. Provost, "Title II," 368. Canon 455 reads as follows:

1. Episcoporum conferentia decreta generalia ferre tantummodo potest in causis, in quibus ius universale id praescripserit aut peculiare Apostolicae Sedis mandatum sive motu proprio sive ad petitionem ipsius conferentiae id statuerit.
2. Decreta de quibus in 1., ut valide ferantur in plenario conventu, per duas saltem ex tribus partibus suffragiorum Praesulum, qui voto deliberativo fruentes ad conferentiam pertinent, proferri debent, atque vim obligandi non obtinent, nisi ab Apostolica Sede recognita, legitime promulgata fuerint.
3. Modus promulgationis et tempus a quo decreta vim suam exserunt, ab ipsa Episcoporum conferentia determinantur.
4. In casibus in quibus nec ius universale nec peculiare Apostolicae Sedis mandatum potestatem, de qua in 1, Episcoporum conferentiae concessit, singuli Episcopi dioecesani competentia integra manet, nec conferentia eiusve praeses nomine omnium Episcoporum agere valet, nisi omnes et singuli Episcopi consensum dederint.

35. See the following commentaries on canons 455-456: Acerbi, "The Development of the Canons on Conferences," 148-51; Arrieta, "De las conferencias episcopales," 324-25; Damizia, "Le conferenze dei vescovi," 267-68; Sanchez, "De las conferencias episcopales," 250-51.

The Decrees Envisioned in Canon 455

Two types of general decrees are mentioned in the code: *general decrees* issued normally by a competent legislator (c. 29) but exceptionally by an administrator with special authorization (c. 30) and *general executory decrees* issued by an administrator (c. 31). While it is occasionally difficult to determine to which type of decree the code refers, there is a fundamental difference between them. General decrees are properly laws and constitute a new regulation in an area with no preexisting norm or with a norm being modified. On the other hand, general executory decrees are subordinate to laws; the purpose of such decrees is to ensure the correct observance of existing laws. At times the code requires the conference to issue a decree (e.g., c. 766 on lay preaching) while at other times such decrees are optional (e.g., c. 891 on an age for confirmation different from the age of discretion).[36] Sometimes the conference is to act on its own (e.g., c. 851, §1 on adapting the ordo for the Christian initiation of adults). At other times, conference activity is mentioned in connection with the normative discretion of the diocesan bishop (e.g., c. 844 regarding norms on sacramental sharing).

The strict requirements of canon 455 including Roman *recognitio* seemed at first to apply only to general decrees (c. 29) since these alone were technically laws as differentiated from general executory decrees. Since canon 455 restricted the conference's normative activity, a strict interpretation seemed warranted (c. 18). However, on May 14, 1985 the Commission for the Authentic Interpretation of the Code surprisingly ruled that canon 455 applied to all general decrees including general executory decrees. This interpretation was confirmed by John Paul II on July 5, 1985.[37]

The conference exercises ordinary proper normative power where it is specified in the code. In other words, it exercises that power as a collegial juridic person in its own name in virtue of the law. The conference has indeed

---

36. On November 8, 1983, just before the new code took effect, the Secretariat of State forwarded to the presidents of episcopal conferences a list of twenty-one instances in which conference decrees were required and twenty-two instances in which such decrees were optional. Unfortunately, the secretariat did not differentiate between general decrees and general executory decrees. See *Communicationes* 15 (1983): 137-39.

37. See *Acta Apostolicae Sedis* 77 (1985): 771.

been established by supreme church authority as a hierarchic instance between the Holy See and the diocesan bishop. Technically, however, the conference is not delegated by the Holy See to issue general decrees nor does it represent the Holy See in exercising the aforementioned normative function. The fact that supreme church authority specifies certain conditions for the exercise of the conference's normative function does not alter its proper character any more than the governmental discretion of the diocesan bishop is necessarily impaired in principle by being subject to certain conditions.

Occasionally the conference may exercise delegated normative authority. Particular legal-pastoral situations in certain territories may suggest the appropriateness of conference norms in areas not provided for in universal law. In this situation a particular mandate may be issued by the Holy See on its own initiative or at the conference's request (e.g., special marriage nullity procedures somewhat comparable to the American Procedural Norms).

The Conference-Diocesan Bishop Relationship

In reflecting on canon 455, Acerbi observes that limitations on the conference's normative prerogatives reflect a code commission desire to respect the legitimate rights of diocesan bishops and the Holy Father.[38] A brief consideration of those other authority figures will help in understanding these limitations.

An understanding of the complex relationship between the diocesan bishop and the episcopal conference requires a thorough analysis of the whole code. Yet a few general observations are pertinent here. First, canon 455 highlights the preeminence of the diocesan bishop's decisions in his particular church. For example, a two-thirds majority is required to approve a general

---

38. See Acerbi, "The Development of Canons on Conferences," 148-51, especially 151:

> the right of an episcopal conference to legislate is regulated according to a principle which does not arise from its intrinsic nature, but from the need to avoid collision with other rights, namely those of the diocesan bishops such as are sanctioned in canon 381 and those of the pope which are recognized in canon 331. The view rejected by the drafters of the code is that the episcopal conference would have all the power necessary to govern a determined portion of the church, between what is reserved to the pope and what is reserved to the diocesan bishop.

decrees unlike the usual provision for a simple majority in such situations (c. 119, §2), e.g., particular council decisions. This two-thirds majority comes from all the conference members with a deliberative vote (c. 454), not simply from those who are present at the plenary session as is customary. Furthermore, such general decrees can be approved only by the plenary assembly and not by a subordinate body such as the permanent council (e.g., NCCB Administrative Committee). Finally, paragraph 4 contained in neither *Christus Dominus* nor *Ecclesiae Sanctae*, states that if the strict conditions in paragraphs 1 through 3 are not verified, the conference or its president can act in its name only if all the members approve. These provisions sharply restrict the options for juridically binding conference decisions. Furthermore, local ordinaries may dispense from conference disciplinary decrees for due cause (c. 88).

The juridically binding force of certain conference decrees should not be unduly emphasized, however important an indicator of conference legal status this may be. The 1973 *Directory on the Pastoral Ministry of Bishops*[39] stressed the morally binding force of conference pastoral orientations in areas other than such general decrees. A spirit of fraternal charity and a concern for ecclesial communion might incline a bishop to follow such orientations in setting diocesan policy even if he did not necessarily favor them during a plenary session. While the revised code carefully protects the diocesan bishop's legitimate pastoral governance autonomy, this hardly means that he can act totally in accord with his own discretion. Quite the contrary, he governs within a network of ministerial relationships within the diocese and necessarily is to collaborate with his fellow bishops in service to the *communio* of the churches.[40]

During the latter stages of the code revision process, questions were

---

39. See Sacra Congregatio pro Episcopis, *Directorium de Pastorali Ministerio Episcoporum*, February 22, 1973 (Vatican City: Typis Polyglottis Vaticanis, 1973), 217, paragraph 212b. Congregation for Bishops, *Directory on the Pastoral Ministry of Bishops* (Ottawa: Canadian Catholic Conference, 1974), 113.

40. For some thoughtful reflections on the necessarily collegial exercise of the episcopal office see Müller, "The Relationship between the Episcopal Conference and the Diocesan Bishop," passim. One should avoid a view of collegiality that is insufficiently sensitive to the importance of the individual bishop's exercising his own personal responsibility in the diocese. See de Lanversin, "De la Loi Générale," 127-28.

raised about the conference impairing the integrity of the episcopal office. Objections were posed against presumably excessive provisions for conference competence in the original code commission schemata. It is difficult to assess precisely the extent and significance of such concerns; however, they clearly moved the code commission toward a gradually more restrictive posture vis-à-vis conference competency in the 1980 schema[41] and subsequent drafts.[42]

The current law seems to reflect somewhat Calvo's view that the normative competency of the diocesan bishop should be seen as the rule and conference competency as the exception. For him the conference fulfills an extraordinary and subsidiary function vis-à-vis the individual bishop in significant issues transcending diocesan boundaries. The principle of subsidiarity is said to be operative in conference-bishop relationships, perhaps even more so than in papal-conference relationships.[43]

However, far from impairing the diocesan bishop's autonomy, the conference may notably support diocesan bishops in their ministry. Since numerous pastoral issues transcend diocesan boundaries, the formulation of

---

41. See Pontificia Commissio Codici Iuris Canonici Recognoscendo, *Schema Codicis Iuris Canonici iuxta animadversiones S.R.E. Cardinalium, Episcoporum Conferentiarum, Dicasteriorum Curiae Romanae, Universitatum Facultatumque ecclesiasticarum necnon Superiorum Institutorum vitae consecratae recognitum* (Vatican City: Libreria Editrice Vaticana, 1980). In the official code commission secretariat response to criticisms of the 1980 schema, it was explicitly mentioned that limitations of the discretion of the diocesan bishop, especially but not exclusively by the episcopal conferences, had been reduced to a minimum in reworking the original schemata. See Pontificia Commissio Codici Iuris Canonici Recognoscendo, *Relatio complectens synthesim animadversionum ab Em.mis atque Ex.mis. Patribus Commissionis ad novissimum Schema CIC exhibitarum, cum responsionibus a Secretaria et Consultoribus datis* (Vatican City: Typis Polyglottis Vaticanis, 1981), 13-14.

42. For example see Acerbi, "The Development of Canons on the Conference," 149-50; Provost, "Title II," 364. Concern about the role of the conference, especially the risk of over-bureaucratization, was forcefully expressed by Gouyon, "Les rélations entre le diocèse et la conférence épiscopale," *L'Année Canonique* 22 (1978): 1-23. He noted that some bishops were somewhat reluctant to speak at plenary sessions, felt somewhat intimidated by the conference staff, and seemed to be prevented from taking proper pastoral initiatives in their own dioceses because they were waiting, perhaps unnecessarily, for conference action in a given area(s). How significantly such apprehensions influenced the structuring of the conference's role in the 1983 code is hard to assess, but they clearly had an impact on the present law.

43. See Calvo, "Las competencias," 663-67. His focus is the exercise of the *munus sanctificandi*, but his observations are probably applicable *mutatis mutandis* to the exercise of the other *munera*.

common pastoral approaches and common norms may enhance an individual bishop's ability to deal responsibly with such issues. Notably different approaches to such issues may actually weaken episcopal authority.[44] In short, the challenge of balancing the values of respect for local autonomy and the necessity of collegial pastoral action is ongoing and defies easy resolution. The present code is one significant stage in that ongoing process.

The Episcopal Conference and the Holy See

The values of affirming papal primacy (c. 331) and fostering church unity underlie several canons stressing the significant role of the Holy See in the establishment and functioning of the conferences. For example, supreme church authority alone may establish, suppress, or change conferences (c. 449, §1), a particularly significant role if the conference does not encompass all the particular churches of a given territory as is customary (c. 448). Furthermore, Holy See *recognitio* is required for both conference statutes (c. 451) and general decrees (cc. 455, §2 and 456).

However necessary such *recognitio* may be regarding the Holy See's overall ecclesial oversight function, it generates significant tensions in Holy See-episcopal conference relationships. This is especially true when conference decrees are substantially changed during the *recognitio* process although technically they still remain episcopal conference documents.

For example, in November 1983 the NCCB voted to permit individual bishops to specify the term of office for pastors (c. 522), yet during the *recognitio* process the Holy See insisted that the term be six years with a possible renewal at the bishop's discretion. Although one may welcome the enhanced protection of the stability ·of pastors, one may also question the failure to respect conference discretion in a significant pastoral matter.[45]

---

44. See Lettman, "Episcopal Conferences in the New Canon Law," *Studia Canonica* 14 (1980): 347-67. A concern for reasonably uniform episcopal policies underlies canon 1316, which calls for neighboring diocesan bishops to strive for uniform penal laws.

45. See J. Janicki, "Chapter VI: Parishes, Pastors, and Parochial Vicars," in *The Code of Canon Law: A Text and Commentary*, ed. Coriden et al., 422-23. Murray questions whether in situations where the Holy See notably modifies conference decrees during the *recognitio* process the whole conference should be asked to discuss and vote on the amended decree. Murray, "The Legislative Authority of the Episcopal Conference," 45.

What is the rationale for the *recognitio*? For some it protects the legitimate autonomy of diocesan bishops who will be bound by conference decrees although they may have opposed their adoption. For others the *recognitio* involves a necessary review of the act of a lower level governmental organ to ensure that its activity corresponds to its competence and respects the hierarchy of norms operative in our legal system (c. 135, §2). For still others the *recognitio* reflects a concern for the harmonious activity of ecclesial communities throughout the world and a needed protection against a possible compromising of the faith, church unity, or episcopal collegiality, though one wonders how significant a concern that is today.

The *recognitio* of a conference decree does not change its nature as a distinctly episcopal conference document. The *recognitio* is a requirement for legitimate conference functioning, yet it implies less significant Roman intervention than the papal *approbatio* of a program of seminary studies (*Ratio institutionis sacerdotalis*, c. 242) or of a conference catechism (c. 775).

Legitimate questions are raised about the need for Roman *recognitio* in so many areas, especially given the code commission's application of such a requirement to both general decrees (c. 29) and general executory decrees (c. 31). This requirement poses serious problems for conferences, especially given the occasional lengthiness of the *recognitio* process. Difficulties also result from Holy See efforts to impose a uniform policy in countries as large and pastorally diverse as the United States and Canada, even when the code itself does not call for such uniformity. Greater flexibility seems warranted if the diverse legal-pastoral needs of the people of God are to be duly met. Hence serious theoretical-practical examination of the continued applicability of this requirement in its present form is imperative.[46]

AN OVERVIEW OF SPECIFIC IMPLICATIONS

After a consideration of some significant features of the general canons on episcopal conferences, I will highlight certain aspects of their normative

---

46. See Morrisey, "Decisions of Episcopal Conferences," 112; Murray, "The Legislative Authority of the Episcopal Conference," 44-46.

role following the order of the code, subdivided according to general headings. At times it is difficult to discern the rationale for the conference's normative competency although frequently the commission simply restates the *ius vigens*. In general, there is a concern to foster deeper communion among neighboring particular churches and to avoid divergent pastoral approaches that might impair legal security and be ecclesially counterproductive. There is also a concern to incarnate the gospel more effectively in various ecclesial contexts with due regard for cultural, social, legal, and religious differences.

There is hardly anything noteworthy to indicate regarding conference normative competency in Book I on general norms or Book VI on sanctions. Hence our attention will be focused on the other five books of the code.

I will not differentiate between general decrees in the strict sense (c. 29) and general executory decrees (c. 31). However, I will specify whether a given normative competency is preceptive or facultative and whether any other church authorities are mentioned in the same context as the conference. Also, in each section I will indicate selected areas in which the conference's proposed normative competency was curtailed during the revision process. This phenomenon was particularly evident in Book III on the church's teaching office, Book V on temporal goods and Book VII on procedures.[47]

Book II: the People of God (cc. 204-746)

The conference's normative role is evident in three general areas: clergy formation and life;[48] the regulation of diocesan consultative bodies, and the governance of parish ministry.

Clergy Formation and Life

Canon 242, §1 requires the conference to determine a program of priestly

---

47. See the Appendix for a comparative listing of references to conference normative competency in the 1983 code, the 1980 schema, the original code commission schemata and the conciliar documents.

48. Unlike the general clerical focus of these provisions, canon 230, §1 requires the conference to specify criteria of eligibility for those men to be formally installed in the lay ministries of lector and acolyte.

formation in light of Holy See norms and subject to subsequent Holy See approval. The conference is also to formulate norms for the formation of permanent deacons (c. 236) and more specifically to determine what part of the breviary they are expected to pray (c. 276, §2, 3º). Finally, the conference is to specify appropriate clerical attire although legitimate local custom will probably be much more influential in this respect (c. 284).

Several explicit references to the conference in the original people of God schema[49] have been dropped.[50] A rather generic norm 83 had indicated various authority figures governing ministerial formation, including the conferences. However, the absence of this provision from the code is probably not overly significant since there is still room for conference normative competency in this area. Several other provisions for conference regulation of ministerial formation and seminary administration are also absent from the current law: norm 85, 2 on permitting nonseminarians in seminaries, norm 85, 3 on training in the humanities, norm 86, 1-2 on spiritual formation, norm 92 on a pastoral internship, norm 112, 1 on seminary government and administration and norm 119, 2 on a seminary tax.

The Regulation of Diocesan Consultative Bodies

Conference norms on presbyteral councils are supposed to guide individual councils in formulating their statutes (c. 496). If local circumstances suggest it, the conference may determine that the chapter of canons function as the college of consultors (c. 502, §3).

A more extensive role for the conference was envisioned in the original people of God schema. For example, the conference was also to specify norms on diocesan finance councils (norm 306, 1) and principles pertinent to the operation of diocesan pastoral councils (norm 328, 1). Although presbyteral councils enjoy only a consultative vote in the current law (c. 500, §2), the conference could have accorded them a deliberative vote in exceptional circumstances according to the original schema (norm 314, 2).

---

49. See Pontificia Commissio Codici Iuris Canonici Recognoscendo, *Schema Canonum Libri II de Populo Dei* (Vatican City: Typis Polyglottis Vaticanis, 1977).

50. In references to the original schemata, the term "norm" is used to differentiate their provisions from the "canons" of the code.

The Governance of Parish Ministry

The conference may authorize limited terms for pastors (c. 522). Either the conference or the diocesan bishop is to specify certain provisions on parish books (c. 535, §1). The conference is to set down some general rules on the support and housing of retired pastors (c. 538, §3).[51]

Book III: the Church's Teaching Office (cc. 747-833)

The conference's normative role is evident in four general areas: ecumenical activities, preaching and doctrinal presentations, the catechumenate, and Catholic education. (At times canons contained in Book IV on the church's sanctifying office will be included for systematic reasons.)

There was a noteworthy curtailment of conference normative competency in Book III, especially in the areas of catechetics and the church's missionary activity. Since relatively little has been published on the activity of the code commission *coetus* working in this area,[52] it is difficult to know precisely the reason(s) for such changes. No postcode canonical source seems to have explored such a development. Perhaps the concerns about the conference's alleged interference in the governmental discretion of diocesan bishops encouraged the commission to limit the role of the conference.

Ecumenical Activities

Canon 755, §2 speaks first of diocesan bishops but also of the conferences' possibly issuing practical norms on ecumenism. The norms should have due regard for the prescriptions of the supreme church authority. Most commentators see supreme church authority as the primary overseer of ecumenism (e.g., 1967 and 1970 ecumenical directories). The conference functions within this broader context, and the individual diocesan bishop has an irreplaceable role in adapting such norms to the specific conditions of local

---

51. Norm 387, 1 had indicated that the conference might provide for special faculties for deans, an option not explicitly noted in the code.

52. For an overview of the work of the specialized code commission *coetus de magisterio ecclesiastico* see *Communicationes* 19 (1987): 281-84.

ecclesial situations. Canon 844, §5 (Book IV) indicates that diocesan bishops or the conference may issue general norms on sacramental sharing with members of other Christian churches or communities. Canon 1126 (Book IV) calls for conference regulation of the declarations and promises required of the Catholic party in a mixed marriage, and canon 1127, §2 provides for conference determination of the formalities for granting dispensations from canonical form in such marriages.

Norm 5 of the original schema on the church's teaching office[53] referred only to the conference (and not to individual bishops) regarding norms both on the ecumenical movement and on common prayer for Christian unity. Norm 2 of the original sacramental law schema[54] spoke first of the conference's and then of individual bishops' discretion regarding norms on sacramental sharing. The code itself focuses more sharply on the individual bishop's ecumenical responsibility and discretion (c. 383, §3).

Preaching and Doctrinal Presentations

Conference norms on lay preaching (c. 766) are to be considered by the bishop in specifying diocesan regulations on preaching (c. 772, §1). The conference is also required to set down norms on doctrinal presentations on radio or TV (c. 772, §2), especially regarding the activity of clerics and religious (c. 831, §2).

Proposed conference norms on extern priests preaching in the diocese (norm 17) and on parish missions (norm 23) are absent from the code. An early proposal envisioning conference norms on preaching in Advent and Lent in light of differing circumstances was not incorporated in the original schema.

During the code revision process, the conference's catechetical role was significantly curtailed, and the educational prerogatives of the diocesan bishop were highlighted commensurately. For example, norm 26, 1 of the original schema envisioned the conference specifying catechetical norms for its

---

53. Pontificia Commissio Codici Iuris Canonici Recognoscendo, *Schema Canonum Libri III de Ecclesiae Munere Docendi* (Vatican City: Typis Polyglottis Vaticanis, 1977).

54. See Pontificia Commissio Codici Iuris Canonici Recognoscendo, *Schema Documenti Pontificii quo Disciplina Canonica de Sacramentis Recognoscitur* (Vatican City: Typis Polyglottis Vaticanis, 1975).

jurisdiction, seeing to the preparation and dissemination of a directory, catechisms, and other catechetical materials and fostering and coordinating various catechetical undertakings.

However, the corresponding canon 775, §1 in the present code refers only to the diocesan bishop in this context. Moreover, the present law does not restate norm 27, 1 of the original schema, which called for diocesan bishops to exercise their normative catechetical role within the context of conference catechetical norms. Nor does the present law restate the original schema's reference to conference norms guiding the diocesan bishop in formulating prescriptions on sacramental preparation and other forms of catechesis (norm 30). Unlike the original schema (norm 26, 1) explicit papal approval is required of conference catechisms (c. 775, §2), but not for the catechetical initiatives of diocesan bishops (c. 775, §1).

Nor must bishops consult the conference before issuing their own catechisms, as had been proposed during the revision process to reconcile the respective catechetical prerogatives of the conference and diocesan bishops. The conference should not impose a distinct 'catechetical line' throughout its jurisdiction, rather it should simply serve individual dioceses through a catechetical office which may be established (c. 775, §3) but need not be as required in the original schema (norm 26, 2). Finally, it is clear that the conference's catechetical role has been sharply reduced in contrast to the 1971 catechetical directory of the Congregation for the Clergy (articles 46, 98, 108, and 128).

The Catechumenate/Missionary Activity

Canon 788, §3 calls for the conference to issue norms regulating the catechumenate, and canon 851, §1 (Book IV) envisions the conference's adaptation of the rite of Christian initiation of adults accordingly. The present law drops proposed conference norms concerning dialogue between missionaries and nonbelievers (norm 36, 1) and episcopal responsibilities in fostering the church's missionary enterprise (norm 40).

Still more surprising is the absence of any explicit reference to the conference in canon 782 on the direction and coordination of missionary endeavors and activities. *Lumen Gentium* 23, *Ad Gentes* 31 and 38, and *Ecclesiae Sanctae* III, 3-11, assigned serious missionary responsibilities to the episcopal conference, which remain in force until explicitly abrogated. The fear of allegedly undue conference power vis-à-vis diocesan bishops is also operative here.[55]

Catholic Education

The only pertinent provision in this connection is canon 804, §1, which calls for conference norms regarding Catholic religious formation and education in schools or in the media. The diocesan bishop is also to regulate such formation and education and to be vigilant regarding the achievement of the church's goals in this area.

Here too there was more extensive provision for conference norms in the original schema, e.g., assisting parents to fulfill their educational responsibilities by sponsoring schools (norm 43, 3), specifying the educational obligations of parents whose children are not in Catholic schools (norm 50, 3), and providing for the establishment of professional and technical schools where appropriate (norm 53, 2).

Book IV: the Church's Sanctifying Office

The conference's normative role is treated most extensively in Book IV (cc. 834-1253) on the church's sanctifying office. With due regard for the conference's adapting the liturgical books (c. 838, §3),[56] those references can be considered under three headings: the sacraments other than marriage, marriage, and sacred times and places.

Sacraments other than marriage

Canon 854 calls for conference norms on baptism by immersion or by

---

55. See J. Coriden, "The Teaching Office of the Church," in *The Code of Canon Law: A Text and Commentary*, ed. Coriden et al., 560.

56. Canon 835, §1 on competent liturgical authorities refers explicitly only to the Holy See and the diocesan bishop whereas norm 90, 1 of the original sacramental law schema also spoke of the episcopal conference. Such an omission in the former canon, however, hardly prejudices the legitimate conference liturgical regulatory role in the code and elsewhere in the liturgical books.

pouring, and canon 877, §3 requires conference provisions on registering the baptism of adopted children. The original schema had specified two other matters involving conference norms, viz., Catholic baptism of the children of mixed marriages (norm 20, 3) and the time of baptism (norm 31).

Canon 891 allows the conference to determine an age for confirmation other than the age of discretion. Canon 895 indicates that either the diocesan bishop or the conference may require parish confirmation registers.

While the conference is not mentioned in the canons on the Eucharist, two canons on penance are noteworthy. Canon 961, §2 refers to the diocesan bishop's determining whether the conditions for general absolution in his diocese meet the criteria agreed upon with the rest of the members of the conference ("*attentis criteriis cum ceteris membris Episcoporum conferentiae concordatis. . .*"). There is no other comparable code formulation regarding the conference. The text (which requires more study) highlights the diocesan bishop's decisional preeminence while indicating the importance of consultation with his peers. But it does not explicitly indicate a distinctive normative role for the conference.[57] Canon 964, §2 calls for conference norms on the arrangement of confessionals.

Canon 1031, §3 authorizes the conference to specify an age for diaconal or presbyteral ordination higher than that specified in paragraphs one and two of the same canon. Only one provision for conference normative competency in the original schema is dropped in the present law (norm 233, 3, 3º on the possible publication of banns for ordination). Several of that schema's provisions on deacons seem to be included under the general rubric of conference norms on diaconal formation in canon 236.

Marriage

As regards the premarriage period, the conference is to regulate engagements where appropriate in light of customs and civil law (c. 1062, §1) and specify rules on prenuptial investigations and banns (c. 1067). Unlike norm 262, 3 of the original schema which authorized the conference to establish marriage impediments, canon 1083, §2 permits it simply to establish

---

57. For a helpful discussion of this whole problematic see J. Manzanares, "De absolutione sacramentali generali in casu gravis necessitatis considerationes," *Periodica* 76 (1987): 130-44.

a higher age for marriage than the code provides (c. 1083, 1), yet only for liceity.

Canon 1120 permits the conference to draw up its own marriage ritual, and canon 1121, §1 calls for either the bishop or the conference to regulate the registration of marriages.

In addition to precluding the conference from establishing marriage impediments, the current law also drops norm 350, 2 empowering the conference to specify the legitimate causes for marital separation.

Sacred Times and Places[58]

The conference approves the statutes of a national shrine (c. 1232). More significantly, it determines holydays of obligations and days of fast and abstinence, although the conference's role is circumscribed in contrast to the original schema. Canon 1246 authorizes the conference with Holy See approval to abolish or transfer to Sunday the observance of the ten holydays specified in the same canon. However, the original norm 45 mandated only two holydays, namely Christmas and a Marian feast to be determined by the conference. Any other holydays were to be determined by the conference. Canon 1251 indicates that the conference may determine that some food other than meat may be the subject of the penitential abstinence obligation. Canon 1253 allows the conference to determine more precisely the implications of the penitential obligations of fast and abstinence (cc. 1249-1252) even to substituting other pious practices. The original schema left even greater latitude to the conference in this regard (norm 48, 2).

Book V: the Temporal Goods of the Church

Periodically the code provides for conference norms regarding temporal goods probably because such norms ensure better coordination of regulations

---

58. In this connection see Pontificia Commissio Codici Iuris Canonici Recognoscendo, *Schema Canonum Libri IV de Ecclesiae Munere, Sanctificandi Pars II De Locis et Temporibus Sacris deque Cultu Divino* (Vatican City: Typis Polyglottis Vaticanis, 1977). One might note the absence in the current law of original norm 28, 2 on conference determination of funeral rites in a given area.

in this complex area (cc. 1254-1310).[59] Conference norms are to regulate the faithful's contributions to the support of the church (c. 1262). The conference may also issue regulations on fund-raising which bind even mendicants (c. 1265, §2). In collaboration with the Holy See the conference is to govern the benefice system with due regard for the specifics of diverse local situations (c. 1272). The meaning of acts of extraordinary administration is also to be determined by the conference. This is a significant issue since the bishop needs the consent of the finance council (cc. 492-493) and the college of consultors (c. 502) to posit such acts validly (c. 1277). The conference helps determine the competent authority for permitting the alienation of church property by specifying minimum and maximum values requiring certain permissions (c. 1292, §1). Finally, the conference is to determine norms for the leasing of church property (c. 1297).

During the revision process, fears were expressed that proposed conference competency unduly restricted episcopal discretion. Hence the *coetus* on temporal goods decided that generally any norm that could be construed as implying such undue restrictions would be dropped, thereby enhancing the legal-pastoral prerogatives of the diocesan bishop in his particular church. For example, norm 5, 2 would have required the conference to regulate the taxing power of local ordinaries. Norm 16, 1 would have required conference norms regarding a diocesan fund for the support of clerics and conference vigilance over episcopal fulfillment of such a responsibility. Norm 16, 3 would have provided for conference specification of a comparable common fund to support other church ministers and to enable richer dioceses to support poorer ones. Finally, norm 37, 2 would have provided a conference office to monitor the bishops' discretion in authorizing the alienation of church property. All were deleted from the schema. This is more an administrative concern than a normative issue; however, it illustrates

---

59. See Pontificia Commissio Codici Iuris Canonici Recognoscendo, *Schema Canonum de Iure Patrimoniali Ecclesiae* (Vatican City: Typis Polyglottis Vaticanis, 1977). For a brief overview of the work of the code commission in this area see *Communicationes* 19 (1987): 294-96. Principle 5 for the revision of the code referred to the law on temporal goods as an area of special applicability of the principle of subsidiarity or legislative decentralization. See *Communicationes* 1 (1969): 81. Hence the commission's approach to the conference's normative role here is of particular interest. In this general context see T. Green, "Subsidiarity during the Code Revision Process," 785-89.

the fear of unwarranted conference centralization. The practical ability of some conferences to carry out such a task efficiently was also questioned.

Book VII: Procedural Law (cc. 1400-1752)[60]

While insisting on a fundamentally unified system of administering justice, principle 5 for the revision of the code expressed a cautious openness to procedural law decentralization. But no explicit reference was made to the episcopal conference in this context. In 1970 an initial report of the procedural law *coetus* referred to possible episcopal conference norms in such areas as tribunal organization and finances, and it envisioned possible conference directories governing matters left open in the code. In 1976 the original schema made no such reference although it provided for modest particular law options. In revising that schema, the *coetus* rejected suggestions that the conference be empowered to issue tribunal regulations and prepare directories governing matters not essential to the validity of the process. There was also a noteworthy curtailment of particular law options provided for in the original schema, e.g., norm 318 enabling the conference to determine instances in which the relatively new oral contentious process might be used. This general issue of conference competency was raised again during the discussion of the 1980 schema, but the commission was unwilling to permit broader infrauniversal normative discretion despite diverse sociocultural factors throughout the church. Perhaps tensions in relationships between the Holy See and countries like the United States in the implementation of procedural law indults in the 1970s influenced the commission in this regard.

Relatively few explicit provisions for conference normative competency are specified in procedural law. Canon 1714 indicates that the episcopal conferences may establish norms for conciliation and arbitration procedures. The conference may also require bishops to set up an office or council to deal with conflict resolution issues; yet even if the bishops' conference does not

---

60. See Pontificia Commissio Codici Iuris Canonici Recognoscendo, *Schema Canonum de Modo Procedendi pro Tutela Iurium seu de Processibus* (Vatican City: Typis Polyglottis Vaticanis, 1976). For a brief overview of code commission activity in this area see *Communicationes* 19 (1987): 300-303. The issues mentioned here are treated in somewhat greater detail in T. Green, "Subsidiarity during the Code Revision Process," 790-94.

require this, individual bishops may take appropriate initiatives on their own (c. 1733, §2).

Finally, a word or two on the problem of administrative tribunals.[61] There was extensive discussion of conference competency in setting up such tribunals and issuing norms to regulate their activity. Several references to such norms occurred in the original 1972 schema on administrative procedure: norm 9, 2 enabling the conference to require bishops to set up diocesan administrative tribunals; norm 13, 2 authorizing the conference to permit deacons or laymen as judges on such tribunals; norm 20, 3 permitting the conference to determine the transition from hierarchic recourse to administrative tribunal recourse and vice versa; and norm 28, 2 empowering the conference to make determinations regarding one-judge administrative tribunals.

Apparently those commenting on the schema differed regarding the conference's relationship to the Holy See and the diocesan bishop. These differences focused on such issues as the extensiveness of conference normative discretion vis-à-vis the Holy See and the appropriateness of subjecting diocesan bishops to the jurisdiction of such tribunals. In any event, at the last stage of the revision process all reference to infrauniversal level administrative tribunals was dropped from the proposed law.

GENERAL CONCLUSIONS

1) The normative role of episcopal conferences should not be unduly emphasized, given the breadth of conference legal-pastoral concerns. However, it is a significant indicator of how the conference is viewed in relationship to other institutes especially at the intermediary level of church governance.

2) The conference's expanded normative competency needs to be situated within the broader context of the 1983 code's efforts to encourage decentralized governance patterns, including an enhanced pastoral governance role for the diocesan bishop.

---

61. See Pontificia Commissio Codici Iuris Canonici Recognoscendo, *Schema canonum de procedura administrativa* (Vatican City: Typis Polyglottis Vaticanis, 1972). For a brief overview of code commission work in this area see *Communicationes* 19 (1987): 304. This issue is treated in slightly greater detail in T. Green, "Subsidiarity during the Code Revision Process," 794-96.

3) The episcopal conference seems viewed primarily as an instrument of pastoral communications and coordination among the bishops of a given territory and secondarily as an institute exercising distinctly governmental authority, e.g., by its issuing of general decrees. In this latter instance, the conference exercises episcopal authority comparable to other intermediary level governmental institutes like particular councils. Such normative authority is ordinary in the areas specified in universal law and delegated in those instances involving a special Holy See mandate.

4) The conference's specifically normative functions need to be situated within the broader context of its fairly comprehensive role in the code. My primary focus has been the conference's issuance of either general decrees or general executory decrees. However, the conference also enjoys certain administrative competencies; it has a right to collaborate with or be consulted by the Holy See in certain areas of Holy See decision making; finally, the conference has rights and duties regarding the sharing of information on issues affecting the conferences, the Holy See, and diocesan bishops.

5) Canon 455 specifies the basic conditions for the conference's issuing general decrees (c. 29), which are properly laws, and general executory decrees (c. 31), which are not technically laws but are geared to their correct observance. Such decrees must be approved by two-thirds of the voting members of the conference, present or not, at a plenary session. Moreover, such decrees must be reviewed by the Holy See (*recognitio*) before they juridically bind in the territory of the conference.

6) The aforementioned limitations on the conference's normative competency reflect the code commission's effort to protect both the diocesan bishop's decisional prerogatives and the oversight role of the Holy See in fostering church unity. Such limitations constitute the commission's response to episcopal concerns during the revision process, especially about allegedly unwarranted conference centralization.

7) The conference's normative role is expressed differently throughout the code. At times one is dealing with general decrees articulating new legal initiatives (c. 29) and at other times with general executory decrees implementing existing higher level norms (c. 31). Such norms are frequently obligatory, yet other times they are facultative. In general, the canons articulating the conference's normative competency refer solely to it, but occasionally the code mentions other church authorities (usually the diocesan bishop) in the same context.

8) The normative role of the conference is a relevant consideration neither in Book I on general norms nor in Book VI on sanctions. However, there are numerous references to such competency in the other books of the code. In all of those areas, however, the conference's normative role is diminished in contrast to the original schemata issued during the revision process. This reflects the aforementioned concerns regarding the conference's status. Such a development is particularly evident in Book III on the church's teaching office, Book V on temporal goods, and Book VII on procedures.

9) The preceding reflections have offered merely a general overview of episcopal conference normative competency in the 1983 code. To assess that competency properly some other lines of inquiry need to be pursued further. One might investigate the relationship between the code and the corresponding conciliar texts and the de facto functioning of various conferences given the different size of such conferences, different sociocultural contexts and different statutes, among other considerations. One might also examine more thoroughly specific areas of conference normative competency, e.g., the exercise of the church's teaching office.

10) Several questions need to be examined regarding the future development of the conference's normative role. A primary issue is whether the conference should enjoy the general normative competency of a particular council without the current constraints of the code. This would put it on a surer footing as a hierarchic institution comparable to the patriarchal synods. This issue cannot be addressed knowledgeably without a more thorough consideration of the conference's relationship to the diocesan bishop and the Holy See and a more careful analysis of the validity of objections to the conference raised during the revision process. Only if the appropriate pastoral autonomy of the conference, the diocesan bishop, and the Holy See is duly respected will there be fostered that healthy institutional diversity which is integral to the communion of churches.

APPENDIX

Areas of Normative Competence for
Episcopal Conferences -- Comparative Listing

P = preceptive	F = facultative
AG = *Ad Gentes*	SC = *Sacrosanctum Concilium*
OT = *Optatam totius*	UR = *Unitatis redintegratio*
PO = *Presbyterorum ordinis*	

1983 Code *Book I*	**1980 Schema** *Book I*	**Original Schemata** *General Norms*
		119, 2 (support of office-holders)
Book II	*Book II*	*People of God*
1) 230, §1 (lector-acolyte; age and qualifications)-P	275, 1	529, 1
		83 (clerical formation)
		85, 2 (nonseminarians in seminaries)
		85, 3 (training in humanities)
		86, 1-2 (spiritual formation)
2) 236 (formation of permanent deacons)-P	207	211, 2
		92 (preordination pastoral probation) (not explicit *OT* 12)
3) 242 (program of priestly formation)-P	213, 1	94, 1 (*OT* 1)
		112, 1 (seminary governance and administration)
		119, 2 (seminary tax)
4) 276, §2, 3° (breviary-permanent deacons)-P	249, 2, 3°	134, 2, 3°

1983 Code *Book II*	**1980 Schema** *Book II*	**Original Schemata** *People of God*
5) 284 (clerical dress)-P	258	144
		242, 1 (liturgical regulations)
		306, 1 (diocesan finance council norms)
6) 496 (presbyteral council norms)-P	416	310
		314, 2 (deliberative competence of presbyteral councils)
7) 502, §3 (cathedral chapter as college of consultors)-F	422, 3	
		325 (canons of honor)
		328, 1 (principles for statutes on diocesan pastoral councils)
8) 522 (limited term for pastors)-F	461	355
9) 535, §1 (parish registers)-F	474, 1	369, 1
10) 538, §3 (support and housing of retired pastors)-P	477, 3	370, 3
		387, 1 (additional faculties for deans)
		Institutes of Consecrated Life
		42 (amount for alienation)

1983 Code *Book III*	1980 Schema *Book III*	Original Schemata *Teaching Office*
11) 755, §2 (ecumenical movement)-F	709, 2	5, 1 (nothing explicit on norms) (*UR* 4)
		5, 2 (prayers for christian unity)
		17 (extradiocesan priests preaching)
12) 766 (lay preaching)-P	721	18
13) 772, §2 (radio-TV preaching)-P	727, 2	13, 3
		23 (parish missions)
		26; 27, 1; 30 (norms on catechesis)
		36, 1 (missionary dialogue with nonbelievers) (*AG* 20)
14) 788, §3 (status of catechumens)-P	743, 3	37, 3
		40 (bishops and missionary activity) (*AG* 32)
		43, 3 (assistance to parents in meeting educational responsibilities)
		50, 3 (educational obligations of parents with children not in Catholic schools)
		53, 2 (establishment of professional and technical schools)

1983 Code *Book III*	1980 Schema *Book III*	Original Schemata *Teaching Office*
15) 804, §1 (norms on religious formation and education in schools)-P	759, 1	55, 1
16) 831, §2 (clerics and religious on radio or TV regarding issues of faith and morals)-P	786, 2	

Book IV	*Book IV*	*Sacramental Law*
17) 838, §3 (preparation and issuance of liturg- ical books in vernacular)-P	792, 3	(*SC* 36, 3-4)
18) 844, §5 (sacramental sharing)-F	797, 5	2, 4 (*UR* 8) 20, 3 (baptism of child in ecumenical marriage)
19) 851, §1 (rite of Christian initiation of adults)-P	804, 1	
20) 854 (mode of baptism)-P	808	22 31 (time of baptism)
21) 877, §3 (registra- tion of baptism of adopted children)-P	831, 3	

1983 Code *Book IV*	**1980 Schema** *Book IV*	**Original Schemata** *Sacramental Law*
22) 891 (age for confir- mation)-F	845	51
23) 895 (parish confir- mation register)-F		
		90 (general liturgical compe- tence) (*SC* 22, 3)
24) 961, §2 (general absolution)	915, 2	132, 3, 1°
25) 964, §2 (confes- sional)-P	918, 2	157, 2
		215, 2 (extension of interstices between acolyte and deacon)
26) 1031, §3 (increased age for ordination)-F	984, 3	219, 3
		220, 1 (diaconal ordination before completion of five years of phil-theo studies)
		233, 3, 3° (banns for ordina- tion)
27) 1062, §1 (engage- ment)-P	1015, 1	247, 1
28) 1067, §1 (prematri- monial investigation, banns, etc.)-P	1020	250
		262, 3 (establishment of marriage impediments)

1983 Code *Book IV*	1980 Schema *Book IV*	Original Schemata *Sacramental Law*
29) 1083, §3 (higher age for marriage)-F	1036, 2	282, 2
30) 1120 (distinctive marriage rite)-F	1074, 2	320, 2 (*SC* 77)
31) 1121, §1 (recording of marriage)-F	1075, 1	321, 1 321, 3 (recording of marriage entered with dispensation from form)
32) 1126 (declarations and promises in ecumenical marriages)-P	1080	278
33) 1127, §2 (dispensation from form)-P	1081, 3	319, 3 350, 2 (causes for marital separation) *Sacred Times and Places/Divine Worship* 28, 2 (determination of funeral rites)
34) 1246, §2 (abolition or transfer of holydays of obligation)-F	1197	45
35) 1251 (abstinence from food other than meat)-F	1202	

1983 Code *Book IV*	**1980 Schema** *Book IV*	**Original Schemata** *Sacramental Law*
36) 1253 (more precise determination of fast and abstinence)-F	1204	48, 2 (*SC* 110)
		52 (Catholics sharing in non-Catholic services and non-Catholic using Catholic facilities)

Book V	*Book V*	*Patrimonial Law*
		5, 2 (norms on episcopal taxing power)
37) 1262 (contributions of faithful)-P	1214	5, 3
38) 1265, §2 (norms on fund-raising even by mendicants)-F	1216, 2	7, 2
		16, 1 (diocesan institute for clergy support) (*PO* 20-21)
		16, 3 (common diocesan fund for various ecclesial needs) (*PO* 21)
		19 (administration of interdiocesan common fund)
39) 1277 (definition of acts of extraordinary administration)		

1983 Code *Book V*	**1980 Schema** *Book V*	**Original Schemata** *Patrimonial Law*
40) 1292, §1 (minimum and maximum sums for alienation purposes)-P	1243, 1	37, 2-3
41) 1297 (leasing of church property)-P	1248	42, 2
Book VI	*Book VI*	*Sanctions*
Nothing relevant	Nothing relevant	Nothing relevant
Book VII	*Book VII*	*Procedures*
		318 (use of summary contentious process)
		333 (appellate court for summary contentious process)
42) 1714 (mediation and arbitration norms)-F	1670	
		Administrative procedure
		3 (particular law competence of episcopal conference)
		22 (possible one judge administrative courts)
43) 1733, §2 (diocesan mediation office and corresponding norms)-F	1693, 2	

Joseph A. Komonchak

The Roman Working Paper on Episcopal Conferences

JOSEPH KOMONCHAK is professor of theology at The Catholic University of America

In January 1988, Cardinal Bernard Gantin, prefect of the Congregation for Bishops, sent the bishops of the world a document entitled "Theological and Juridical Status of Episcopal Conferences."[1] An accompanying letter recalled that the "Final Report" of the 1985 synod of bishops had suggested a study of the theological status of episcopal conferences and especially of their doctrinal authority.[2] On May 19, 1986, Pope John Paul II had entrusted this task to the Congregation for Bishops, which was to undertake it in close cooperation with the Congregations for the Doctrine of the Faith, for the Oriental Churches, and for the Evangelization of Peoples, and with the General Secretariat of the synod of bishops. A study group was set up which with the help of experts produced the *instrumentum laboris*, or working document, now sent out to the bishops.

---

1. The typed copy received by the U.S. bishops was published as "Draft Statement on Episcopal Conferences," *Origins* 17 (1987-88): 731-37. Recognizing the inadequacy of the English translation provided, Archbishop John May, president of the NCCB, requested and received a copy of the original Italian text of the document. This has since been published in *Il regno-documenti* 23 (1988): 390-96. (Note: All citations of the *instrumentum laboris* are from my own translation of the Italian original, but the references are to the pages and columns of the *Origins* version.)

2. "Final Report," II, C, 8, b, *Origins* 15 (December 19, 1985): 449. Cardinal Gantin also explained that another statement of the same synod was also taken into account: "In the procedures of the Conference of Bishops, account must be taken both of the good of the Church, that is, the service of unity, and of the inalienable responsibility of each bishop for the universal Church and for his particular Church" (II, C, 5; *Origins* 15: 449).

The cardinal went on to state that the text was not to be considered definitive and that the bishops, singly or collectively, were free to correct and emend it. The questions added at the end of the text were designed to provoke "additions or descriptions which would be inserted into the text itself." After the study group has examined all the responses received, it will make appropriate revisions of the text and submit it to the pope.[3]

This is all that is publicly known about the origin and preparation of the working paper.[4] The names of the members of the study group or of the experts they consulted have never been made public. While internal inconsistencies suggest that the document was written by more than one hand, frequent nearly verbatim borrowings from several articles published in *Civiltà Cattolica*, some of them before the 1985 synod, tempt one to believe that their author had a prominent role in the preparation of the *instrumentum laboris*.[5]

Outline of the Argument

After a brief introduction, the *instrumentum laboris* is divided into two parts. The first, "The Theological Status of Episcopal Conferences," has five sections, the first three of which discuss the notions of *communio* and collegiality, the bases and realizations of collegiality, and collegiality as realized by bishops individually or when gathered in groups. Conclusions are then

---

3. The last paragraph of the introduction to the text itself confirms the provisional character of the working paper: "While seeking to be complete, it is not intended to be definitive. The very questions collected together at the end show the open character of a text which would seek to make assertions that are theologically and canonically grounded, but which may also evoke reactions capable of making this document serve its purpose more adequately, which is precisely to deepen the study of the status of episcopal conferences and above all of their magisterial authority." "Draft Statement," 731B-732A.

4. The last page of the typed text indicates that the text was finished in Rome on July 1, 1987. No explanation is available why it was sent out to the bishops only six months later.

5. See the three unsigned editorials, "La dottrina dell'episcopato prima e dopo la 'Lumen Gentium,'" *Civiltà Cattolica* 136/1 (1985): 313-24; "Conferenze episcopali e corresponsabilità dei vescovi," 136/2 (1985): 417-29; "Il Sinodo dei Vescovi come sviluppo della collegialità episcopale," 136/4 (1985): 105-17; and three articles by Giandomenico Mucci, "Il principio di sussidiarietà e la teologia del collegio episcopale," 137/2 (1986): 428-42; "Le conferenze episcopali e l'autorità del magistero," 138/1 (1987): 327-37; "Concili particolari e conferenze episcopali," 138/2 (1987): 340-48. Internal evidence suggests that Mucci was also the author of the editorials.

deduced with regard to the episcopal conferences and in particular to their teaching role.

The second section, "The Juridical Status of Episcopal Conferences," briefly discusses the legislative power and pastoral authority of the conferences, the relationship between them and the individual bishop, and the relationship between the plenary assembly of the conferences and their permanent administrative organs. The document concludes with a set of eleven questions which largely presuppose the arguments given in the text and ask how certain practical problems may be avoided or corrected.

Although the introduction briefly notes the importance assigned to episcopal conferences by Pope John Paul II, the rest of the text, especially when read in the light of the history of discussions about episcopal conferences at and since Vatican II, clearly comes down on the side of those who have wanted to restrict as much as possible the theological and juridical status of the institution. It argues that the conferences cannot properly be considered collegial in character. They have instead a primarily practical and consultative character. They are regarded as posing potential threats to the authority of individual bishops and of the pope. They do not, as collective bodies, have any magisterial role. All of these positions are presented as if they are required by the texts of Vatican II and by the revised Code of Canon Law. The argument bears striking resemblances to, and at times even verbal dependence on, the fears and warnings articulated in the critical literature summarized in the introduction to this volume.

Since that introduction has already reviewed the development of the practical critique of episcopal conferences, I will restrict myself in this article to a consideration of the central theological arguments advanced in the *instrumentum laboris* as a foundation for its restrictive assessment of the theological status of the conferences. I will return at the end of this essay, however, to the question of the relationship between the practical and the theological dimensions of the problem.

The Notion of *Communio*

The Roman text begins its argument with a discussion of the notions of ecclesial *communio* and episcopal collegiality, which the working paper rightly regards as interdependent realities. It is, therefore, not surprising that the implications which Vatican document draws with regard to the collegial character of episcopal conferences are grounded in its view of ecclesial *communio*.

The *instrumentum laboris* begins its theological argument with a brief definition of the church as *communio*: "In fact, the Church is not merely a human society; in its deepest essence it is a mysterious but real communion among those who, having received the Word of God in faith and gathered together by that same Word in the Eucharist, form in Christ a communion with God himself." In its internal and invisible reality the work of the Holy Trinity, the church is realized as a visible communion of faith, sacraments, and common life whose external principle is the episcopal college with its head, the Roman pontiff. "The invisible communion produces, preserves, and strengthens the visible communion in the Church, whether at the level of the individual believers or at that of the particular Churches." This communion grounds the equal dignity of all members while not excluding the variety of ministries.[6]

By beginning with the notion of the church as *communio*, the text echoes both the council and the 1985 synod. The description is rather rapid, however, and does not develop at all its single reference to the Eucharist as the realization of communion in particular assemblies of believers. The standpoint instead is consistently that of the universal church, a choice whose motive, it seems, is revealed later in the text when it deplores a tendency "to ignore the ontological and even historical priority of the universal Church over the particular Churches," argues that "the Church is first of all a single and universal-catholic reality. . . , the single '*communio*,' people of God and body of Christ," and defends "the primacy of the one and universal Church over the particular and local Churches."[7]

---

6. "Draft Statement," 732A-B.

7. "Draft Statement," 735A-B. The telegraphically brief argument here may depend on a speech given by Cardinal Joseph Ratzinger to the meeting of the college of cardinals in the fall of 1985 where he argued that "the unity of the Catholic church preceded the plurality of the particular churches which are born of it and receive their ecclesial character from it." This precedence, he went on to argue, is not simply ontological but historical, as evidenced in the description of the church on the day of Pentecost. See Joseph Ratzinger, "De Romano Pontifice deque collegio episcoporum" (Rome: 1985, photocopy), 3 (my translation). This argument seems to overlook that the universal church, already realized in the plurality of languages, was also a *local* church. It was the at once local and universal church *of Jerusalem* that was the mother of all other churches; see Louis Bouyer, *The Church of God: Body of Christ and Temple of the*

The issue here, of course, is not *whether* the church is a universal *communio*, but *how* it is such, that is, what it means. As the later passage shows, the question turns on the interpretation of what has been called "the most important ecclesiological formula of the Council,"[8] the statement that particular churches are "formed in the image of the universal Church" and that "it is in and out of them that the one and only catholic Church exists" (*Lumen Gentium* 23, my translation). This text has led some authors to ask which of these, the universal church or the particular churches, is to be considered to have "priority" or "primacy."[9] If there are no particular churches except as "formed in the image of the universal Church," then the latter appears to have priority. But if the universal church does not exist except as realized in and out of the particular churches, the latter appear to have priority. But if *both* statements are true, then perhaps it is best to abandon the language of "priority" or "primacy" in order to recognize the inadequacy of the distinction between the universal church and the particular churches in a recognition of their mutual interiority or, as some theologians even call it, their circumincession.[10]

The *instrumentum laboris* has not chosen this path, however, and instead assigns priority to the universal church. This fatal choice is reflected particularly in its almost total neglect of the spiritual and sacramental realization

---

Spirit (Chicago: Franciscan Herald Press, 1982), 278-79; and Henri de Lubac, *The Motherhood of the Church followed by Particular Churches in the Universal Church* (San Francisco: Ignatius Press, 1982), 207-208: "A prior universal Church, or one alleged to be existing on her own, apart from all the other churches, is only *un être de raison*."

8. Eugenio Corecco, "Aspects of the Reception of Vatican II in the Code of Canon Law," in *The Reception of Vatican II*, ed. G. Alberigo, J.-P. Jossua, and J. A. Komonchak (Washington, DC: The Catholic University of America Press, 1988), 274.

9. For two examples, compare Bruno Forte, *La chiesa, icona della Trinità: Breve ecclesiologia* (Brescia: Queriniana, 1988), 48-62, and Battista Mondin, *La Chiesa primizia del Regno* (Bologna: Dehoniane, 1986), 405-18.

10. The real issue, it seems to me, is whether the theological principles of the church's self-constitution are purely formal (and therefore abstractly universal) or must also include their material realization in specific local communities which make the one church's catholicity *concretely* universal. An ecclesiology of the church's concrete self-realization cannot regard its local character as a secondary theological principle. I have argued the point in "Towards a Theology of the Local Church," FABC [Federation of Asian Bishops' Conferences] Papers no. 42 (Hong Kong: FABC, 1986). For the inappropriateness of asking about the "priority" of one over the other, see de Lubac, *The Motherhood of the Church*, 203-208.

of the one church in the local and particular churches. It is symptomatic that the text either ignores or underplays (1) the role of the bishop as head of a particular church, representing it to the universal church, (2) the idea of the universal church as a *corpus Ecclesiarum* (*LG* 23) or communion of communions, and (3) the powerful conciliar theme of various kinds of "organic groups" of churches, in which the "*Ecclesiarum localium in unum conspirans varietas* more splendidly displays the catholicity of an undivided Church" (*LG* 23; see *Orientalium Ecclesiarum* 2-3). The result is a one-sidedly universalistic view of the church as *communio* which neglects the horizontal and reciprocal relationships among the churches because of its stress on the vertical relationship between them and the universal church.[11]

The authors of the *instrumentum laboris* appear to have been led to this choice by a fear of an emphasis on the local church which they say has recently been denounced by Pope John Paul II. The texts which they adduce, however, are far more balanced than their use of them would make one believe;[12] and they might have found in another papal address a remarkable validation of the ecclesial significance of groups of particular churches.[13]

In that speech, the pope describes dimensions of the church which are quite absent from the *instrumentum laboris*, particularly the anthropological, cultural, and historical experiences in which in various times and places the concretely catholic church comes to be in and out of the particular churches. His remarks are a commentary on the organic groupings of churches

---

11. "Like the extraordinary synod of bishops, the draft sees in episcopal collegiality the imprint of the *communio*-character of the church. But a persistent emphasis is here striking: the *universalistic vision* which displays this communion-character almost exclusively on the level of the universal church. The draft speaks of the ontological and historical priority of the universal church over the particular church. The organic mutual interiority (*Ineinander*) of local church and universal church, which the council's eucharistic ecclesiology of communion stressed, is hardly appreciated. Another emphasis follows from this: the one-sided stress on the *vertical aspect* of collegiality, while the horizontal aspect is less taken into account." Hermann-Josef Pottmeyer, "Was ist eine Bischofskonferenz? Zur Diskussion um den theologischen Status der Bischofskonferenzen," *Stimmen der Zeit* 1988: 440 (my translation).

12. The three texts mentioned in the "Draft Statement," 735A, can be found in *Insegnamenti di Giovanni Paolo II*, 8/1 (Vatican City: Libreria Editrice Vaticana, 1985), 991-98; *Insegnamenti* 9/1 (1986): 1133-34; and *L'Osservatore Romano*, December 12, 1986, 5.

13. "One Church, Many Cultures," address to the college of cardinals, December 21, 1984, *Origins* 14 (1984-85): 498-502; for the original Italian text, see *Acta Apostolicae Sedis* 77 (1985): 503-514.

described in *Lumen Gentium* 13 and 23, where the council sought to revalidate intermediate associations of churches whose ecclesial significance had been obscured, particularly in the Western church.[14] While he does not ignore the dangers of a dissolution of catholic unity, the pope provides a powerful description of "the 'special' Christian experiences" within different sociocultural contexts and of how they affect such central and basic dimensions of the church's existence as its reception of the Word of God, its worship, its theological reflection, and its unfolding of ecclesial *communio*. The papal role itself is seen as in the service of this *catholic unity*, to help assure the mutual communication of all the gifts God has given to the various particular churches for the enrichment of all and the realization of "fullness in unity."

It is the utter absence of these ecclesiological themes of the council that is so startling in the *instrumentum laboris*, particularly since it was precisely an evocation of the providential emergence of such organic groups of churches which supplied the context in which *Lumen Gentium* makes its only reference to episcopal conferences (*LG* 23). Because they ignore the reality of such organic groups and understate the significance of the local diocesan churches, it is not surprising that the authors of the *instrumentum laboris* have such difficulties in appreciating the theological status of episcopal conferences.

---

14. "The integration of the diocese into the unity of the universal church does not usually occur in an immediate way, but through larger circumscriptions or groups of particular churches, whose importance for the unity of the universal church can hardly be exaggerated. But in fact, in the Latin church for various reasons, among which church-state relations played no small role, a juridical and constitutional situation developed in which, because of the weakening of intermediate instances, in particular the office of the metropolitan, and the consequent centralization of the church's governance in the hands of the Roman curia, the room left for the development of autonomous associations of particular churches was greatly reduced. The Second Vatican Council, with regard to the question of the church's organization, was chiefly inspired by this ecclesial situation. It also, however, proposed important new ideas which take more adequate account of the demand for a distinctive life for particular churches united in larger associations. Signs of this new orientation are the anticipated restoration of the office of the metropolitan and especially the institution, however qualified, of episcopal conferences as hierarchical instances of an ecclesiastical region. Of great help in this effort, of course, was the attention given to the Oriental churches in union with the Holy See, the autonomy of which was recognized to such a degree as to ground hope for ecumenically fruitful developments." Klaus Mörsdorf, "L'autonomia della chiesa locale," in *La Chiesa dopo il Concilio*, Atti del Congresso Internazionale di Diritto Canonico, Rome 14-19 gennaio 1970 (Milan: Giuffre, 1972), I, 179 (my translation).

The Notion of Collegiality

The same fault mars the presentation of the notion of collegiality in the *instrumentum laboris*. This begins well enough, presenting collegiality as *communio* on the level of the church's pastors and rooted in the sacrament of ordination. Collegiality is not, therefore, simply a matter of external organization, but "an ontological and sacramental reality which derives from episcopal consecration and from hierarchical communion."[15]

Questions begin to arise, however, when one recognizes that the *instrumentum laboris* has chosen as the key to its exposition of Vatican II's teaching on collegiality the same universalistic view that marks its presentation of ecclesial *communio*. If I may put it this way, the text assigns priority or primacy to the whole college of bishops, presiding in the universal church, over the individual diocesan bishop, presiding in his particular church. Let me illustrate.

1. The "external principle" of the universal *communio* is said to be the whole episcopal college,[16] with little recognition that "the individual bishops are the visible principle and foundation of unity in their particular Churches" (*LG* 23).[17]

2. The effect of episcopal consecration is several times said to be insertion into the college of bishops,[18] but only once is it said to be the constitution of a bishop as "the authoritative teacher of the faith for his particular Church."[19] For a text which claims to be defending his rights, there are remarkably few references to a bishop as head of his particular church.[20] The stress falls overwhelmingly on the role of the bishop as an agent or embodiment of the universal college. This may account for the fact that the

---

15. "Draft Statement," 732B-733B.

16. "Draft Statement," 732A.

17. This conciliar text is alluded to in "Draft Statement," 733C, but in a universalistic perspective.

18. "Draft Statement," 732B, 733A, 733B.

19. "Draft Statement," 735C. For the issues at stake here, see Yves Congar, "La consécration épiscopale et la succession apostolique constituent-elles chef d'une Église locale ou membre du collège," in *Ministères et communion ecclésiale* (Paris: du Cerf, 1971), 123-40.

20. See "Draft Statement," 733C, 734A, 734C-735A.

council's careful description of how one becomes a member of the college is rather muddled in the Vatican text[21] and, as the German bishops have noted, that the word "bishop" is used with great imprecision, leaving it unclear whether it refers only or primarily to diocesan bishops or also to titular bishops.[22]

3. Although the text states that "the episcopal office is by its nature *collegial*,"[23] it says so weakly that the "personal" acts of bishops are only "open to an at least implicit collegiality" insofar as they have repercussions on other churches or on the whole church.[24] Indeed, it even says that most of their acts are not collegial, becoming so only when integrated into the higher authority of the college when this is exercised in full or partial fashion.[25] To distinguish "collegial" from "personal" in this fashion is to overlook the full *ecclesial* character of the bishop's role as head of a particular *church*.

4. This is further illustrated when the "personal" character of the bishop's authority is explained by the fact that "sacramental consecration establishes a relationship between Christ and the individual bishop, in virtue of which he alone represents and makes present the Lord as Head of his people. The episcopal college..., while remaining subject to the supreme power over the whole Church, has instead the task of representing the Church herself."[26] Being "collegial," then, means being an embodiment of the whole college, while "personal" means representing Christ.

---

21. Whereas the council had said that "one is constituted a member of the episcopal body in virtue of sacramental consecration and by hierarchical communion with the head and members of the college" (*LG* 22) and that episcopal consecration confers the three *munera Christi*, the *instrumentum laboris* maintains that "by incorporating them into the college, the imposition of hands confers upon bishops as well as the *munus docendi et sanctificandi* the *munus regendi* also." "Draft Statement," 733A. What in the council were distinguished as cause and condition here are confused together.

22. See "Stellungnahme der Deutschen Bischofskonferenz zum Instrumentum laboris 'Der theologische und juridische Status der Bischofskonferenzen,'" #2.1.

23. "Draft Statement," 733B.

24. "Draft Statement," 733C.

25. "Draft Statement," 734A.

26. "Draft Statement," 733C; for configuration with Christ as the chief "personal" effect of ordination, see also 735A, 735B.

In all of this what dominates is the role of the bishop as a member of the episcopal college rather than as head of a particular church. That the bishop is the head of a particular church is not denied, of course, but he appears to be this principally as an embodiment of the apostolic authority which is continued in the college of bishops. That this college is composed of, and perhaps could be said to exist only "in and out of" heads of particular churches is not considered. As with *communio*, the college is seen principally as "one indivisible, universal reality"[27] which precedes and grounds the identity of the individual diocesan bishop.

Important elements in the council's teaching about the college are thus neglected. The *instrumentum laboris*, for example, never cites the council statement that "this college, insofar as it is composed of many members, expresses the variety and universality of the People of God, while, insofar as it is assembled under one head, it expresses the unity of the flock of Christ. In it bishops, while faithfully respecting the primacy and pre-eminence of their head, exercise their own power for the good of their faithful, indeed for the good of the whole Church, with the Holy Spirit constantly strengthening its organic structure and harmony" (*LG* 22). Also missing is the assertion that "individual bishops represent their own Churches, while all of them, together with the pope, represent the whole Church in the bond of peace, love, and unity" (*LG* 23). Finally, the discussion of the "personal" and "collegial" character of the bishop's office falls far short of the perspectives of the council's description:

> As members of the episcopal college and legitimate successors of the Apostles, individual bishops are, by Christ's arrangement and decree, bound to have that concern for the whole Church which, although it is not exercised through an act of jurisdiction, nonetheless supremely contributes to the advantage of the universal Church. For all the bishops must promote and defend the unity of the faith and the discipline which is common to the whole Church; they must instruct the faithful in a love of the whole mystical Body of Christ and especially of the members who are poor, suffering, and undergoing persecution for the sake of justice (see Mt 5:10); they must, finally, promote all that activity which is

---

27. "Draft Statement," 733A.

common to the whole Church, especially so that faith may increase and the light of the full truth may arise upon all men. Besides, it is an established fact that by ruling well their own Churches as portions of the universal Church, bishops contribute effectively to the good of the whole mystical Body of Christ, which is itself a body of Churches (*LG* 23, my translation).

To appreciate the hermeneutical option taken by the authors of this document in interpreting Vatican II, it is helpful to recall the acute analysis of two opposing ideas of collegiality which Joseph Ratzinger discerned in the conciliar debates.[28] The modern view begins from the universal church and from the whole college. It focuses on the full and supreme power of the college, which is conceived as "the supreme governing board of the Church,"[29] and it is mainly concerned with comparing this power to the pope's full and supreme power. It derives its notion of collegiality less from the history of the church than from speculation.

The other view Ratzinger found in the church fathers. It begins with the particular church, seen not as a "part" of the church but precisely as truly the church. The head of a particular church has by that fact itself significance for the whole church which exists only in the particular churches. Correspondingly, the special role of the pope is intrinsically related to his being the head of a particular church. The chief concern of a patristically oriented notion will thus be to recover the organic role of the particular churches in the unity of the whole church.

Ratzinger noted that both of these views can be found in the conciliar documents, and that for the future much will depend on which of these is emphasized by interpreters. It seems clear that the *instrumentum laboris* has chosen to interpret the council in the light of the modern notion of collegiality. The governing perspective is consistently that of the universal church and of

---

28. Joseph Ratzinger, "Die bischöfliche Kollegialität nach der Lehre des Zweiten Vatikanischen Konzils," in *Das neue Volk Gottes: Entwürfe zur Ekklesiologie* (Dusseldorf: Patmos-Verlag, 1970), 171-200, at 184-87.

29. Ratzinger here refers to Karl Rahner's much-disputed view of the college of bishops as "the supreme governing board of the Church." See Karl Rahner, "The Episcopal Office," in *Theological Investigations*, vol. 6 (Baltimore: Helicon, 1969), 313-60. Rahner's position has been vigorously criticized by such theologians as Ratzinger, Strotmann, Bouyer, and Legrand.

the whole college of bishops. The latter is in effect seen as "the supreme governing body of the universal Church,"[30] into which members are brought by episcopal ordination, and by participating in which individual bishops have authority over particular churches. As the effect of ordination, insertion into the college takes great precedence over appointment to lead a particular church. The papal primacy is left without connection with the bishopric of the church of Rome and seen only as an implication of "the primacy of the universal Church over the particular and local Churches."

These basic perspectives on communion and collegiality govern the more precise descriptions which the *instrumentum laboris* offers of episcopal collegiality and the conclusions it draws with regard to episcopal conferences.

"Effective" and "Affective" Collegiality

Two fundamental realizations of collegiality are distinguished in the *instrumentum laboris*, those which involve the whole college and those which do not. The first are said to express collegiality "in the strict sense" and to effect an *actio collegialis*, while the second derive from the *affectus collegialis* and can only be said to be collegial in "an analogical, theologically improper sense." "In the first case, there is an effective collegiality which is not without but is indeed enriched by the *'affectus,'* while in the second case, one can speak of affective collegiality, even if some *'effectus'* cannot be excluded." Collegiality is only used properly of the first type; of the second it is better to speak of "coresponsibility." In the strict sense, collegiality is exercised only in two ways: in an ecumenical council or in a united action of all bishops called for or at least received by the pope.[31]

This programmatic statement seems clear enough, but other passages in the *instrumentum laboris* muddy the water. If bishops are led to express their coresponsibility for the governance of the whole church, through such means as the synod of bishops, this is said to represent a case of "true, but partial collegiality."[32] "A certain partial collegiality" is also ascribed to episcopal

---

30. This phrase is not found in the *instrumentum laboris*, but can be found in G. Mucci, "Concili particolari e conferenze episcopali," *Civiltà Cattolica* 138/2 (1987): 345.

31. "Draft Statement," 733A-B.

32. "Draft Statement," 733B.

acts effected within episcopal structures such as the synod and the national conferences.[33] If the conferences are later said to "express collegiality, but only in an analogous sense," a few lines later it is said that "it is not exact to speak of a collegial exercise of episcopal power in the case of the episcopal conference,"[34] and their acts are then said never to be "acts of the college."[35] The theological section of the *instrumentum laboris* concludes with the statement that a conference is "a contingent structure, of a collective, non-collegial character."[36]

The incoherence of the text's statements about the collegial character of episcopal conferences is itself an indication of the problematic character of the sharp distinction with which it begins. Because the starting point is the whole college, everything must be determined by it. When all the bishops are involved in an action, there is collegiality in the strict, true, and proper sense. Logically, it must follow therefore that certain other joint actions of bishops can be called collegial only in improper, inexact, or analogous senses.[37] That this all or nothing logic is betrayed by referring nonetheless to some of these actions as "true, but partial collegiality" is perhaps to be explained by the fact that the council, the 1985 synod, and Pope John Paul II all do speak of those other actions as collegial.[38]

---

33. "Draft Statement," 734A.
34. "Draft Statement," 734C.
35. "Draft Statement," 735C.
36. "Draft Statement," 735C.

37. The authors of the *instrumentum laboris*, like some others, may have been led to deny collegial character to the episcopal conferences by the fact that *Christus Dominus* says that they are a means by which bishops exercise their pastoral role *"coniunctim."* If the council does not use the term *"collegialiter"* here, it is not because it wished to exclude this possibility, but because the conciliar debates revealed that the question remains open. They chose, therefore, a generic term, *"coniunctim."* See Giorgio Feliciani, *Le conferenze episcopali* (Bologna: Il Mulino, 1974), 374-77, and Remigiusz Sobanski, "The Theology and the Juridic Status of Episcopal Conferences at the Second Vatican Council," in *The Nature and Future of Episcopal Conferences*, ed. H. Legrand, J. Manzanares, and A. García y García (Washington, DC: The Catholic University of America Press, 1988), 68-106.

38. For the pope's view, see Josef Tomko, "Il Sinodo dei Vescovi e Giovanni Paolo II," in *Sinodo dei Vescovi: Natura, Metodo, Prospettive* (Vatican City: Libreria Editrice Vaticana, 1985), 13-44, esp. 33-36; Giorgio Feliciani, "Le Conferenze episcopali nel magistero di Giovanni Paolo II," *Aggiornamenti sociali* 38 (1987): 141-54. It may also be, of course, that the *instrumentum laboris* had multiple authors.

It may help to clarify things to investigate the origin of the sharp initial distinction made between "effective" and "affective" collegiality. The *instrumentum laboris* correctly notes that the noun "collegiality" does not appear in the texts of Vatican II, but does not point out that neither do the two adjectives "effective" and "affective." This distinction appears to have arisen out of a postconciliar concern to put some system into the description of collegiality found in *Lumen Gentium* 22-23 and to bring it into accord with the *Nota explicativa praevia*.

In *Lumen Gentium* 22-23, a careful rereading will discover the following points: (1) the "collegial character" of the episcopal order illustrated historically; (2) its "supreme authority over the whole Church," which is exercised (3) solemnly in an ecumenical council, but can be exercised also when a (4) "united action" of the bishops around the world becomes, at least by papal reception, (5) a "collegial action" or a "true collegial act" (*LG* 22). But (6) "collegial union" is also displayed in "the mutual relationships of individual bishops with the particular Churches and with the universal Church," this being displayed in (7) the bishops' "concern for the whole Church," (8) their concern to see the gospel preached throughout the world, (9) their "universal fellowship of love" by which they come to one another's aid. Moreover, (10) organically united groups of churches have arisen by divine providence, constituting "a unity-intending variety of local Churches," in the context of which are mentioned (11) the ancient patriarchal churches and (12) episcopal conferences today, the latter being fruitful and effective realizations of (13) "collegial spirit" (*LG* 23).

Clearly these two paragraphs present a very rich and varied notion of collegiality which encompasses a broad range of experiences and activities. Some of their statements are historical, e.g., the instantiations of collegiality in the early church and the development of organic groupings of churches; some of them are quite technical, e.g., the description of what constitutes a "true collegial act"; some of them are prospective, e.g., what is hoped for from the episcopal conferences.

This rich and varied notion of collegiality was differentiated to some degree in the *Nota explicativa praevia*, which distinguished "*strictly* collegial action," occurring only occasionally, from activities in which the college, although always existing, is not "in full act." This distinction could be taken to mean that all the other instances of collegiality invoked in *Lumen Gentium* 22-23 are collegial only in some loose sense, "partial" acts of collegiality.

The history of the tendency to express these distinctions in terms of "effective" and "affective" collegiality remains to be written. To the best of my knowledge, no one at the council nor in the commentaries published immediately afterwards used this language. It began to appear in connection with the 1969 synod of bishops, where it was used, it seems, without the technical meaning it has since assumed. It served rather as a way of insisting that the "*affectus collegialis*" not be considered simply a vague sentiment but rather be put into effect, that is, rendered "effective."[39] As the tendency increased to force the council's broad and rich teaching into precise distinctions, not to say disjunctions, between "truly" or "strictly" collegial acts involving the whole college and other acts deriving "only" from the *affectus collegialis*, the adjectives "effective" and "affective" began, almost imperceptibly, to be assigned to the two kinds of acts.[40]

This shift was quite clear around the time of the 1985 synod. It appeared in commentaries on the Final Report of the synod, has been taken up in the

---

39. See René Laurentin's book, written before the Synod, *Enjeu du deuxième Synode et contestation dans l'Église* (Paris: du Seuil, 1969), 281; Angel Antón's book, *Primado y colegialidad: Sus relaciones a la luz del primer Sinodo extraordinario* (Madrid: B.A.C., 1970), 101-107, expresses the interpretation of the man who served as the synod's special secretary. I do not find elsewhere in his book or in Caprile's *Il Sinodo dei Vescovi: Prima assemblea straordinaria* (Rome: Ed. "Civiltà Cattolica," 1970) any indication that the terms "affective" and "effective" were actually used in the synodal debates. Antón's article, published just before the synod, "Sinodo e collegialità extraconciliare dei vescovi," in *La collegialità episcopale per il futuro della Chiesa* (Florence: Vallecchi, 1969), 62-78, does not use the distinction.

40. Henri de Lubac made much of this distinction in *The Motherhood of the Church*, 257-73, appealing to Willy Onclin's article, "Collegiality and the Individual Bishop," in *Pastoral Reform in Church Government*, vol. 8 of *Concilium* (New York: Paulist Press, 1965), 81-91. But neither here nor in a later article, "Le pouvoir de l'évêque et le principe de la collégialité," *La Chiesa dopo il Concilio*, vol. 1, 135-61, does Onclin deny collegiality of less than full acts of the college, as de Lubac seems to imply. By 1976, however, Jerome Hamer was arguing that the council itself had made a clear distinction between an "*actio collegialis*" and the "*affectus collegialis*." See "Chiesa locale e comunione ecclesiale," in *La chiesa locale: Prospettive teologiche e pastorali*, ed. A. Amato (Rome: Libreria Ateneo Salesiano, 1976), 29-45, at 43. Hamer reproduced this argument twice later, in "La responsabilité collégiale de chaque évêque," *Nouvelle Revue Théologique* 105 (1983): 641-54, and at the 1985 meeting of the college of cardinals; see *Synode Extraordinaire: Célébration de Vatican II* (Paris: du Cerf, 1986), 600-602. Giuseppe Alberigo was one of the few to criticize the sharp distinction and the use of "affective" and "effective" to express it; see "Istituzioni per la comunione tra l'episcopato universale e il vescovo di Roma," in *L'ecclesiologia del Vaticano II: dinamismi e prospettive*, ed. G. Alberigo (Bologna: Dehoniane, 1981), 235-62, at 249.

Vatican *instrumentum laboris*, and now threatens to become canonical. Thus, for example, the International Theological Commission (ITC), although not using the adjectives themselves, proposes the distinction to which they are applied:

> Episcopal collegiality, which succeeds to the collegiality of the Apostles, is *universal*. In relation to the *whole* of the church, it belongs to the *totality* of the episcopal body in hierarchical communion with the Roman pontiff. These conditions are fully verified in an ecumenical council and can be verified in a united action of the bishops throughout the world according to what is set down in *Christus Dominus* 4 (see *Lumen Gentium* 22). To some degree they can also be verified in the synod of bishops, because "representing the whole catholic episcopate, it at the same time indicates that all bishops participate in hierarchical communion in the concern for the whole church" (*CD* 5; see *LG* 23). On the other hand, institutions such as episcopal conferences (and their continental groups) belong to the organization and to the concrete or historical form of the church (*iure ecclesiastico*). If words such as "college," "collegiality," "collegial" are applied to them, they are being used in an analogous and theologically improper sense.[41]

While refusing the ITC's conclusion, the Final Report of the 1985 synod of bishops says that "the *affectus collegialis* is broader than effective collegiality understood in a merely juridical sense. The *affectus collegialis* is the soul of collaboration among bishops on the regional, national, and international levels."[42]

---

41. Commissio Theologica Internationalis, *Themata Selecta de Ecclesiologia* (Vatican City: Libreria Editrice Vaticana, 1985), 34 (my translation). For the controversial history of this paragraph, see Giuseppe Ruggieri, "Le conferenze episcopali viste da Roma: Collegialità affettiva ma non effettiva," *Il regno-Attualità* 33 (1988): 297 n. 2. Antón is incorrect in stating that the ITC used the words "effective" and "affective"; see "The Theological 'Status' of Episcopal Conferences," in *The Nature and Future of Episcopal Conferences*, 205.

42. "The Final Report," II, C, 4; *Origins* 15: 448C. As Antón points out, however, it is unclear, first, why effective collegiality should ever be considered purely juridically and, second, why the Final Report will later say that partial realizations of collegiality "cannot be deduced directly from the theological principle of collegiality; they are rather governed by ecclesiastical law." See Antón, "The Theological 'Status,'" 207-209.

Two authoritative commentators on the question have recently applied the two adjectives rather strictly. Walter Kasper, who helped write the Final Report, distinguishes between "effective" and "affective":

> Because of this ontological and sacramental basis, the collegiality of bishops is not only a juridical reality; it cannot be limited to effective collegiality. Consequently, affective collegiality also cannot be understood as a purely emotional reality, as a mere collegial sentiment. Affective collegiality is rather an expression of the ontological and sacramental reality of collegiality, and to that degree it is related to effective collegiality as the latter's basis.[43]

Similarly, Angel Antón repeats his distinction "between collegiality in the *strict* sense (effective) and the *affectus collegialis* (affective collegiality)."[44] It is symptomatic of the problem that both Kasper and Antón must go to some lengths to insist that the *affectus collegialis*, so far from being mere sentiment, is an ontological and sacramental reality which is the basis of "effective" collegiality.

The effect of these developments is not very fortunate. Although often presented as representing the teaching of Vatican II, the underlying distinction in fact forces the council's broad range of collegial possibilities and historical experiences into a rigid framework, derived from the *Nota praevia*'s concern about the question of supreme power in the church. The supreme exercise of collegial responsibility is taken to be the norm against which all other exercises are to be compared. Found lacking by this norm, they are almost inevitably considered, despite protests to the contrary, as "second-rate" instances of collegiality. This tendency is further aided by using the terms "effective" and "affective," which suggest that the supreme exercise of collegiality is the only one with genuine effects and that the others rest simply upon some vague

---

43. Walter Kasper, "Der theologische Status der Bischofskonferenzen," *Theologische Quartalschrift* 167 (1987): 3 (my translation).

44. Angel Antón, "La collegialità nel Sinodo dei Vescovi," in *Il Sinodo dei Vescovi*, 59-111, at 92; see also his comment: "Vatican II intended *affectus collegialis* not as a mere sentiment but as an ontological reality derived from the sacramental ordination of bishops and ordered towards *collegial action*, to 'effective collegiality.'" This position is repeated in his article, "The Theological 'Status,'" 205.

fellow-feeling among bishops. (I have heard bishops speak in this way.) The labored sentence in the *instrumentum laboris* is a perfect example: "In the first case, there is an effective collegiality which is not without but is indeed enriched by the *'affectus,'* while in the second case, one can speak of affective collegiality, even if some *'effectus'* cannot be excluded."[45] The banality of this statement is sufficient indication that the distinction between "effective" and "affective" collegiality should be abandoned.

If distinctions need to be made, there are other ways of expressing them. The council's texts would support the differentiation of "supreme" exercises of collegiality, in or outside an ecumenical council. The *Nota praevia* legitimates calling this "strict" or, better, "full" collegiality. To speak of supreme or full exercises of collegiality leaves much room for the many different ways in which the council spoke of the collegial character of the episcopal office to be recognized in their importance for the life of the church.[46] A distinction between "full" and "partial" expressions of collegiality can thus be justified, provided that the latter are not considered to be "theologically improper." Whatever distinctions are employed, however, they must be such as do not relegate to a secondary or exceptional role what the council regarded as historical and contemporary expressions of the "collegial character" of the episcopal office itself, of the "collegial union" among bishops, and of the "collegial spirit." Winfried Aymans put the issue pointedly:

> It must always be remembered that Vatican II's basis or historical proof for its teaching on the college of bishops or the "collegial nature and character of the episcopate" refers to particular synods before the council points to "the ecumenical councils celebrated in the course of history." One cannot, then, prove the principle of collegiality in the church on the

---

45. "Draft Statement," 733B.

46. Ratzinger interpreted the *Nota praevia*'s distinctions as meaning that the acts involving the full authority of the whole college "are not typical and may not even be the most important feature of collegiality, which is rather designed to recall the essentially plural *communio*-structure of the Church, so that the limits of centralization and the significance of the particular Churches are kept in mind, that is, those collegial acts which do not fulfill the conditions of an *actus stricte collegialis*." Joseph Ratzinger, "Announcements and Prefatory Notes of Explanation," in *Commentary on the Documents of Vatican II*, vol. 1, ed. H. Vorgrimler (New York: Herder and Herder, 1967), 304.

basis of particular councils in order then to maintain that the principle thus discovered is valid only on the level of the universal church.[47]

The issue remains the one which Ratzinger pointed out in 1964: Is collegiality to be considered primarily systematically and juridically, with a concentration on the question of "supreme power" over the whole church, or in a way which at once respects the full reality of the many churches within the one church and constructs its theology of church order on the basis of the church's history? As he put it then:

> The meaning of collegiality cannot in fact be that of putting a parliament in place of a monarchy, for example, but rather of restoring the value and the effectiveness of the *Ecclesiae* in the *Ecclesia*, in other words, of promoting "partial collegiality," which is, of course, as such of central significance also for the whole and gives life to the conciliar structure of the church and which at a given time can and will be exercised in ecumenical councils as the highest form of collegial activity in the church of God.[48]

And this introduces a final set of reflections on the *instrumentum laboris*.

Historical Perspectives

One of the main weaknesses of the *instrumentum laboris* is the lack of consideration of the history of the church's collegial structures which Joseph Ratzinger criticized during the conciliar debates.[49] Only one paragraph is devoted to the history of episcopal conferences. Their "remote foundation" is said to be the very ancient conviction that bishops, besides responsibility for their own churches, have "the duty of concern for the universal Church." This

---

47. Winfried Aymans, *Das synodale Element in der Kirchenverfassung* (München: Hueber-verlag, 1970), 204 (my translation).

48. Joseph Ratzinger, "Die bischöfliche Kollegialität," *Das neue Volk Gottes*, 196-97 (my translation).

49. Joseph Ratzinger, "Konkrete Formen bischöflicher Kollegialität," in *Ende der Gegenreformation?*, ed. J.C. Hampe (Berlin:Kreuz-verlag, 1964), 155-63.

led to their gathering in particular councils to discuss common problems. This promising beginning, however, is followed immediately by a description whose effect is to question the relevance of the "remote foundation":

> The same conviction also inspired in our epoch the creation and development of episcopal conferences, even if their *proximate foundation* is rather of a practical and pastoral nature (the sharing of experiences) and one which in some cases tended to make possible a unified and effective attitude among bishops confronting challenges coming from various political and social circumstances. (The solidarity of the hierarchy has been and remains, in given situations, a guarantee of the Church's autonomy and freedom of action.)[50]

The text then goes on to stress the differences in current canon law between particular councils and episcopal conferences.

Two comments may be made about this argument. First, by comparison with *Lumen Gentium*, the history is rather thin in its evocation of a sense of collegiality in the early church. The practice of holding particular councils preceded the first ecumenical council and revealed a different sense of the word "college" than that proposed in the *instrumentum laboris*. As Ratzinger notes:

> For the early church, the idea of the whole college was secondary and appeared only quite late. At least in the first four centuries, one will look in vain for the comprehensive idea that the whole college of bishops is as such the successor to the college of apostles. It is instead the particular colleges, in the local churches themselves and in the ecclesiastical provinces, which are in the foreground. That is why particular councils precede the ecumenical councils and represent the *via ordinaria* while the latter are the *via extraordinaria*.[51]

Nor does the apparent contrast implied in the suggestion that conferences emerged for "practical and pastoral" purposes in particular "political

---

50. "Draft Statement," 734A-B.
51. Ratzinger, "Die bischöfliche Kollegialität," 185-86.

and social circumstances" hold up. The agendas of the ancient regional synods reveal many items of a "practical and pastoral nature" occasioned by "political and social circumstances."[52] The similarities are greater than the differences, it seems, so that Joseph Ratzinger and Yves Congar have seen the episcopal conferences as expressions of the same spirit of episcopal solidarity that inspired the regional and national synods.[53]

Moreover, as Feliciani has made clear, this proposed distinction is also not accurate for the last 150 years during which episcopal conferences have emerged and developed. The roles played by both particular councils and episcopal conferences, the topics they considered, and the motives for which the Holy See recommended them were often identical. In at least one text, the Congregation for the Council even said that "meetings of bishops, which today are called 'conferences,' as it were take the place of synods." The relationship between the episcopal conferences and particular councils was often differently evaluated by the popes of the last two centuries as also by various fathers at Vatican II.[54]

Finally, if, as the *instrumentum laboris* points out,[55] *Christus Dominus* 36

---

52. See Hermann J. Sieben, "Episcopal Conferences in Light of Particular Councils during the First Millennium," in *The Nature and Future of Episcopal Conferences*, 30-56; Antonio García y García, "Episcopal Conferences in Light of Particular Councils during the Second Millennium," ibid., 57-67.

53. "Insofar as the bishops' conference relates back to the ancient church's synodal structure, it can and must be conceived as also an expression of the collegial structural element. In its concrete form, of course, a variable institution of ecclesiastical law, it is basically, nevertheless, an expression and form of realization of a basic given in the church: of the mutual collegial linkage among bishops, which represents an essential element of their office." Ratzinger, "Konkrete Formen bischöflicher Kollegialität," 162 (my translation); see also "The Pastoral Implications of Episcopal Collegiality," 62-63, and *Theological Highlights of Vatican II* (New York: Paulist Press, 1966), 130: "The early Church established the various synods and instituted the patriarchate; today the same reality takes a new form in episcopal conferences." For Yves Congar, see "Collège, primauté . . . Conférences épiscopales: quelques notes," *Esprit et vie* 96 (1986): 385-90. In a recent interview Congar commented: "What the episcopal colleges are doing today is the same thing. I am convinced that in the Middle Ages they would have been called 'councils.'" "La sinodalità e una forma essenziale della chiesa cattolica," *Il regno-Attualità* 31 (1986): 252 (my translation).

54. See Feliciani, *Le conferenze episcopali*, 133-35, 165-70, 279, 305, 383; the quotation is from p. 166.

55. "Draft Statement," 734B.

did express the hope that particular synods and councils "may flourish with renewed vigor," it gives no help in understanding why this ancient institution has atrophied[56] and what theological and practical considerations support its revival.

A second and more important criticism of the neglect of history in the *instrumentum laboris* recalls a point made earlier, the significance of the early councils as expressions of regional communions of churches. The text completely ignores the development, which the council called providentially guided, of organic groups of churches bound together by distinctive disciplines, liturgical usages, and theological and spiritual heritages (*LG* 23). In a fine phrase the council said that this "*Ecclesiarum localium in unum conspirans varietas* gives a more splendid demonstration of the unity of an undivided Church" (*LG* 23). The council was to echo this respect for the existence of groups of churches within the one church in its decrees on Eastern Catholic churches (*Orientalium Ecclesiarum* 2-3), on ecumenism (*Unitatis Redintegratio* 14-18), and on the church's missionary activity (*Ad Gentes* 21-22), texts which clearly demonstrate the ecumenical and missionary significance of this vision of catholicity as a *communio Ecclesiarum*. As John Paul noted in the speech cited earlier, these groups of churches have been the concrete means by which the church has become concretely Catholic as, in the words of the council, it seeks to "recapitulate all of humanity, with all of its goods, under Christ the Head, in the unity of his Spirit. In virtue of this catholicity, the individual parts bring their own gifts to the other parts and to the whole Church, so that the whole and the individual parts are increased by all sharing in and with one another and striving together towards fullness in unity" (*LG* 13).

During the council, the recovery of the ecclesial value of these intermediate associations of churches was often linked closely with the question of the role of episcopal conferences. Joseph Ratzinger, for example, pointed out the need to disentangle the confusion between the patriarchal and primatial roles of the bishop of Rome and to break up the Latin patriarchate, replacing it with a number of "patriarchal areas," that is, regions with an autonomy similar

---

56. See Eugenio Corecco, *La formazione della Chiesa cattolica negli Stati Unite d'America attraverso l'attività sinodale* (Brescia: Morcelliana, 1970), 65-84, where he discusses what he calls "a total decay of the institution of councils." An illustrative example: despite Trent's prescription of a provincial council every three years, the average province held only three councils in the last 350 years!

to that of the ancient patriarchates, but under the direction of the episcopal conferences.[57]

In an essay entitled "Primacy and Episcopacy," Ratzinger developed the theme at greater length:

> The image of a centralized state which the Catholic church presented right up to the council does not flow only from the Petrine office, but from its strict amalgamation with the patriarchal function which grew ever stronger in the course of history and which fell to the bishop of Rome for the whole of Latin Christendom. The uniform canon law, the uniform liturgy, the uniform appointment of bishops by the Roman center: all these are things which are not necessarily part of the primacy but result from the close union of the two offices. For that reason, the task to consider for the future will be to distinguish again and more clearly between the proper function of the successor of Peter and the patriarchal office and, where necessary, to create new patriarchates and to detach them from the Latin church. To embrace unity with the pope would then no longer mean being incorporated into a uniform administration, but only being inserted into a unity of faith and *communio*, in which the pope is acknowledged to have the power to give binding interpretations of the revelation given in Christ whose authority is accepted whenever it is given in definitive form.

After exploring the ecumenical implications of this vision, Ratzinger concluded: "Finally, in the not too distant future one could consider whether the churches of Asia and Africa, like those of the East, should not present their own forms as autonomous 'patriarchates' or 'great churches' or whatever such *ecclesiae* in the *Ecclesia* might be called in the future."[58] Although Ratzinger himself no longer repeats such suggestions,[59] his earlier comparison

---

57. Ratzinger, "Konkrete Formen," 158-62.

58. Ratzinger, "Primat und Episkopat," in *Das neue Volk Gottes*, 142-43 (my translation).

59. In his latest writings, Ratzinger barely takes note of the regional groupings of churches and of the particular conciliar activities of bishops which he once so extolled. Now collegiality basically means "transcending the local horizon in what is common to catholic unity," so that "particularizations basically contradict the idea of collegiality." See *Church, Ecumenism and Politics* (New York: Crossroad, 1988), 13-14, and 74-77.

of the ancient patriarchates and episcopal conferences continues to be echoed.[60]

This proposal requires, of course, as Ratzinger once admitted, recognizing the inadequacy of the simple and unhistorical distinction between episcopal and papal rights and the variability of possible expressions of collegiality.[61] The *instrumentum laboris*, however, appears content with the distinction between universal church and particular church. Its only even oblique reference to groups of churches is in the warning that episcopal conferences might give rise to "ecclesiastical instances which would claim an undue autonomy from the Apostolic See and would thus end up by setting themselves against it and its doctrinal and disciplinary directives."[62] This is followed by a repudiation of the proposal advanced by Klaus Mörsdorf on the basis of a recognition of the importance of intermediate associations of churches, namely that the conferences be given "a generalized competence in legislative matters." This, the text says, would give the conferences "the same dignity and authoritative character as particular councils and Oriental synods and could, in addition, lead to an excessive limitation of the authority of individual bishops."[63] To consider some sort of legislative autonomy for episcopal conferences as a sort of modern equivalent of ancient groupings of churches, in other words, is seen simply as a threat to the pope and to the bishop.

Because the history of particular councils and the practice of Oriental synods thus are considered to have nothing to offer to a discussion of episcopal conferences,[64] the *instrumentum laboris* can be content with a

---

60. See, for example, Hervé Legrand, "La réalisation de l'Église en un lieu," in *Initiation à la pratique de la théologie*, vol. 3, ed. B. Lauret and F. Refoulé (Paris: du Cerf, 1983), 278-87, 321-22; J.- M. Tillard, "The Theological Significance of Local Churches for Episcopal Conferences," in *The Nature and Future of Episcopal Conferences*, 226.

61. Ratzinger, "Konkrete Formen," 162.

62. "Draft Statement," 735A.

63. "Draft Statement," 735B. This section is textually dependent on Mucci's articles, "Conferenze episcopali e corresponsabilità dei vescovi," *Civiltà Cattolica* 136/2 (1985): 421-22, and "Il principio di sussidiarietà e la teologia del collegio episcopale," ibid. 137/2 (1986): 441. Morsdorf's proposal was made in "L'autonomia della Chiesa locale," 184-85.

64. The Roman text thus ignores the associations between the conferences and the Oriental synods which were made at Vatican II, in the *motu proprio, Ecclesiae sanctae*, and at the 1969 synod of bishops.

positivistic description of the differences between councils and conferences in the *ius vigens*. The latter have a primarily practical role, "within the sphere of the concrete problems of time and place, a role centered on the exchange of opinions and experiences, the purpose of which is to create a consensus about the general lines of pastoral action." Only later is this sentence, which comes close to reducing the conferences to consultative bodies, qualified with the admission that the conferences do have legislative authority within certain limits.[65] The theology behind the *instrumentum laboris*, however, offers no real reason why the conferences should ever have such authority.

It is now perhaps clear why the *instrumentum laboris* is so lacking in historical information and perspective. The history of the church's structures shows a great deal of variety in the ways in which what Ratzinger called "the collegial structural element" in the church's constitution has been expressed. The strictly juridical approach of the Roman document, focused on the supreme and universal exercise of the college's authority, represents a modern emphasis, characteristic of an ecclesiology which has departed from the more balanced ecclesiology of the first millennium and ignores the horizontal or reciprocal relationships among churches and among their heads in favor of a simple dichotomy which knows only the distinction between the universal church, presided over by the pope, and the particular church, presided over by the bishop. The essential synodality of the church in the churches thus has disappeared from view.

Conclusions

The effect of all this is a very reductionistic view of the nature and role of episcopal conferences. Since they do not involve the whole college of bishops, they cannot be considered, in the strict and proper sense, institutions expressive of collegiality. They have no theological consistency of their own, but serve only practical functions of communication and support.[66] Unless kept

---

65. "Draft Statement," 734B-C.

66. Cardinal Ratzinger precisely and forcefully stated the import of this text: "We must not forget that the episcopal conferences have no theological basis; they do not belong to the indispensable structure of the Church as Christ willed it; they have only a practical, concrete function." Ratzinger, *The Ratzinger Report*, 59. This sentence is most effectively addressed in the

carefully within these functional limits, they can only pose a threat to the authority of the individual bishop or to that of the pope. At the end of the document, one is left wondering how it is that the present pope could have ever called them "very necessary, useful and sometimes absolutely indispensable."[67]

The great question remains how could such a document ever have been considered an adequate response to the 1985 synod's call for a fuller and deeper study of the episcopal conference. The text shows no signs that the vast literature on episcopal collegiality has been reviewed,[68] that the teaching of Vatican II has been carefully and thoroughly restudied, that the ecclesiological issues at stake have been more than superficially evaluated, that the contrary opinions of other theologians and canonists have been taken into account. The *instrumentum laboris* simply reproduces as if they go without question a set of fears and criticisms with regard to episcopal conferences which, after circulating for the last fifteen years or so, were neatly summarized recently in the series of articles in *Civiltà Cattolica* on which the text draws so freely and extensively.

One may perhaps be permitted to advance the hypothesis that the real issues behind the document are not primarily theological at all, but practical and church-political. Criticisms that *some* conferences are compromising the personal authority of individual bishops appear to have been taken at face value.[69] The inevitable tensions involved in a relaxation of the centralization and uniformity of modern Roman Catholicism appear to have been one-sidedly interpreted as illegitimate calls for autonomy. Rather than addressing these practical criticisms and evaluating their accuracy, the authors of the *instrumentum laboris* have assumed their validity and rushed in with a

---

article written in 1964 in which Ratzinger criticized the view that "the bishops' conferences lack all theological basis" in order to defend the view that they are "one of the possible forms of collegiality." See "The Pastoral Implications of Episcopal Collegiality," 63-64.

67. "Draft Statement," 731B.

68. Compare the treatment of the subject in the *instrumentum laboris* with the material Aymans assembled in his book, *Das synodale Element in der Kirchenverfassung*, and his book was published in 1970!

69. A review of the reports and interventions made at the 1985 synod would reveal a generally positive assessment of the conferences as important supports for the work of individual bishops; see *Synode extraordinaire*.

theological diagnosis of the problem and a hasty solution in the form of an ecclesiology they seem to think goes without saying.

Something similar happened at Vatican II, as Joseph Ratzinger observed at the time. The debates on collegiality were being oversimplified because pragmatic concerns were being confused with theological questions, with the result that theological statements were coming close to functioning as ideological supra- or infrastructures. Desired or feared practices were being invested with divine-right status and so exempted from criticism. Ratzinger proposed an intelligent solution to this problem:

> The correct attitude must rather be to let the pragmatic remain pragmatic and clearly to see how narrow the real sphere of divine law is in the church and how wide the space left to opinion. Not least of all, it should also attempt to hinder an ideologizing of the pragmatic, a problem under which we suffer today, by which the past covered all possible practical givens with the slogan "Sanctum" and so removed them from discussion and from the play of pragmatic forces.[70]

Whether Ratzinger himself would still see things the same way is not known, but there was wisdom in his comments then, and the contemporary debate would be much elevated by remembering it. If there are practical problems with some of the episcopal conferences, they should be pointed out by all concerned and addressed practically. It should be noted that many of the ones adduced can be dealt with by a revision of the statutes of the conferences, a task which the Code of Canon Law assigns to the diocesan bishops themselves.[71] It is difficult to see how it will be a defense of the latter's

---

70. Ratzinger, "Konkrete Formen," 155-56.

71. This point has been made very clearly by Hubert Müller: "If individual problems surface which actually lie within the canonical arena, the solution is not to take recourse to the highest authority but rather for the diocesan bishops to exercise their proper responsibility according to canon 454, §2 (second half of text). They are to consider possible changes in the statutes which will ensure the proper balance between the legitimate autonomy of the particular church and the necessary collaboration of the bishops of a particular grouping of churches in view of the salvation of souls." Hubert Müller, "The Relationship between the Episcopal Conference and the Diocesan Bishop," in *The Nature and Future of Episcopal Conferences*, 129; see Hervé Legrand's comments on this article, "Reflections on Conferences and Diocesan Bishops," ibid., 132-33.

authority to deprive them of their practical self-responsibility by removing the question to the realm of higher authority.

It might also be recalled that the 1985 synod's suggestion of a fuller and deeper study of episcopal conferences does not have to be considered a call for an authoritative church document. In fact, there is much that argues against such a solution. *None* of the articulations of the theological principles found in the *instrumentum laboris* enjoys the scholarly consensus necessary before an authoritative determination.[72] Issues which the council and even the new code deliberately left unresolved need not and, it can be argued, cannot be resolved at the present time. The synod's suggestion would be most appropriately met if the basic theological questions concerning the nature of *communio*, collegiality, the magisterial role of the conferences, etc., were left for resolution by the normal course of scholarly debate among theologians, canonists, historians, and sociologists.

---

72. The best proof of this statement would be a reading of the acts of the 1988 Salamanca colloquium on episcopal conferences, held before the *instrumentum laboris* was released, as found in *The Nature and Future of Episcopal Conferences*.

Part III:

Theological

Studies

Avery Dulles, S.J.

Doctrinal Authority of Episcopal Conferences

AVERY DULLES holds the Laurence J. McGinley Chair in Religion and Society at Fordham University

The doctrinal authority of episcopal conferences could be assessed in the light of many sources. In a complete treatment it would be necessary to discuss all of the following: Vatican Council II, the revised Code of Canon Law, the statements of recent popes, those of Roman congregations, those of synods of bishops (notably the synods of 1967, 1969, and 1985, including the interventions of members of those synods), the 1987 *instrumentum laboris* circulated by the Congregation of Bishops, the approved statutes of episcopal conferences, the *praenotanda* to liturgical books promulgated by the conferences, the statements of conferences and conference officers that refer to teaching authority, the actual practice of the conferences with regard to teaching, and the opinions of theologians. In a relatively brief article it would not be possible to cover all these sources except in a very superficial way. I shall therefore severely limit my scope. In the first part of this article I shall analyze the principal statements of Vatican Council II and of the 1983 Code of Canon Law on the subject. In the second part I shall discuss the self-understanding of the United States episcopal conference as illustrated by its actual practice since 1967. Then I shall give some brief concluding reflections.

Vatican II on Episcopal Conferences

According to an ancient tradition, councils were supposed to declare the faith by a morally unanimous vote of the bishops in the Catholic communion.

A mere majority was never considered sufficient. Vatican Council II, adhering to this tradition, sought to decide controversies not by simple majorities but only by consensus. Unlike most earlier councils, however, Vatican II did not limit itself to defining the Catholic faith; it involved itself in prudential tasks of establishing contingent structures. Predictably, no real unanimity could be attained on some of these issues. On many controversial subjects the council gave only rather vague directives, leaving the specifics to be sorted out in the postconciliar period. The popes and bishops of the past generation have been struggling to clarify what Vatican II left unsettled.

Vatican II's initiatives regarding episcopal conferences are a case in point. *The Decree on the Bishops' Pastoral Office in the Church* (*Christus Dominus*) in its chapter on cooperation among bishops, strongly recommended the formation of episcopal conferences for an exchange of insights and experiences resulting in a "holy union of energies" (*sancta . . . virium conspiratio*) for the common good (*CD* 37, my translation). It then proceeded to define such a conference as "a kind of assembly [*coetus*] in which the bishops of a given nation or territory jointly exercise their pastoral office [*munus pastorale*] by way of promoting the greater good which the church offers to human beings, especially through forms and methods of the apostolate suitably adapted to the circumstances of the times" (*CD* 38.1). After specifying to some extent the membership and offices of the conferences, the decree went on to speak of their activity. "Decisions [*decisiones*] of the episcopal conferences," it declared, "provided they have been legitimately approved by at least two-thirds of the votes of the prelates who have a deliberative vote in the conference, and provided they have been reviewed [*recognitae*] by the Apostolic See, shall have juridically binding force, but only in those cases prescribed by the common law of the church or determined by a special mandate from the Apostolic See issued either on its own initiative [*motu proprio*] or in response to a petition of the conference itself" (*CD* 38.4).

Neither in these clauses nor elsewhere in the documents of Vatican II is there any explicit mention of the teaching function of the conferences. Not surprisingly, therefore, this has become a bone of contention in the postconciliar period.

Current Differences of Opinion

One group of authors, representing a negative position, denies that the episcopal conferences as such possess any teaching authority. Cardinal Joseph Ratzinger, if he is correctly reported, may be judged as holding this position. At a Roman consultation on January 18-19, 1983, he allegedly stated: "A bishops' conference as such does not have a *mandatum docendi*. This belongs only to the individual bishops or to the college of bishops with the pope. When a bishop exercises his teaching authority for his diocese, his statements are binding in conscience."[1] Once again, in *The Ratzinger Report*, the cardinal is quoted as holding: "No episcopal conference, as such, has a teaching mission; its documents have no weight of their own save that of the consent given to them by the individual bishops."[2]

A similar position is taken by James P. Green in his dissertation on the *mandatum docendi* of the episcopal conferences, and by his mentor, Gianfranco Ghirlanda, S.J., of the canon law faculty at the Gregorian University.[3] They distinguish between the *munus docendi* (teaching office) and the *potestas magisterii authentici* (authoritative teaching power). While granting that the bishops of a territory can teach conjointly through their conference, they deny that the conferences have a power to teach authoritatively unless this is conferred by special mandate from the Holy See.

A position strongly favorable to the teaching authority of episcopal conferences is taken by another canon law professor at the Gregorian University, Francisco Javier Urrutia, S.J. He asserts: "When the conference teaches, it teaches as such, and not the individual bishops insofar as they adhere to the opinions contained in the declaration. For this reason religious submission (*obsequium religiosum*) is due to the opinions proposed by the conference both on the part of the bishops themselves and on the part of the faithful of their churches."[4]

At the Salamanca consultation on episcopal conferences on January 2-9, 1988, Julio Manzanares took approximately the same position as Urrutia:

---

1. Jan Schotte, "A Vatican Synthesis," *Origins* 12 (April 7, 1983): 692.
2. Cardinal Joseph Ratzinger with Vittorio Messori, *The Ratzinger Report*, trans. Salvator Attanasio and Graham Harrison (San Francisco: Ignatius Press, 1985), 60.
3. James P. Green, *Conferences of Bishops and the Exercise of the "Munus Docendi" of the Church* (Rome: P. Graziani, 1987); Gianfranco Ghirlanda, S.J., "De Episcoporum Conferentiis deque exercitio potestatis magisterii," *Periodica* 76 (1987): 573-603.
4. Francisco Javier Urrutia, S.J., "De exercitio muneris docendi a Conferentiis Episcoporum," *Periodica* 76 (1987): 607 (my translation).

"The episcopal conference legitimately established as a unity and acting according to its statutes, is capable of exercising an authoritative magisterium and is juridically empowered to exercise this de facto."[5]

A mediating view, taken by a third group of theologians, is that episcopal conferences perform an important teaching function but that they cannot directly impose any obligation on the faithful to accept their teaching. Ladislas Orsy, S.J., for example, holds that the Holy Spirit may act through the conferences, giving new insights to the bishops, but the degree of supernatural assistance can never be measured in advance. Accordingly, their statements should be received with "religious respect," but at the same time pondered and subjected to critical examination. The teaching of the conference must in each case be assessed in the light of its harmony with Scripture, tradition, and the living faith of the universal church.[6]

The Discussion at Vatican II

The arguments for and against the teaching power of episcopal conferences generally appeal not only to the final text of the Vatican II *Decree on the Bishops' Pastoral Office* but also to the earlier drafts of that decree and to the views expressed in the debate at the council. The initial schema, *De episcoporum et de diocesium regimine* of February 1962, referred to the need for teaching on the national or territorial level because of problems that occasionally arise affecting many dioceses in a region. According to Cardinal Paolo Marella, the official reporter, "it is for it [the conference] to declare, defend, and promote those aspects of faith, morals, or law which are suited to the whole nation in the particular circumstances and to oppose the more dangerous errors and deviations."[7] The revised schema of 1963 went even further, stating that declarations of the conference would under certain conditions have binding force even for the bishops of the territory "when it is

---

5. Julio Manzanares, "The Teaching Authority of Episcopal Conferences," *Jurist* 48 (1988): 234-63.

6. Ladislas Orsy, S.J., "Episcopal Conferences: Their Theological Standing and Their Doctrinal Authority," *America* 155 (November 8, 1986): 282-85.

7. *Acta et Documenta, periodus praeparatoria*, II. 2.526 (*Relatio* of Cardinal Paolo Marella; cf. schema, I, 1, p. 520). (My translation.)

a question of publishing declarations of major importance in the name of the national conference of bishops."[8]

Some of the council fathers sent in written observations during the summer of 1963.[9] Then, on November 5-15 the matter came up for discussion in the conciliar aula. In these written and oral exchanges a number of prominent bishops, including Cardinal Albert Meyer of Chicago,[10] the then Archbishop John Krol of Philadelphia,[11] and Bishop Luigi Carli of Segni, Italy,[12] warned against assigning doctrinal responsibilities to the conference on the grounds that the conference would thereby be overburdened and that the legitimate authority of the diocesan bishops would be undercut. A much greater number of bishops, however, spoke in favor of assigning a magisterial role to the conferences, both because a doctrinal instance was needed between the Holy See and the individual diocese and because the analogies of particular councils and patriarchates suggested the appropriateness of that function.[13]

The subsequent redactions of the schema on bishops omitted any explicit mention of the teaching functions of the conference, except in a footnote asserting, in part: "Sometimes public declarations, which may on occasion be of the greatest importance, will have to be made in the name of all the bishops."[14] The official reporter, Bishop H. Schäufele, gave as the reason for omitting the previous material on the teaching functions the requirement to produce a briefer text.[15] In the final version even the explanatory note was omitted, apparently because of a policy decision to attach no notes to the decree except those referring to the sources and authorities.

What is decisive for the interpretation of the council is, of course, the final text. The dispute about the meaning of the text turns upon two rather

---

8. "Schema decreti de episcopis ac de diocesium regimine," *Acta synodalia* (*AS*) II.4.374. (My translation.)

9. *AS* II. 5. 271-401.

10. *AS* II. 5. 41-42.

11. *AS* II. 4. 424, in a written memorandum prior to the discussion in the aula.

12. *AS* II. 5. 72. 75.

13. Manzanares, "Teaching Authority," 241.

14. *AS* IV. 2. 604.

15. *AS* III. 6. 204.

ambiguous terms, *munus pastorale* and *decisiones*. The first of these terms, "pastoral," can be used in either a narrow or a broad sense. In the narrow sense, pastoral is opposed to dogmatic or doctrinal. Understood in this way, the term would imply that the conferences are devices for collaboration and consultation among the bishops as they carry on their practical tasks. According to the *instrumentum laboris* circulated in 1988, the episcopal conferences "are proposed, by their own nature, as operative, pastoral, and social means, and not directly as doctrinal means."[16] They would be on the interdiocesan level primarily consultative organs, as are pastoral councils on the diocesan level (cf. *CD* 27 and *Ecclesiam Suam* 16).

The term "pastoral," however, may also be used, and was sometimes used by Vatican II, in the broader sense that includes the doctrinal. *Christus Dominus*, as we have seen, is designated as a decree "on the pastoral office (*munus pastorale*) of the bishops," but in the text the pastoral office is explained as including the threefold function of teaching, sanctifying, and governing (*CD* 11). A case can therefore be made for holding that when the term "pastoral" recurs in *Christus Dominus* 38.1 it must include the teaching function. Even so, the conferences are not said to perform *all* the pastoral functions of diocesan bishops, and thus it remains debatable whether the term "pastoral" in *Christus Dominus* 38.1 implies that the conferences as such have doctrinal functions.

A similar ambiguity attends the term *decisiones* in *Christus Dominus* 38.4. The term can be understood in the narrow sense, to mean laws and administrative positions, or in a broad sense, as including doctrinal determinations. In view of the references to the teaching role of conferences in earlier drafts, some argue that the broader sense is more probable.[17] But it is also possible that the revision was intended to modify the meaning of the earlier version so that the definitive text would accord only practical functions to the conference. I conclude, therefore, that the current debate about the doctrinal functions of the conferences cannot be settled by appeal to the text of *Christus Dominus*, even in light of the schemas and the history of the discussion at the council.

---

16. Vatican Congregation for Bishops, "Draft Statement on Episcopal Conferences," *Origins* 17 (April 7, 1988): 735.

17. Manzanares, "Teaching Authority," 242.

The passing references to episcopal conferences in other documents of Vatican II are no more conclusive for our question. *Lumen Gentium* (*The Dogmatic Constitution on the Church*) 23, after hinting at some analogy between contemporary episcopal conferences and the ancient patriarchates, states only that through the conferences the collegial sense (*collegialis affectus*) of the episcopate can be brought to concrete application. *Sacrosanctum Concilium* assigns to the conferences important functions in the practical regulation of the liturgy, but does not deal with their doctrinal role. The same may be said regarding the missionary functions of the conferences in *Ad Gentes*. In all probability the commissions that drew up these texts did not consider the doctrinal function of the episcopal conference ripe for conciliar decision, and deliberately kept this question open.

The 1983 Code

If the council left the doctrinal role of the conferences unsettled, it must be asked whether the 1983 revised *Code of Canon Law* offers material that can be used to support either side of the debate. Those opposed to doctrinal functions generally base their case on book II, part 2 of the code, which contains a chapter on episcopal conferences (canons 447-459) in which no mention is made of teaching. For present purposes the crucial canons in this chapter are canon 447, dealing with the nature of the conferences, and canon 455, dealing with their decision-making powers.

Canon 447 practically repeats *Christus Dominus* 38.1, except that it describes the conference as an *institutum permanens* and states rather vaguely that it exercises *certain* pastoral functions (*munera quaedam pastoralia*) without specifying whether teaching is one of the functions of the conference. Thus the canon does not seem to settle any points about the teaching role of conferences that are currently under discussion.

Canon 455 corresponds to *Christus Dominus* 38.4, but where the council had spoken of *decisiones*, canon 455, §1, mentions "general decrees" (*decreta generalia*). Even though elsewhere (canon 341, §1) the code uses the term *decreta* to include all decisions of an ecumenical council, whether doctrinal or preceptive, the present canon apparently has reference only to laws and administrative dispositions.[18] The Commission for the Authentic Interpretation of the Code has interpreted the canon as applying not only to laws but also to general executory decrees.[19] Canon 455 may, however be relevant for the theme of this chapter since the logic of the restrictions on the legislative powers of the conference set forth in this canon could be applied in some measure to doctrinal determinations. I shall return to this point when I take up the question of the conditions under which the conferences can impose obligatory doctrine.

Commentators favoring the teaching authority of episcopal conferences generally base their case primarily on "Book III, on the Teaching Office of the Church," and especially on canon 753, which deals with the teaching authority of bishops. It reads:

> Although they do not enjoy infallibility in teaching, the bishops in communion with the head and members of the college, whether as individuals or gathered in conferences of bishops or in particular councils, are authoritative teachers and masters of the faith (*authentici sunt fidei doctores et magistri*) for the faithful entrusted to their care, who are bound to adhere to this authoritative teaching (*authentico magisterio*) of their bishops with religious submission of mind (*religioso animi obsequio*). [My translation].

The canon just quoted gives rise to two major schools of interpretation. One school (represented by Urrutia and Manzanares) interprets it as giving authoritative magisterial powers to the conferences as such; the other

---

18. On this point there is agreement even among many canonists who disagree about whether the conferences have teaching authority. See J. P. Green, *Conferences of Bishops*, 100; Ghirlanda, "De Episcoporum Conferentiis," 591; Urrutia, "De exercitio muneris," 617-21; Manzanares, "Teaching Authority," 342. James H. Provost, commenting on canons 455 and 456, lists "exercising authentic magisterium (c. 753)" among the activities of the conference mentioned by the code, but not as one of the cases in which the conferences are empowered to issue general decrees. See *The Code of Canon Law: A Text and Commentary Commissioned by the Canon Law Society of America*, ed. James A. Coriden, et al. (New York: Paulist Press, 1985), 370-71.

19. See the contribution of Thomas J. Green to this volume. He refers to a ruling of May 14, 1985, confirmed by Pope John Paul II on July 5, 1985 (*Acta apostolicae Sedis* 77 [1985]: 771).

(represented by J. P. Green and Ghirlanda) holds that the canon simply presents two modes by which the diocesan bishops may teach: either as individuals in their own dioceses or conjointly with others in particular councils or conferences. On the second interpretation this canon would confer no doctrinal powers either on particular councils or on episcopal conferences as such.

Bracketing for the moment the question of the obligatory force of the teaching, we may first concentrate on the subject, the teacher. Three arguments may be given for holding that the conferences are here accorded the power to teach. First, this is the obvious sense of the canon itself. Admittedly, the grammatical subject of the sentence just quoted is the bishops, not the conferences, but the bishops are described as teaching in conferences, not as individuals. What they do unitedly in the conference, the conference itself does. To take a parallel case, one may refer to canon 749, §2 dealing with ecumenical councils. It speaks of the infallible magisterium that the bishops possess either when united in an ecumenical council (in *Concilio Oecumenico coadunati*) or when dispersed throughout the world (*per orbem dispersi*). No one would deny that the code here recognizes the infallible teaching powers of ecumenical councils.[20] Thus it is difficult to deny that canon 753 accords some kind of teaching power to episcopal conferences.

A second argument is from the parallelism with particular councils. It is generally admitted that when the bishops of a province or nation gather in council they exercise, under certain conditions, an authentic magisterium. In the history of the church, particular councils have played an important role in the development of doctrine. The Third Council of Carthage in 397 drew up an authoritative list of the canonical books of Scripture. A series of African particular councils from 411 to 418 condemned the Pelagian heresy. The Second Council of Orange in 529 rejected what has come to be called semi-Pelagianism. The Council of Braga in 675 condemned the Priscillianists. The Fourth Council of Toledo in 633 declared: "If a question about the faith arises, a synod of all Spain is to be convoked." A number of councils in Toledo, including that of 675, drew up important confessions of faith. This list could be greatly lengthened.[21]

---

20. Urrutia, "De exercitio muneris," 610-611.
21. For further points on the material in this paragraph see Hermann J. Sieben, "Episcopal

Although the doctrinal role of particular councils has been less prominent in the second millennium, it is still, in principle, recognized. Canon 445 of the 1983 code gives particular councils a role in decreeing what seems appropriate for increasing faith and directing morals. This canon and canon 291 of the 1917 code make it clear that the decrees of particular councils affect the whole territory, including bishops who were absent or were in disagreement with the decisions reached. Thus the interpretation given by J. P. Green and Ghirlanda to canon 753 encounters major difficulties when applied to particular councils.[22]

The third argument, more speculative, is taken from the collegial character of episcopal conferences. The term "collegial" in canon law and theology has at least two different senses. The juridical sense is illustrated by canon 115, §2, and canon 119. The latter states that juridical persons in the church, when they act corporately in certain legitimate ways, perform "collegial acts," i.e., acts imputable to a public or corporate person. Since, according to canon 449, §2, episcopal conferences are juridical persons, it follows that their acts can be, in the juridical sense, collegial; they are not just the sum of the individual acts.

The question whether episcopal conferences are collegial in the theological sense is more complex. In the full and strict sense collegiality, as a theological term, applies to acts of the whole body of bishops in hierarchical communion with the pope as head of the college. The *nota explicativa praevia* attached to chapter 3 of *Lumen Gentium* makes it clear that the bishops cannot act in a strictly collegial way except when the whole body of bishops, together with the pope as its head, is involved.[23]

It may be argued, however, that the theological concept of collegiality is partially yet truly verified when some of the bishops, coming together for

---

Conferences in Light of Particular Councils during the First Millennium," *Jurist* 48 (1988): 30-46; Brian Daley, S.J., "Structures of Charity," in the present volume; Yves Congar, "Collège, primauté . . . Conférences épiscopales: Quelques notes," *Esprit et vie* 96 (1986): 388-89; and Avery Dulles, S.J., *The Reshaping of Catholicism* (San Francisco: Harper & Row, 1988), 215.

22. I here repeat in substance the criticism made by Antonio García y García in "Episcopal Conferences in Light of Particular Councils during the Second Millennium," *Jurist* 48 (1988): 60-62.

23. "Prefatory Note of Explanation" in *The Documents of Vatican II*, ed. Walter M. Abbott, S.J., and trans. Joseph Gallagher (New York: America Press, 1966), 98-101.

common action, implement their solidarity with a view to the totality. *Lumen Gentium* 22 seems to support this wider interpretation when it asserts that collegiality is suggested by the practice of summoning several bishops to take part in the ordination of a new bishop. *Lumen Gentium* 23, moreover, states that the collegiate sense is put into practical application by institutions such as the patriarchates of ancient times and "the episcopal bodies (*coetus*)" of today.

Taking up the term here used for "collegiate sense," *affectus collegialis*, some recent authors distinguish between two kinds of collegiality, effective and affective. This distinction, which was used at the extraordinary synods of 1969 and 1985, is quite legitimate, provided that it is recognized that "affective collegiality" is not sterile and ineffective; it has practical effects.[24]

We may conclude, therefore, that collegiality, in a true theological sense, is partially and analogously verified when a group of bishops come together to serve the unity of the whole church by their joint ministry.[25] Since collegiality includes the power of the episcopal body to teach, it seems to follow, at least *prima facie*, that conferences, as partial gatherings of the college, participate in the teaching office. This third argument, however, does not seem sufficiently cogent to yield a firm conclusion except as supported by the two previous arguments.

To escape the conclusion that canon 753 accords teaching authority to episcopal conferences, canonists such as J. P. Green and Ghirlanda hold that the bishops in conference teach simply as individuals addressing the people of their dioceses. This, as explained above, seems contrary to the obvious meaning of the canon. It is also contrary to the practice of the conferences. In accordance with canon 454, §2, conference statements are commonly issued not only in the name of the diocesan bishops and coadjutors who happen to

---

24. Affective collegiality, according to Angel Antón, "is not to be reduced to a mere sentiment, but, expressing the same ontological sacramental reality as effective collegiality, it preceded it in the historical development of the synodal element in the church and is ordered to it." Antón, "Theological 'Status' of Episcopal Conferences," *Jurist* 48 (1988): 205.

25. Ibid., 204. Many other authors have made essentially the same point: Walter Kasper, "Der theologische Status der Bischofskonferenzen," *Theologische Quartalschrift* 167 (1987): 3; Hermann J. Pottmeyer, "Was ist eine Bischofskonferenz?," *Stimmen der Zeit* 206 (July 1988): 441; and Bernard Sesboüé, "Les Conférences épiscopales en question," *Études* 369 (July-August 1988): 102.

have voted in favor of them, but in the name of the whole conference, including some nonbishops and some bishops who have only titular status. The documents, moreover, are addressed to all the faithful of the territory, and not simply to the subjects of the bishops who have signified their agreement.

What Obligatory Force?

Once it is established that episcopal conferences have teaching authority, further questions arise about the obligatory force of their pronouncements. Obviously the conferences cannot require the unconditional assent of faith. As incomplete realizations of the college, they cannot claim the authority proper to the college as a whole. But Vatican II's *Lumen Gentium* 25 acknowledged two other kinds of authority in episcopal teaching.[26] It stated that all bishops who teach in communion with the Roman pontiff "are to be respected (*venerandi*) by all as witnesses to divine and Catholic truth." It also stated that the formal teaching of the pope, even when he is not speaking *ex cathedra*, and that of one's own bishop, when he speaks in the name of Christ, is to be accepted with religious submission (*religioso animi obsequio*). It seems evident that bishops speaking in conference possess the first of these two types of authority. Whether they possess the second, the council did not say.

Here, however, the new code goes beyond the council. As quoted above, canon 753 states that when the bishops in conference teach authoritatively, their teaching is to be accepted with religious submission of mind (*religioso animi obsequio*). At least under some circumstances, therefore, the faithful are bound to accept the teaching of the conference with that ready allegiance of mind that is owed to the teaching of the pope and to their own diocesan bishop.

At this point a whole series of further questions arises. What happens in the case of a conflict between the conference and the diocesan bishop, who is an authentic teacher in his own diocese? Can he teach differently than the conference or is he bound to conform to the decision of his colleagues? Must

---

26. J. P. Green, *Conferences of Bishops*, 143 notes the distinction made by *Lumen Gentium* between the "reverence" due to all the bishops and the "submission and adherence" due to one's own proper bishop. This distinction is lucidly explained by Gérard Philips, in his authoritative commentary, *L'Église et son mystère au IIe Concile du Vatican*, vol. 1 (Paris: Desclée, 1967), 322.

there be a two-thirds majority, as for binding legislation, or a moral unanimity, or can a simple majority suffice? Must there be any kind of papal approval or review?

On all these points opinions differ. Ghirlanda takes the position that the conference does not by itself have power to impose obligatory doctrine, but that the Holy See might be able to give it such power under certain conditions. Against Urrutia he argues that if the conference could bind its own members to assent to its teaching without any special mandate or review from the Holy See, there would be a lack of parity between the legislative and the doctrinal powers of the conference. According to canon 455, the conference cannot legislate except on certain specific matters, as mandated by general legislation or by special action of the Apostolic See, and even in those cases the law must be passed by two-thirds of the members who have deliberative voice, and must, in addition, be reviewed by the Holy See. That the conferences should be able to make binding doctrinal statements without similar safeguards would appear, in Ghirlanda's eyes, to be inconsistent.[27]

Urrutia responds that the necessary safeguards are built into the very nature of doctrinal decrees, which do not depend, as legislation does, upon the mere will of the legislator, but rather upon the revelation given in Christ, which all Christians are bound to respect. Of course it is possible that the conference, not being infallible, might err, but in that case the usual principles for dissent from noninfallible teaching would sufficiently protect the rights of individuals who disagreed with the conference.[28]

Unlike Urrutia, I would hold that when an episcopal conference is not simply reiterating the doctrine of the universal church, but attempting to develop doctrine by a binding declaration, some safeguards should be imposed to prevent a regional hierarchy from diverging doctrinally from the universal church and to protect the freedom of the bishops and faithful of the region from undue restrictions in matters of belief. When witnessing to the faith the bishops should strive for moral unanimity. At a minimum something analogous to the conditions for binding legislation in canon 455 should apply. Vatican II may, in fact, have envisaged such restrictions on the conferences' power to

---

27. Ghirlanda, "De Episcoporum Conferentiis," 593-603; and "Responsio P. F. J. Urrutia animadversionibus," *Periodica* 76 (1987): 642.

28. Urrutia, "De exercitio muneris," 621-25.

teach if the *decisiones* of *Christus Dominus* 38.4 include, as Manzanares maintains, doctrinal decrees.

For certain doctrinal activities of episcopal conferences, approval or *recognitio* by the Holy See is explicitly required by the code. For example, canon 775, §2 permits episcopal conferences to supervise the preparation of catechisms for their territory, but only with previous approbation by the Holy See. Similar restrictions are imposed for the preparation of liturgical books and commentaries on them. According to canon 838, §3 translations and adaptations of the rites may not be published without prior review (*recognitio*) by the Apostolic See. It would be anomalous if lesser safeguards were exacted for the promulgation of new doctrine than for these more disciplinary regulations, both because doctrine is by its nature more universal than discipline (and thus less specific to particular regions) and because authentic doctrine calls for internal assent as well as external conformity. Review or reception by the Holy See would add an element of universality that would otherwise be lacking.[29]

Even if prior approval and subsequent review by the Holy See are necessary for their authoritative doctrinal statements, the conferences do not thereby lose their power to teach in their own name, any more than the *mandatum* and *recognitio* required for certain legislative acts by canon 455 deprives the conferences of legislative power. Conference statements that have been reviewed by the Holy See remain acts of the conference and do not become acts of the Holy See.

Dissent by Bishops from Their Conference

One reason for restricting the teaching authority of episcopal conferences is to preserve the functions of diocesan bishops as teachers in their own dioceses. The teaching ministry of the diocesan bishop, as shepherd of the faithful committed to his care, should not be eclipsed by that of the conference. On the comparatively rare occasions where the conference does feel it

---

29. Herman J. Pottmeyer is of the opinion that *recognitio* of conference teaching by the Holy See would be unnecessary and burdensome. See his article, "Das Lehramt der Bischofskonferenz," in *Die Bischofskonferenz: Theologischer and juridischer Status*, ed. Hubert Müller and Herman J. Pottmeyer (Düsseldorf: Patmos, 1989), 116-33, esp. 132.

necessary to issue binding declarations of doctrine, bishops, like other members of the church, have the freedom to dissent conscientiously. But public dissent should be exercised very sparingly because of the danger of scandal and division. The *Directory on the Pastoral Ministry of Bishops* issued by the Congregation for Bishops in 1973 dealt with this problem, without specific reference to doctrinal decisions. It stated:

(a) The bishop accepts with loyal submission the decisions legitimately taken by the conference and reviewed by the Apostolic See, for they have the force of the law through the Church's highest authority, and he puts them into practice in his diocese although he may not previously have agreed with them or they may cause him some inconvenience.

(b) There are other decisions and regulations of the conference which do not have a juridical binding force; and as a rule the bishop makes them his own with a view to unity and charity with his brother bishops, unless serious reasons he has carefully considered in the Lord prevent it. . . .[30]

Applying these provisions analogously to points of doctrine, one may say that when the episcopal conference issues authoritative pronouncements the individual bishop is in principle bound to agree, but that he may conscientiously dissent--either internally or externally--under the same conditions that other Catholics may dissent from noninfallible teaching.[31] When the conference teaches unauthoritatively, neither the bishop nor the faithful in general are obliged to yield internal assent. Even in cases of unauthoritative conference teaching, however, the individual bishop will be reluctant to dissent publicly because of the desirability to maintain unity and solidarity with his brother bishops.

From these principles a corollary would seem to follow. The same concern for unity that moves individual bishops not to dissent from the

---

30. Sacred Congregation for Bishops, *Directory on the Pastoral Ministry of Bishops* (Ottawa, Ontario: Canadian Catholic Conference, 1974), article 212, p. 113.

31. In its collective pastoral, "Human Life in Our Day" (Washington, DC: USCC, 1968), the United States hierarchy spelled out its norms of licit dissent (pp. 18-19).

conference should deter the conference itself from issuing controversial statements, even of a nonbinding character, that lack clear doctrinal warrants in the Catholic tradition. Except where urgent necessity demands, the conference should avoid placing its members in the dilemma of either concealing their honest disagreement or impairing the bonds of unity by public dissent.

Statements by Officers and Committees of the Conference

In all that has been said thus far, the point under discussion has been the doctrinal weight of statements issued by the conference as such. Somewhat different considerations would apply to statements made by officers, boards, or committees of the conference. The conference has no power to delegate its teaching authority, and thus the pronouncements of organs of the conference cannot be clothed with the authority of the conference itself.[32] This is not to say that they lack all authority. Such statements are to be seen as emanating from individuals or groups whom the conference judges competent for the positions they hold, and thus as enjoying a certain presumptive authority. This presumption may in an individual case be rebutted by opposition coming from within the conference, as occurred in the case of the statement, "The Many Faces of AIDS," issued by the Administrative Board of the USCC in December 1987.[33] The amount of opposition in that case, while it did not prove that the statement was wrong, deprived it of the authority normally attached to documents issued by the Administrative Board.

The Larger Context: Vatican II and Adaptation

Thus far the present essay has attempted to determine, with the help of canon lawyers, whether and to what extent episcopal conferences may issue binding declarations of doctrine. The primary criteria have been normative

---

32. Manzanares remarks that the proper functions of the plenary assembly are nondelegable ("Teaching Authority," 262). Ghirlanda in his "De Episcoporum Conferentiis," p. 595, says the same. Both authors cite the authoritative declarations published in *AAS* 60 (1968): 361 and *AAS* 72 (1980): 106.

33. "The Many Faces of AIDS," *Origins* 17 (December 24, 1987): 481-89, followed by a series of reactions, 489-93.

texts from Vatican II and the Code of Canon Law. The results of this investigation, though significant, have been meager. The recent discussion, especially in canonical circles, seems to be based on the questionable assumption that the conferences are seeking to impose their assertions by appeal to their own teaching authority. This concept of teaching does not correspond well with the usual practice of the conferences. For a more realistic approach it will be helpful to situate the conferences in the context of contemporary ecclesiology, and in that light to consider the kind of teaching in which the conferences actually engage.

Episcopal conferences, in the form in which we know them, have arisen in the context of a new vision of the church as a universal but internally diversified community of faith.[34] Anticipated to some extent before the council, this vision came into its own with Vatican II. *Lumen Gentium* proposed a concept of catholicity in which each region was seen as contributing through its special gifts to the other regions and to the whole. The task of the Holy See, in this vision, is to protect legitimate differences while seeing to it that such differences do not hinder unity but rather contribute to it (*LG* 13). Breaking with the rather monolithic ecclesiology of recent centuries, *Lumen Gentium* endorsed a moderate pluralism. It recognized that particular churches had in the course of time coalesced into organically united groups with their own canonical, liturgical, theological, and spiritual heritage (*LG* 23). This, according to the council, was a providential development of great importance for our own day. Vatican II spoke approvingly of the ancient patriarchates, with their synodal forms of government, and added that similar benefits might be expected from the episcopal conferences that had recently sprung into existence in various regions (*LG* 23; *Orientalium Ecclesiarum* 7).

The pastoral constitution, *Gaudium et Spes*, emphasized the need for adaptation in the sphere of evangelization. "The accommodated preaching of the gospel," it stated, "ought to remain the law of all evangelization. For thus each nation develops the ability to express Christ's message in its own way. At the same time a living exchange is fostered between the church and the diverse cultures of people" (*GS* 44, my translation).

A similar concern for diversity pervades *Ad Gentes*, the *Decree on the*

---

34. In the remainder of this paper I follow in part what I have written in "What Is the Role of a Bishops' Conference?" *Origins* 17 (April 28, 1988): 789-96.

Church's Missionary Activity. The church, we there read, borrows from the customs and traditions of each people, from their wisdom and learning, all that can contribute to the glory of the Creator. "If this goal is to be achieved," the decree continues, "theological investigation must necessarily be stirred up in each major sociocultural area" (*AG* 22).

The council did not suggest that different regional churches should profess different beliefs, but it insisted that the one faith ought to be proposed with different accents and nuances corresponding to the abilities, resources, and customs of each people and the variety of historical situations.

The Pastoral Magisterium

To clarify the kind of teaching that should be distinctive to a given time or place it may be helpful to distinguish between a strictly doctrinal and pastoral magisterium.[35] In its strictly doctrinal activity the magisterium is concerned to establish permanent and universal truth as something to be accepted with firm intellectual assent. In its pastoral activity the magisterium seeks to make the truth of the gospel accessible and fruitful in the lives of the faithful. The attention is not so much on the objective content of the doctrine (which is presupposed) as on the subject to whom it is being proclaimed.

This distinction has a basis in Vatican II. *Gaudium et Spes* is officially designated as a "*pastoral* constitution" to distinguish it from the two "dogmatic constitutions," *Lumen Gentium* and *Dei Verbum*, and from *Sacrosanctum Concilium* (which is simply called a "constitution"). The first footnote to *Gaudium et Spes* explains that the constitution is called pastoral because it does not directly teach doctrine but, presupposing certain doctrines, applies them to the world and to contemporary society. The same footnote distinguishes between the "pastoral intention" and the "doctrinal intention," stating that both are present, though in different proportions, in the two parts of *Gaudium et Spes*.

Reflecting on the nature of a "pastoral constitution," Karl Rahner, S.J. concludes:

The essence of a Pastoral Constitution consists in instructions issued by

---

35. Ibid., 793.

the Church primarily for her own members, and to some extent over and above this for all men who are ready to pay attention to the Church. These instructions are issued in view of the contemporary situation as evaluated under the charismatic influence of the Spirit and in response to the charismatic summons of God.[36]

Such instructions, Rahner explains, "do not have the character of a mere 'doctrine' (with external validity) or of binding laws in the strict sense of the term," but do pertain to the tasks of the pastoral office.[37]

Pastoral, to be sure, should not be opposed to doctrinal. In all their teaching activity the pastors seek to feed the flock of Christ with the salutary food of sacred doctrine. Vatican II was a pastoral council because it sought to follow the exhortation of Pope John XXIII, in his opening allocution, to take into account the characteristics of modern thought and communication, "everything being measured in the forms and properties of a magisterium which is predominantly pastoral in character."[38] The council concerned itself with eliciting people's free and eager participation in the community of faith and with showing how the radiance of the gospel could shine more brilliantly in the contemporary world. To this end it advocated respectful dialogue and prudent adaptation, seeking to place the church's message, without any diminution or distortion, within the grasp of different audiences who had not yet heard it, or had not given it a favorable hearing.

Need for a Pastoral Magisterium in the U.S.A.

For many reasons it is important for the Catholic church in the United States to have a body that can regularly engage in pastoral teaching on the national level. The individual bishop cannot effectively teach in isolation. Since communications are today very rapid and travel is frequent, the individual Catholic does not feel as closely bound to the residential bishop as would formerly have been the case. The local bishop, of course, has an inalienable

---

36. Karl Rahner, S.J., "On the Theological Problems Entailed in a 'Pastoral Constitution'" in *Theological Investigations*, vol. 10 (New York: Herder and Herder, 1973), 311-12.

37. Ibid., 295.

38. John XXIII, "Opening Speech to the Council," in *Documents*, ed. Abbott, 715.

responsibility for structuring the transmission of Christian doctrine in his diocese and for exercising doctrinal vigilance. In addition he should, in principle, personally engage in preaching and teaching. But his efforts will often be more effective if pursued in conjunction with bishops in neighboring dioceses. Common statements emanating from the episcopate of the region or nation are sometimes called for.

At the other end of the spectrum, the universal teaching authority of popes and councils, including that of the Vatican congregations, while indispensable for clarifying the obligatory content of Catholic belief, cannot adequately serve the pastoral needs of every region. Quite properly the universal agencies deal with problems that are general in the church. Usually they are issued in the style and language customary to the Roman church. In recent years the pope has attempted to meet the needs of various regions by pastoral journeys in which he addresses concerns specific to a given area. But such trips, which are occasional by their very nature, cannot relieve the bishops of the region of their ordinary doctrinal responsibilities.

It is almost essential, therefore, that there be a pastoral teaching agency intermediate between the residential bishop and the Holy See. This could, in principle, be a particular council, but since plenary and provincial councils have become exceedingly rare, and are now regarded primarily as legislative assemblies, it is clearly advantageous for the episcopal conferences to assume the pastoral teaching role on the regional or national level.

The magisterial role of the episcopal conference varies in relation to the distinctive spiritual and religious heritage of the nation or territory. Americans have their own national characteristics. They generally set a high value on freedom and independence. They expect communications to be free, frank, and open. They want their public officials to explain why they take the positions they do and to be accountable in their actions. Catholics are inevitably, and to some degree rightly, influenced by these national traits. American church authorities therefore have to speak and act in a style that respects these tendencies. Roman documents, which often show signs of emanating from a more hierarchical and authoritarian mentality, must be adapted to the American situation in order to be well accepted. This is the more important because the church in this country receives virtually no public funding or legal privileges. For its effective functioning it depends almost entirely on the free consent of the faithful and on the good will of the general public.

Religious pluralism in the United States has gone further than in most other countries. It is therefore possible to achieve a large degree of ecumenical collaboration, provided that care be taken to respect the sensitivities of other religious groups. Occasionally it may be necessary for the bishops to warn against some non-Catholic religious movements, such as militant fundamentalism. A teaching authority centered in Rome could scarcely be expected to respond adequately to these local conditions.

A further characteristic of our national culture is the high development of science and technology, which is evident in fields such as genetics, medicine, energy, and weaponry. The church has the possibility of engaging in serious dialogue with scientists and industrialists, as well as with government officials, on the moral and religious implications of new theories and technologies.

Finally, mention should be made of the position of women in American society. The important roles played by women in various professions and in public life arouse different expectations regarding ecclesiastical government and practice. The procedures taken for granted in some other parts of the world, where decision-making power is lodged in the hands of men alone, are a source of tension for many Catholics in the United States.

Response of the NCCB

Responding to the ecclesiastical vision of the Second Vatican Council and the actualities of the current situation in the United States, the National Conference of Catholic Bishops has engaged predominantly in pastoral teaching. Almost immediately after the end of the council it began to address the spiritual needs and possibilities of the American situation. In 1967 the United States hierarchy issued its first collective pastoral letter, "The Church in Our Day." The president of the NCCB, Cardinal John F. Dearden, in his preface, explained this letter as a commentary on the Vatican II *Constitution on the Church*, with special reference to areas of concern in this country. "As its very name implies," said the cardinal, "the pastoral letter is intended to have as its first objective and as its guiding principle the care of souls."[39]

In a few cases the NCCB has concerned itself with formally doctrinal questions, but always with a view to particular pastoral situations. For

---

39. "The Church in Our Day" (Washington, DC: USCC, 1968), 3.

example, it has drawn up a list of "Basic Teachings for Catholic Religious Education" (January 11, 1973), followed, in November 1977, by the national catechetical directory, *Sharing the Light of Faith*. On several occasions the United States bishops have sought, in pastoral letters, to transmit Catholic moral teaching in a pastorally sensitive and compassionate manner.[40] Likewise doctrinal in tenor is the pastoral letter, "Behold Your Mother: Woman of Faith" (November 1973), which presents Catholic teaching concerning the Blessed Virgin Mary in a light attractive to many Americans of our day.

The United States episcopal conference has a doctrinal committee that has been active in supervising publications in this country and has occasionally given warnings that certain books were considered doctrinally unsound or dangerous to faith or morals. The doctrinal committee, in collaboration with the bishops' ecumenical committee, has often engaged in evaluations of ecumenical dialogue statements.

The most highly publicized sphere of activity of the NCCB has undoubtedly been its teaching on social issues. Under this heading should be mentioned its frequent pronouncements on abortion, its letter on Marxist Communism (1980), and its two lengthy letters, "The Challenge of Peace" (1983) and "Economic Justice for All" (1986). These letters, especially the last two, well illustrate the kind of degree of authority that pertains to the pastoral magisterium.

In "The Challenge of Peace" the bishops distinguished three types of statements in their own document: declarations of universal moral principles that are presumably accessible to all through reason and conscience, reiterations of Catholic social teachings as found in papal and conciliar documents, and prudential applications of these principles to the particular circumstances of the day. They stated explicitly that the applications were prudential judgments not binding on the conscience of the faithful, but added that Catholics should give serious attention and consideration to these applications as they attempted to form moral judgments consistent with the gospel (CP 10). A similar disclaimer is contained in "Economic Justice for All." Except where they were reiterating universal moral principles or formal church teaching, the bishops explained, their recommendations required only

---

40. E.g., "Human Life in Our Day" (Washington, DC: USCC, 1968); "To Live in Christ Jesus: A Pastoral Reflection on the Moral Life," *Origins* 6 (November 25, 1976): 357-72.

serious consideration "by Catholics as they determine whether their own moral judgments are consistent with the gospel and with Catholic social teaching" (EJ 135).

The social teaching of the NCCB, and of its policy arm, the USCC, has been variously evaluated. Some have welcomed the high degree of specificity with which the bishops have addressed divisive social issues. Others have felt that these statements have caused polarization and alienation in the church itself and have somewhat undermined the teaching authority of the conferences. No matter what position one takes on this debatable matter, the principles set forth in this paper would seem to hold.[41]

Value of the Consultative Process

The juridical authority of documents is important when the bishops are establishing official doctrine to be preached and taught as part of the apostolic faith, as frequently happens in councils. But such formal authority is a relatively minor consideration when the bishops are making pastoral applications to the changeable circumstances of the day. The effectiveness of such pastoral documents depends less on the authority of the speakers than on the credibility and persuasiveness of what they say. The faithful will assess the contents of the documents in the light of their sense of the faith, their total life-experience, and the force they perceive in the argumentation.

For all these reasons, a different methodology is appropriate for the preparation of pastoral, as contrasted with strictly doctrinal, statements. This difference is already hinted at in the Vatican II pastoral constitution *Gaudium et Spes*, which points out that the clergy do not have, and should not be expected to have, ready answers to all the complex questions of the day (*GS* 43). "It is the task of the entire People of God, especially the pastors and theologians, to hear, distinguish, and interpret the many voices of our age, and to judge them in the light of the divine Word" (*GS* 44).

It follows, therefore, that pastoral instructions, which aim to discern the signs of the times, need not be issued with oracular finality from a lofty eminence. The United States bishops, in their recent pastoral letters, have adopted what may be called a consultative magisterium. They have publicized

---

41. For further discussion see Avery Dulles, *The Reshaping of Catholicism*, 154-83.

the names of the priests, religious, and lay persons used as staff and consultants. They have held numerous public hearings, published preliminary drafts, invited comment, and revised their statements in view of the feedback. This consultative process involves a certain risk that the statements will be politicized, reflecting the agendas of various interest groups. But it also assures a broader exposure to data and problems that might otherwise escape attention.

An assessment of the pastoral magisterium of the episcopal conference should not overlook the educational value of the consultative process itself. By inviting participation and engaging in dialogue with morally and religious concerned persons, the bishops stimulate reflection on the issues of the day in the light of the gospel. By means such as this they can perform a true teaching role even before they formulate the conclusions to which, in their judgment, the process leads.

Conclusions

The preceding discussion of the actual practice of the NCCB enables us to go beyond the rather modest conclusions suggested by the earlier, more canonical, part of this article. The episcopal conference in this country has never sought to change or extend Catholic doctrine. It has never tried to oblige the faithful of its region to assent to anything not taught in the whole Catholic church. On the other hand, it has engaged vigorously in teaching. It has reminded people of the official teaching, presented that teaching in an attractive light, called attention to deviations, and suggested concrete applications, especially in the socioeconomic area. Through consultations and hearings, the NCCB has raised certain important issues, relating the gospel to public life. The doctrinal function of the conference, therefore, cannot be adequately understood in juridical and canonical terms alone.

The findings of this paper may be summarized as follows:

(1) An episcopal conference is never able to define doctrine in a way that engages the unconditional assent of faith.

(2) Under certain rather exceptional conditions it may be appropriate for an episcopal conference to formulate obligatory doctrine for the faithful of its own nation or region. This, however, should not be done without

safeguards equivalent to those set forth in *Christus Dominus* 38.4 and in canon 455 of the 1983 code. Such authoritative teaching, while not infallible, may call for religious submission (*religiosum animi obsequium*).

(3) Bishops, like other members of the faithful, are free to dissent from authoritative teaching of their own conference under the usual principles governing dissent from authentic, noninfallible teaching. But they will not dissent publicly except for serious reasons, bearing in mind the importance of maintaining solidarity in the episcopal body.

(4) The teaching of an episcopal conference carries with it the authority of whatever official teaching or traditional doctrine the conference may incorporate by reference in its own statements.

(5) When an episcopal conference makes pastoral applications of ethical principles or Catholic doctrine to the particular circumstances of the time and place, the applications do not carry with them a direct or automatic obligation to assent. On the other hand, the Christian faithful, respectful of the moral and religious authority of their bishops, will take such statement into serious account as they form their own consciences.

(6) Solicitous to preserve concord within the church, the episcopal conference will avoid issuing even nonbinding statements that are divisive unless there are clear warrants in the Catholic tradition or some urgent necessity requires.

(7) Episcopal conferences teach not only by issuing official pronouncements but also by raising certain issues, by stimulating discussion, and by inviting serious reflection on the implications of the gospel for the present day.

(8) The de facto authority of a conference statement or document will depend in great part on the reception given to it by the faithful, who will appraise it in light of their own sense of the faith. Statements enjoying little or no juridical authority may gain great influence and be cited with approval for generations to come.

Ladislas Orsy, S.J.

Reflections on the Teaching Authority of the Episcopal Conferences

LADISLAS ORSY is professor of canon law at
The Catholic University of America

The purpose of these reflections is to offer some insights concerning the authority of the episcopal conferences in doctrinal matters and the corresponding obligation of the faithful in responding to their teaching. They are presented as a contribution to an ongoing debate which in many ways is still in an initial stage.

Let the reflections start from an empirical fact: episcopal conferences the world over issue statements and declarations which to all intents and purposes appear as teaching activity. As this happens, quite naturally a theoretical question arises: do those conferences have an authority to teach?

The fact cannot be doubted: conferences do teach. The question is then legitimate: by what authority?

To avoid any ambiguity, we must be clear from the beginning (and throughout) that our inquiry is about an authority vested in the conferences *as such*; an authority beyond that which individual bishops can bring into their assemblies.

In order to proceed correctly, we must before anything else determine the proper field for our investigation. Is the question theological? Or is it canonical? To have the right answer here is of capital importance because the sources and the methods of the two sciences are different. To commit ourselves to the wrong direction in the beginning may well lead us the wrong exit at the end.[1]

---

1. The purpose of a theological investigation is to know more about a mystery of faith; the purpose of canonical legislation is to establish norms of action for the support and appropriation of a value. There is a hierarchy between the two operations: values are determined by theological investigation, rules for their protection and acquisition are given by legislation. This

The rightful allocation of the question to a specific field, however, can be determined only by taking cognizance of the nature of the realities themselves to which it refers; it refers to the proclamation of the evangelical message and to the assemblies of bishops that we call conferences.

Teaching by Bishops is a Theological Activity

The roots of any teaching in the church are in the Word of God, no matter who is doing it, the bishops or any others. When a teacher proclaims the mighty deeds of God, the Holy Spirit is present and active and brings testimony in the hearts of the hearers to the truth of the message.[2]

The preservation and development of the message never was, of course, the exclusive task of the bishops: our belief is that the revelation has been entrusted to the whole church. Yet, our tradition has attributed, from the earliest time, a special role to the bishops: when the community was divided over a point of doctrine, the bishops had the capacity to recognize the correct position; they had the task and power to proclaim the truth to which all the contending parties had to surrender. Moreover, the same tradition has liked to compare the call of the bishops to that of the apostles: both were sent to be heralds of the gospel.[3]

---

hierarchy must be always respected in inquiries which refer to realities which are part of a mystery but are also objects of canonical regulations. If the correct sequence is reversed, mystery is measured by our laws, and speculations take the place of clear courses of action. The former leads to legalism, the latter to disorder.

Canonical documents have their own hermeneutics: the method of interpreting theological texts must never be transferred to them. Communications for knowledge and norms for action were not born from the same intention.

Thus, the Code of Canon Law was not conceived, written, or promulgated with the aim of defining doctrine. For this we have ample evidence from the commission itself, which proclaimed repeatedly during the revision process that it had no intention of entering into doctrinal issues (see note 17). It follows that to use a text from the code to argue a theological point is likely to be inappropriate. It may involve projecting a meaning into the law, a meaning that was never there.

2. We speak of the "sacrament" of the Word precisely because of its mysterious connection with the presence and operations of the Holy Spirit--a belief that in substance goes back to apostolic times.

3. This ancient and permanent tradition has been proclaimed anew by Vatican Council II:

As a matter of practical procedure, the bishops exercised their power of being judges in matters concerning Christian doctrine in synods or councils. In the beginning there were no laws about the structure and authority of such assemblies: they were created by the good sense of the bishops and others, and recognized by the church at large as indispensable instruments for preserving the authentic message.

Now this exceptional capacity of the bishops to be judges of the truth has always been attributed to the assistance of the Holy Spirit--a charism in the Pauline sense. Theologians, however, distinguished carefully this assistance from inspiration: the "determinations" and "canons" of a council were not thought to be the Word of God in the same way as the Scriptures were. Assistance meant mainly protection against error, although positive help in the process was not excluded. Full protection, of course, was granted to the "great synods" only; that is, to the ecumenical councils. But in no way did theologians rule out the partial help of the Spirit to particular councils.

This being our tradition, the teaching or "judging" by the bishops cannot be understood in any other way than as a theological activity.

Assemblies of Bishops for an Ecclesial Purpose are Theological Realities

We turn now to the question concerning the nature of the conferences. Are they theological realities or merely legal institutions? If the former, they participate intimately in the mystery of the church; if the latter, they are ultimately human creations for convenience's sake.[4]

Among the principal duties of bishops, the preaching of the Gospel occupies an eminent place. For bishops are preachers of the faith who lead new disciples to Christ. They are authentic teachers, that is, teachers endowed with the authority of Christ, who preach to the people committed to them the faith they must believe and put into practice. By the light of the Holy Spirit, they make that faith clear, bringing forth from the treasury of revelation new things and old (cf. Mt. 13:52), making faith bear fruit and vigilantly warding off any errors which threaten their flock (cf. 2 Tim. 4:1-4). (*LG* 25)

4. In this essay I shall repeatedly refer to the "episcopal college." To avoid any misunderstanding, I wish to make clear that I understand it as Vatican Council II understood it: "The order of bishops is the successor to the college of the apostles in teaching authority and pastoral rule; or, rather, in the episcopal order the apostolic body continues without a break. Together with its head, the Roman Pontiff, and never without this head, the episcopal order

As a starting point, we must obviously hold that ecumenical councils are theological realities: the whole church believes that they have the capacity to witness to the truth *in the Spirit.*[5] Every time we say the Nicene-Constantino-politan Creed, we acknowledge a divine authority in the great councils.

Now it would be absurd to assume that the assistance of the Spirit arises instantaneously whenever an ecumenical council opens but before that the episcopal body is devoid of the same help. Such an understanding would be close to a magical interpretation of the role of the Spirit.

A far more satisfactory explanation can be found through the concept of *communio.*[6] Let us recall some foundational principles in ecclesiology.

The entrance into Christian life is baptism. Now baptism is often conceived as an individual gift: the person who receives it must keep and treasure the grace that the sacrament signifies and gives. But this is a one-sided and incomplete understanding: baptism is the entry into the living body of Christ that is the church sustained by the Spirit. Through him and in him, there is a mysterious bond among the baptized: the one Spirit of God animates many human persons.[7]

---

is the subject of supreme and full power over the universal Church." (*LG* 22)

From the earliest times *dynamis, potestas,* "power", in the church was understood to be a gift of the Spirit. It is only in the twelfth century that the purely legal concept of jurisdiction appears.

It would be difficult to assume that the church had always attributed full power to the college of bishops but no power at all to their smaller gatherings. The evidence points to the contrary: precisely because the church quietly believed in the presence of *dynamis* or *potestas* in the smaller assemblies, the custom of particular synods grew up and prospered in many regions and through many ages.

Now, if there was power there had to be authority.

5. So have the bishops living dispersed in all parts of the world, provided that the head of the college calls them to collegiate action (cf. *LG* 22). In this essay I shall refer several times to ecumenical councils as the prototype of the full exercise of the collegiate power but, needless to say, I am aware that the same fullness is present in the episcopal body when the members are dispersed but are acting together.

6. There is the crux of the issue: is collegiality a particular form of *communio,* or not? If it is, there can be degrees in it. If not, it is a *sui generis* reality which (for practical purposes) functions with great rarity. When it does, there are no organic antecedents to it, and it is not followed by any organic process.

7. See Heribert Muehlen, *Una mystica persona: Eine Person in vielen Personen* (Munich: Schoeningh, 1967).

No wonder the gatherings of Christians for an ecclesial purpose have always been considered an external expression of an internal unity. The faithful kept believing, on scriptural grounds, that when a group of them came together to profess their faith and to pray, the Spirit was with them with an intensity that exceeded his gifts to individual persons.

The sacrament of confirmation is a continuation or extension of the baptismal gift, a deeper insertion into the body of Christ that is the church.

Similarly, the participation in the Eucharist cannot be conceived adequately as the "receiving of holy communion," a passive act of receiving the body and blood of Christ. The other aspect of this sacrament is far more important: the faithful are received into Christ, into a unity that is *communio* with the head and all the members.[8]

This leads us to the sacrament of orders. Is it simply a gift to an individual (granted, for the sake of the community), or is it the reception of the individual into the communion of bishops, a communion sustained by the Spirit?

Many signs in our tradition point toward the latter: the ordination of a bishop is an incorporation into a special communion in the larger communion of the whole church, into the episcopal "order."[9] The full implications of the

---

8. See Louis Dussaut, *L'Eucharistie, Pâque de toute la vie* (Paris: Cerf, 1972).

9. A great deal in the history of the sacrament of order points toward the episcopal ordination being a reception into a collective body. For instance, the Council of Nicea in the East and in the fourth century, decreed (canon 4): "The bishop shall be appointed by all (the bishops) of the eparchy (province); if that is not possible on account of pressing necessity, or on account of the length of journeys, three (bishops) at the least shall meet, and proceed to the imposition of hands (consecration) with the permission of those absent in writing. The confirmation of what is done belongs by right, in each eparchy, to the metropolitan." See Charles Joseph Hefele, *A History of the Councils of the Church* (Edinburgh: T. & T. Clark, 1883)

Similar rules are found in Gratian's *Decretum,* in the West and in the twelfth century: ". . . conventu totius provinciae episcoporum, maximeque metropolitani vel auctoritate, vel presentia ordinetur episcopus. . . ." (Distinctio XXIII, c. II [*Corpus Iuris Cononici,* ed. Aemilins L. Richter and Aemilins Friedberg, 1879, col. 809]). Again: "Ab omnibus conprovincialibus episcopi ordinentur. . . ." (D. LXIV, c. I [Richter and Friedberg, 247]). Even more strongly: "Quod autem episcopi non sint, qui minus quam a tribus episcopis ordinati sunt, omnibus patet." (*c.5,D.LXVIII; Friedberg: 255*).

There are many other texts in Gratian referring to the ordination of bishops as a collective action by the episcopate.

Taking into consideration also the texts about synods, one could make a good case for the hypothesis that the practical rules in the *Decretum* concerning the episcopate have been

doctrine of Vatican Council II concerning the necessary participation of all diocesan bishops in the *sollicitudo omnium ecclesiarum* remain to be worked out.[10]

No less than the communion of the faithful, this special communion of the bishops is an ontological reality because it is grounded in the Spirit. Obviously it is not anything separated from the main body of the church, but is part of it.

This special communion exists all the time. It can manifest itself externally in different degrees. It does so at the highest degree when the bishops are assembled in an ecumenical council; it reveals itself to lesser degrees whenever bishops legitimately gather for an ecclesiastical purpose, no matter what name they may give to their assemblies. The conferences are precisely the expressions of such a theological reality.

Teaching Authority is Rooted in the Word and in the Spirit

To have authority means to have the power to create an obligation binding another person. That other person can be bound to various attitudes or actions: the response must depend on the content of the call.

---

inspired by the belief that a group of bishops legitimately assembled is endowed with a special authority.

10. Vatican Council II declared: "By virtue of sacramental consecration and hierarchical communion with the head and other members of the college, a bishop becomes part of the episcopal body." (*CD* 4)

Further: "As lawful successors of the apostles and as members of the episcopal college, bishops should always realize that they are linked one to the other, and should show concern for all the churches. For by divine institution and the requirement of their apostolic office, each one in concert with his fellow bishops is responsible for the Church." (*CD* 6)

The council certainly suggests that every ordination is for the universal church as well as for a particular church; every ordination is an entry into the college.

Theologically it is difficult to see why this divine duty of solicitude that goes beyond the borders of a diocese can be exercised with collective authority on the highest level (ecumenical council) but not in smaller assemblies of bishops (synods, conferences).

If the bishops of Africa decided to fulfill their divine duty of solicitude for all churches in that continent by deliberating and deciding together, and they did so remaining in communion with the see of Rome, it is fitting to say that in their doings a significant part of the universal college has come to life. Such arguments *ex convenientia* must not be lightly dismissed: Aquinas used them a great deal.

We are on solid ground by affirming that when an assembly of bishops, including a conference, makes a doctrinal statement, the ultimate authority to bind the faithful must be in the Word of God, not in the human beings who proclaim it. The response to the Word itself cannot be anything else than its acceptance. Obedience of faith is due to a proclamation only insofar as it speaks the very Word of God.

Episcopal conferences, however, do not have the capacity to proclaim the Word infallibly, hence the response of the faithful cannot be an unconditional surrender to the truth of their statement. But it does not follow that there is no obligation in the faithful to respond. Their response, however, must be two faceted: it must contain a readiness to accept the Word, and it must contain a measure of prudence to verify the statement through its reception by larger communions than a conference can be, such as by the full episcopal college, or by the entire church at large, pope and bishops included.

The authority of the conferences in doctrinal matters is rooted therefore in the authority of the Word of God, and in the Spirit who assists the bishops who speak it. But the conferences do not have the charism of infallibility, hence their statements ought to be further authenticated by the church universal. In practice this can mean authentication by an ecumenical council, by all the bishops dispersed but acting together, or by a papal declaration with special solemnity.

The response required on the part of the faithful has been described several times by Vatican Council II and by the new Code of Canon Law. But here I wish to discuss one term only, used by both; perhaps the most important one in this context. It is *obsequium*, a word that has suffered much from mistranslations, especially into languages which have no precise equivalent for it. English is one of them.[11]

---

11. Xaverius Ochoa's well known *Index Verborum Concilii Vaticani Secundi* (Rome: Commentarium pro Religiosis, 1967) gives twenty references under the entry *Obsequens, obsequor, obsequium*.

The word is used four times in the new code; see canons 218 (toward the magisterium in general), 678 (from the part of religious toward the local bishop), 752 (toward a non-definitive proclamation of the pope or the college of bishops), and 753 (toward the teaching of the bishops). Canon 753 explicitly mentions the conferences: "Episcopi qui sunt in communione cum Collegii capite et membris, sive singuli sive in conferentiis Episcoporum aut in conciliis particularibus congregati, licet infallibilitate in docendo non polleant, christifidelium suae curae commissorum authentici sunt fidei doctores et magistri; cui authentico magisterio suorum

To understand *obsequium* it is necessary to realize that it does not mean a specific act; it is one step removed from a precisely definable action. It means an attitude which in its turn ought to bring forth a specific act, but the nature of this act will have to be determined by the content of the statement that introduces the obligation.[12]

Thus, *obsequium* may bind to "obedience in faith" when it is clear that the conference simply proclaimed anew a long held belief, or it may bind to "respect for the declaration" while the process of reception (or sometimes rejection) is gradually developing in the church universal.

Confirmation by Reception

A particular assembly of bishops cannot be in itself the ultimate guarantee of the authenticity of their message in the same way as an ecumenical council can. The guarantee, therefore, must come from the rest of the church: from the full episcopal college, the see of Rome, or the universal community of the faithful. They too have the Spirit![13]

Thus, to assess the value of a document or pastoral letter issued by a conference is a delicate operation. To assume some capacity to speak *in the Spirit* is very much in harmony with our traditions. Yet for a fuller assessment one has to wait and see the reception of the proclamation. The conference is an organic part in a larger body, and the full truth is with the entire body.

While one can say *yes* to the question, "Do conferences have authority to teach?", one cannot give a simple and uniform answer to the question "What specific acts can this authority command?" It depends on the content of their teaching. Yet, because bishops gathered together *for an ecclesial purpose* are not without some assistance of the Spirit, *obsequium* (in the sense I explained) should always be the first response to their teaching.

Episcoporum christifideles religioso animi obsequio adhaerere tenentur."

12. "Loyalty" is a similar term in English: it expresses an attitude which can bring forth various acts--from sacrificing one's life for a cause to faithful disagreement.

13. "They too have the Spirit!": an exclamation attributed to Pope John XXIII. He would have spoken it in answer to complaints that the bishops "were running away with the council" since they kept rejecting most of the preparatory work done under the supervision of the pope.

Teaching is not Disciplinary Legislation

Confusion sometimes arises from treating the act of teaching and the obligation that it generates in the same way as an act of disciplinary legislation and the duty that it engenders. Teaching is then regarded as the "will of the superior," and the assent to it as "an act of obedience." The role of the intelligence of faith is not mentioned.

In the church there is *an authority to teach, a doctrinal authority*; it is the authority to proclaim the Word. In the church there is also an *authority to impose an action*, which is mostly known under the name of *juridical authority*. The task of the former is to communicate knowledge that saves; the task of the latter is to establish well-measured balances in the community, so that all can live, pray, and work in peace.

The distinction between these two types of authority is of epistemological origin. Philosophically (and, *mutatis mutandis,* theologically) there is a radical difference between affirming the truth and imposing an action, and correspondingly, between surrendering to the truth and carrying out an order.

Balancing the Abstract Theory with Existential Realities

These reflections would remain substantially incomplete if they did not mention the need to balance the abstract theory concerning the conferences' authority to teach with the concrete circumstances of each of such assemblies. In a mysterious way, divine assistance and human limitations are present in every conference. Thus, in the existential order many factors can arise which ought to be taken into consideration in assessing the binding force of a declaration. Let me mention some of them.

There are episcopal conferences which are not free from government interference that may vary from mild pressure to downright oppression. When this happens, the bishops cannot speak as they wish, a factor to be taken into consideration in interpreting their pronouncements.

Further, the statements issued by various conferences will always be marked by the human qualities of the members: the degree of their learning and wisdom will be reflected in all that they say; this is another hermeneutical factor.

Also, some conferences may be unduly influenced by public opinion, or by nationalism, or by theological trends: all such factors must be balanced by prudent interpretation.

In none of these cases do I assume that a conference places itself outside of the Catholic communion; all I am suggesting is that in granting *obsequium* the faithful should not be unaware of the human elements that play a part in its teaching.[14]

Conferences by Divine Design?

If assemblies of bishops are endowed with authority, it is legitimate to ask by what right, human or divine? If by human right, it must be through some kind of delegation coming from the pope, if by divine right it must come from God.

There are difficulties with both positions. If such assemblies have their power by delegation, who delegated their power to early particular councils or to patriarchal synods? Certainly not the pope.

But if they have it from God, where is the evidence for it? Vatican Council II confirmed the opinion that diocesan bishops have their power by divine right; it said the same for the college of bishops. But it did not speak about synods and conferences "by divine right."

The answer lies in abandoning the somewhat simplistic distinction that assumes that ecclesiastical institutions fall neatly into one of those two categories. Reality is more complex than that.

There are institutions in the church which undoubtedly exist by divine right but the modality of their existence has always been determined by the church's legislation. For instance, the sacraments of penance, of the infirm, of marriage, certainly exist by divine right, yet the modality of their administration, including the structure of the sign, has been shaped by the church. At times, it is difficult to say where the divine dispensation ends and the human regulation begins.

---

14. This is not the place to deal with the delicate problems of individual bishops and assemblies of bishops breaking their communion with the church or abandoning the integrity of their Catholic faith. Such cases occurred throughout history.

When such bishops break the bond of unity, they obviously lose the authority they possessed in the body of the church; they *exit* from the community which is endowed with power.

We say that a diocesan bishop rules his diocese by divine right. But the need for several bishops (of a province, of a region, of a nation) to get together and provide pastoral care for the faithful that is beyond the resources of the individual pastors, may be indeed part of their divinely imposed obligation. In other terms, the divine law may be binding the bishops to seek collective action. And when we know from other sources that the many assembled are sustained and assisted by one Spirit, a divine design becomes even more evident.

This is to postulate a more sophisticated understanding of divine and human rights which blend in many institutions, among them the assemblies of bishops.

Perhaps what I could say at this point--pending further investigation and reflection--is that particular assemblies of bishops existed and continue to exist in the church by divine design, but the forms and structures of such gatherings were always shaped by ecclesiastical customs, ordinations, or legislations.[15]

The fact stands that throughout its history the church kept respecting, upholding, and promoting--without fail--particular assemblies of bishops. Question: is this attitude a significant theological fact? If it is, can it signify an intuitive perception that such particular communions of bishops were indeed part of a divine design?

Unsatisfactory Theories

The following is a report on some theories which I find unsatisfactory. Even if they seem to resolve some problems, they leave many questions without convincing answers.

1. The theory that episcopal conferences and particular synods (so

---

15. For a detailed and tightly reasoned explanation of the theory of church institutions by "divine design," see the talk given by Gisbert Greshake, professor of theology at the University of Freiburg in Br., "Die Stellung des *Protos* in der Sicht der romisch-katholischen Dogmatischen Theologie," at the meeting of the Society for the Law of the Eastern Churches, in 1987, at Santiago de Compostela, Spain. The proceedings of the meeting were scheduled to be published in the 1988 issue of *Kanon*, the journal of the same society published by the University of Vienna, Austria.

frequent in history) are radically different; they are not analogous institutions. It follows that from the history of the synods nothing (or hardly anything) can be learned about the nature of the conferences; they do not constitute a precedent for the conferences.

Response: This theory is based on the assumption that the modern episcopal conferences are purely juridical creations. It does not take into account at all the ontological communion which exists in the episcopal body, a communion which can have different manifestations. Logically, if our conferences are purely legal creations, particular synods, as they are described in the Code of Canon Law and as they existed and operated in history, could not be anything else either. But there is ample evidence in our tradition that the church attributed a special force to the teachings and disciplinary decrees of particular synods. Such synods played an important role in the shaping of the beliefs and structures of the church; they were second only to the "great councils." There is no reason to deny a similar role for the conferences.

This theory really sees the conferences as a kind of "association of bishops," or as an organization for some administrative purposes. No wonder that in this conception episcopal conferences are described as public *fora* for the exchange of ideas among local bishops.[16]

2. The theory that allows collegial action in the proper sense on the level of an ecumenical council only.

Response: This theory does not conceive of the episcopal body as a *communio* which can operate on different levels with different intensity. It perceives two distinct realities only: the individual bishops and their full assembly. I am not sure how far it concedes the assistance of the Spirit to individual bishops, but it certainly affirms that when the college is assembled, the assistance is there in full intensity. Such a sudden appearance of the Spirit is pointing toward something magical. Why could he not assist particular groups of the bishops *as a collectivity* to a lesser degree?

---

16. The Code of Canon Law speaks of both institutions: synods and conferences. It is a canonical distinction, perhaps more a compliment to our past traditions than a description of our present practices, since synods above the diocesan level are not frequent in the present, nor are they likely to become so in the future. The conferences are obviously taking over their role. Theologically the distinction cannot have much significance once the ontological reality of the *communio* of the episcopate is accepted.

If this theory is pushed to its ultimate consequences, it should be extended to the whole church: the *sensus fidelium* and the *sensus fidei* in the faithful, who are able to recognize infallibly the truth, are operating only when the whole church has arrived at a conclusion, not when new insights are gently and gradually developing in the various parts of the body of the faithful.

3. The theory that sharply distinguishes between effective and affective collegiality, the former alone being collegiality in the proper sense.

Response: The ghost that haunted the fathers of Vatican Council II is still with us: an ambivalence in the understanding of what "college" is. One perception of it originates in Roman law: it understands college as a juridical entity, which either exists in its fullness or not at all--a conception on which Cardinal Dino Staffa's rejection of collegiality was based. Another sees college as *communio* which can exist in different degrees--an approach that Karl Rahner kept explaining and defending.

Those who operate with the first definition can admit a collegial action in one case only: when all are convoked and all are acting in a collegial fashion. Those who work with the second definition see the college as capable of operating at different levels and with varying intensity. Then, all its actions are rooted in communion and have a significance and value that comes from this communion, an underlying ontological reality sustained by the Spirit.

4. The theory that equates the authority to teach with the authority to issue disciplinary norms.

Response: Admittedly, I am touching a complex issue with roots that extend far and wide. There is the philosophical issue of how human persons come to know the truth, and there is the theological issue of how they receive the revealed truth. In either case, the reaching of the truth by human effort, or the reception of it by divine grace, is not simply an act of the will that orders the intellect to accept a statement blindly. On the natural level the intelligence rests in truth when rational arguments support it; on the level of faith the mind comes to rest when the Spirit testifies to the truth of the message--that is certainly the doctrine of Paul the Apostle.

Undoubtedly, the temptation still persists to go back to a theory that saw the *potestas magisterii* as part of the *potestas iurisdictionis*. The proponents of such a theory failed to see that no one can surrender to the truth of a statement or belief on the basis of a disciplinary order alone, without some support for the intelligence--support that in matters of faith must come from the Spirit.[17]

Laws dealing with the *munus docendi* of the church (and there are plenty of them in the new Code of Canon Law) must be explained in function of their theological foundations. To take the laws as normative for doctrine is to subvert the hierarchy between theology and canon law--besides positioning against the intention of the legislator.[18]

5. The theory that draws a sharp distinction between doctrinal and pastoral teaching.

Response: This is a distinction which is difficult to sustain since it would postulate two types of truth, one doctrinal, the other pastoral. Admittedly, some teaching may look more doctrinal than pastoral, such as the definition of *homoousios*, yet the pastoral implications of its acceptance are reaching far and wide--touching on every single prayer addressed to the Father *through* our Lord Jesus Christ. Conversely, some teaching may appear more pastoral than

---

17. The theory that regarded the *potestas magisterii* as part of the *potestas iurisdictionis* gained wide acceptance after the Council of Trent and endured well into our century. A clear description of it can be found in the (once) widely used and highly authoritative manual of canon law by Wernz and Vidal: "Universa potestas ecclesiastica in duas tantum dividitur species scl. in potestatem *iurisdictionis* et potestatem *ordinis*. Quae potestas iurisdictionis generice spectata denuo subdividitur in potestatem *magisterii* circa credenda et in potestatem *iurisdictionis* circa agenda. . . ." (p. 4). Further: "At utraque potestas in hoc *convenit*, quod unaquaeque proxime *voluntati* imponit *praecepta*" (ibid., note 2). See Franciscus Wernz and Petrus Vidal, *Ius Canonicum*, tomus IV, vol. 2 (Rome: Universitas Gregoriana, 1935).

Behind this theory there is a voluntaristic conception of the theological act of faith.

18. There could not be a more eloquent testimony to the fact that the intention of the legislator was not to make any doctrinal statement through legislation than a declaration sent to the episcopal conferences by the authority of Cardinal Pericle Felici, then president of the Pontifical Commission for the Revision of the Code of Canon Law. His text: "Theologicae definitiones atque considerationes plerumque in canonibus recognitis desunt, cum Codicis canonum non sit doctrinam exponere, sed disciplinam ecclesiasticam referre. Doctrina theologica, licet fundamentum sit legislationis canonicae, in ipsa hac legislatione praeberi non debet, nisi quatenus opportunum videatur ut significatio normarum aptius intelligatur earumque momentum peculiari modo sublineetur."

The last sentence in particular shows that the canons are not there to proclaim or explain any doctrine but to establish a discipline. They must be interpreted on the basis of previously existing doctrine.

See "De schemate documenti. . . de sacramentis," *Communicationes* 7 (1975): 27.

doctrinal, such as statements on peace or the economy, yet such teaching too must be rooted in evangelical morality--which is doctrine in the strictest sense of the term even if our comprehension of it is limited.

True, Vatican Council II entitled one constitution on the church *dogmatic* and the other *pastoral*, but there is no evidence to show that the fathers intended to differentiate between two types of truth; in all probability they meant only that the so-called "pastoral" document contained a great number of prudential directions for action. But as a matter of fact the pastoral constitution contains a significant amount of dogmatic teaching; e.g., the section on marriage is a systematic exposition of the theology of marriage-- as we never had it before.[19] And the dogmatic constitution is very pastorally oriented in its chapters on the "Call to Holiness" and on "Religious."

The distinction should not really be between doctrinal and pastoral teaching but between doctrinal teaching and pastoral action. The former is concerned with truth, the latter with prudent courses of action. In fact, both constitutions on the church contain doctrinal statements and directions for prudential action but not in the same measure.

---

19. An explanatory note appended to *Gaudium et Spes* by the council fathers is very much to the point:

> The pastoral constitution "*De Ecclesia in Mundo Huius Temporis*" is made up of two parts; yet it constitutes an organic unity.
> By way of explanation: the constitution is called "pastoral" because, while resting on doctrinal principles, it seeks to express the relation of the Church to the world and mondern mankind. The result is that, on the one hand, a pastoral slant is present in the first part, and, on the other hand, a doctrinal slant is present in the second part
> In the first part, the Church develops her teaching on man, on the world which is the enveloping context of man's existence, and on man's relations to his fellow men. In part two, the Church gives closer consideration to various aspects of modern life and human society; special consideration is given to those questions and problems which, in this general area, seem to have a greater urgency in our day. As a result, in part two the subject matter which is viewed in the light of doctrinal principles is made up of diverse elements. Some elements have a permanent value; others, only a transitory one.
> Consequently, the Constitution must be interpreted according to the general norms of theological interpretation. Interpreters must bear in mind--expecially in part two--the changeable circumstances which the subject matter, by its very nature, involves. (Abbot, *Documents*, 199 n2.)

In other terms *Gaudium et spes* is as much doctrinal as it is pastoral.

Reflections on a Specific Theory

There is nothing that is more helpful for promoting the development of our understanding of a theological issue than prolonged debates among the searchers and researchers. To date, the issue of the teaching authority of the conferences has not benefited much from such discussions, since the problem has just begun to penetrate into the consciousness of canonists and theologians. Nonetheless, the contributions are on the rise. One of them is by Gianfranco Ghirlanda, professor at the Faculty of Canon Law at the Gregorian University in Rome.[20] In the following I wish to examine his theory, both for its content and for its methodological foundations.

The content of his theory can be summed up in a number of "theses." They are of my own formulation, and my summaries obviously cannot render all the nuances that he brings into his own exposition. The reader is advised to study the original text.

1. The episcopal ordination confers the *munus docendi*; the insertion of a bishop by the pope into the hierarchical structure of the church confers the *mandatum docendi*.[21]

---

20. See Gianfranco Ghirlanda, "De Episcoporum conferentia deque exercitio potestatis magisterii," *Periodica* 76 (1987): 573-603.

Ghirlanda in his article refers extensively to a doctoral dissertation written under his direction by James P. Green, *Conferences of Bishops and Exercise of the "Munus Docendi" of the Church* (Rome: [author's own publication], 1987), to the extent that his article appears as a confirmation of the positions taken by Green. In these reflections, however, I wish to respond to Ghirlanda's article only.

See also the critical evaluation (*impugnatio*) of Ghirlanda's position by his colleague at the Gregorian University, Francisco Xavier Urrutia (ibid., 605-36).

21. It is interesting to compare this statement with the position of another canonist (and well-qualified theologian), Winfried Aymans, professor at the University of Munich: "Aufgrund von Taufe und Firmung haben alle Gläubigen Anteil an der *Lehraufgabe* ("munus docendi") der Kirche. Die Kirchenkonstitution "Lumen Gentium" bringt dies durch den Hinweis darauf zum Ausdruck, dass Christus sein prophetisches Amt nicht nur durch die Hierarchie, sondern auch durch die Laien erfüllt."

Ghirlanda sees the source of *munus docendi* in the episcopal ordination; Aymans finds it in what makes a Christian, baptism and profession of faith. The two authors clearly operate out of two different ecclesiologies. Winfried Aymans, "Begriff, Aufgabe und Träger des Lehramts," in *Handbuch des katholischen Kirchenrechts*, ed. Joseph Listl et al. (Regensburg: Pustet, 1983), 533.

2. There are two types of collegiality: effective and affective. Effective collegiality is exercised only when the full body of bishops acts collegially; affective collegiality is present when several bishops (in small and large groups) act *coniunctim*, together.[22]

3. All gatherings of bishops below the level of an ecumenical council and in whatever form (conferences, synods of various types) are the manifestations of collegial *affectus*.

4. The principal purpose of the conferences is consultative and pastoral: not jurisdictional, not legislative.

5. The conferences do not have the *potestas authentice docendi*, which is granted by the pope through canonical mission; for such grant no evidence exists either in the conciliar documents or in the Code of Canon Law.

6. In the conferences the bishops exercise their power of teaching *coniunctim*, which word means that distinct individuals act together on the strength of the power of each, but the collectivity as such has no power of its own.

7. If there is any authority in a doctrinal statement made by a conference, it can only be because the local bishop makes it his own or because the Holy See supports it. Hence, proper *obsequium* cannot be due to the conference as such, only to an individual bishop or to the See of Rome.

In summary, Ghirlanda conceives the episcopal conferences as merely legal entities instituted for the purposes of friendly exchanges and joint actions among the bishops. Since no power exists outside the whole college and the office of the individual bishops, conferences as such cannot have any power to teach; if they have some legislative power it is only by delegation.

To evaluate this theory methodologically, we should begin by raising the question about the extent of the horizon of the author. One is struck

---

22. This terminology is not easy to understand. "Effective collegiality" clearly refers to a bond and to a pattern of operations which are manifest and verifiable at an ecumenical council or in virtually identical situations; "affective collegiality" appears to refer to an internal disposition in persons--and no more.

One wonders if this terminology was inspired by Roman Law which held that *affectus maritalis* was necessary for *matrimonium*.

A more correct way of speaking would have been to say that *affectus collegialis* is the necessary internal disposition for any type of collegial action, admitting that the *effectus* can be of different degree and intensity.

immediately by the absence of a historical horizon. Conferences appear as modern creations, with no similarity to any earlier institution in the church. Yet the particular synods which arose from the second century are very similar indeed to our modern conferences. After all, when the bishops of a particular province, in the East or in the West, got together (and with great frequency in certain regions and in certain epochs), they did nothing else than what our conferences are doing. It was not on the basis of any legislation or delegation that those assemblies gathered, deliberated, taught the faithful, and issued disciplinary laws. The bishops met, compelled by their solicitude for their churches and their *sensus fidei*, to which the churches responded by due *obsequium* out of their own *sensus fidei*. The analogy of those synods with the conferences is inescapable.

There is a total absence of ecumenical perspective. The Eastern church has remained faithful to its early tradition of synodal government, a most certainly catholic practice even if the Latin church has not embraced it to the same extent. If we say that the assemblies of bishops as such cannot have any authority to teach, are we not rejecting the authentic tradition of a sister church--part of the one church of Christ? In doing so, are we not rejecting our own tradition; after all, what is theirs was also ours![23]

The theory was not conceived within a broad theological horizon either. Since Ghirlanda does not perceive the permanent theological bond between *communio* and collegiality within the episcopal order, he cannot but distinguish sharply between "effective" and "affective" collegiality. The former alone can be collegiality in the proper sense of the term; the latter cannot have any theological content, it being no more than the manifestation of mutual good will and some *ad hoc* cooperation. The problem with this perception is that it fails to see the episcopal college as a living body, assembled and sustained by the one Spirit whom the bishops receive at their ordination. This Spirit is the one who holds them together and gives a special character and authority to their assemblies.

Once the conferences are seen as deprived of any theological foundation,

---

23. To say that particular synods in the Eastern church (or in the Western church for that matter) had the authority to teach is not to imply that such assemblies ever could claim the same authority as the "great synods" (ecumenical councils). Particular synods were recognized as far as they were acting within the universal communion of bishops, which implied also that their teaching had to be received by the same communion.

it is logical to understand and explain them in legal terms only, and to seek out canonical sources to explain them. The authority to teach becomes a legal authority, the imposition of a teaching a merely disciplinary matter. The faithful are then expected to respond accordingly: their duty is to obey. But canon law itself cannot give any assistance to the bishops to find the correct doctrine, nor could it increase their capacity to be authentic judges of our tradition. Nor could canon law prompt the conscience of the faithful in the same way as the Spirit does.

There is a further observation concerning methodology: Ghirlanda tends to use too exclusively (virtually in isolation) the texts of Vatican Council II and other official texts after the council. The guiding hermeneutical principle in interpreting such texts should be that they can reveal their full meaning only when they are integrated into our ancient tradition. Thus to argue only from modern texts about the nature and power of an ecclesiastical institution which has parallels in history cannot be the correct method for reaching the right conclusion.[24]

Conclusion

If a unified conclusion can be formulated at the end of these reflections, it is this: the clue to understanding the teaching authority of the episcopal conferences is in the concept of *communio*, which is an ontological reality in the church. It exists all the time independently of any human endeavor, sustained by the Spirit who created it. Episcopal collegiality is a specific manifestation of this *communio*. It can reach perfection and completeness in the case of an ecumenical council. It can manifest itself to lesser degrees in other legitimate assemblies of the bishops for an ecclesial purpose. All such assemblies carry an authority but, again, in different degrees.

Whenever an ecumenical council proclaims a point of doctrine with the

---

24. It is obvious to everybody today that the constitution *Pastor aeternus* of Vatican Council I cannot be correctly interpreted unless it is balanced by the constitution *Lumen Gentium* of Vatican II. An explanation of the primacy on the basis of the words of Vatican I *alone* would be misleading; it would be a sort of theological reductionism; a kind of fundamentalism on the basis of a selected text.

What would be an unsatisfactory method for handling the texts of Vatican I is also an unsatisfactory method for using the texts of Vatican II.

required solemnity, the whole church is bound to follow its teaching; the very existence of the council guarantees the authenticity of its message. Whenever a particular assembly of the bishops makes a doctrinal declaration, their message is not without authority, although the historical event of the gathering cannot be the final guarantee of the truth of it. The response of the faithful, therefore, should be *obsequium* on the one hand, and prudent waiting for the authentication of the message through its reception, on the other hand.

The issue of the authority of the episcopal conferences is ultimately a theological question. It can be properly handled and resolved only by exploring the full extent of the history of episcopal assemblies of whatever nature, provided that they were legitimate; by taking into account the catholic traditions that have been and are alive in the Eastern church; by interpreting every text of Vatican Council II within the context of broad historical and ecumenical horizons. Once all such dimensions are explored and the conclusions are in place, they can help us to find the correct meaning of the canonical texts; never vice versa. There is no evidence that the church intended to define theological realities by legislation; in fact there is overwhelming evidence to the contrary.

The author of these reflections submits that there are good reasons to assert that episcopal conferences have an authority to teach, but such authority is a complex theological reality that admits many shades and variations, reflects analogous situations, and is not easily captured by positive legislation. One could hardly expect anything else if those assemblies of bishops are somehow living manifestations of the mystery of the church.[25]

---

25. Some other conclusions are also emerging from this debate: (1) the outcome of the search concerning the teaching authority of the conferences is conditioned by previously taken positions in ecclesiology; and (2) the choice of the method in the inquiry (especially the choice between the theological and the canonical) virtually determines the conclusions.

Michael A. Fahey, S.J.

Eastern Synodal Traditions: Pertinence for Western Collegial Institutions

MICHAEL FAHEY is Dean of the University of St. Michael's College, Toronto

Roman Catholics, trained in the ecclesiology of the West, frequently identify Eastern Orthodox and Ancient Oriental Orthodox Christians in terms of what doctrines or church polity they do not accept. From a Roman perspective, these Christians are often seen as believers who deny the procession of the Holy Spirit from the Father and from the Son or who reject universal papal primacy of jurisdiction in the worldwide church.

Such categorizing is clearly inadequate in any serious attempt to understand another Christian community of faith. Would it not be more helpful to approach these Christians with a more positive attitude, and to ask whether in the convictions of Eastern Orthodox and pre-Chalcedonian Christians there might not be truths or practices of pastoral care that have become forgotten within our own church? In fact, the churches of the Christian East, for all their problems with caesaro-papism, triumphalism, ethnocentrism, and immobilism, have preserved a profound understanding of the church's conciliar or synodal (sometimes called synodical) character.[1] The

---

1. The Orthodox theologian John Meyendorff, at a 1980 symposium in Bologna, noted the dangerous evolution of legitimate canonical regionalism in the East into ecclesiastical nationalism and a factor of division. John Meyendorff, "Régionalisme ecclésiastique, structures de communion ou couverture de séparatisme?" in *Les Églises après Vatican II: Dynamisme et prospective*, ed. Giuseppe Alberigo, vol. 61 of *Théologie historique* (Paris: Beauchesne, 1981), 329-45.

present unrest in the Roman Catholic church over what governing force to assign to episcopal conferences and how to preserve national or cultural distinctiveness in the worldwide church arises from a reduction of synodal structures in the life of the Roman church.

Synods

In Greek theological language, as Lumpe has explained so well, the word *synodos* has the double function of describing what the Latin church calls either a *concilium* or a *synodus*.[2] In ecclesiastical Greek, *synodos* is closely allied to the biblical term *ekklēsia* and has roots in Jewish religious practices.[3] In the consciousness of today's Eastern Christians, including Eastern Catholics in full communion with the Roman See who have not lost their ecclesial distinctiveness through Romanization, the church must always exist synodically or in synod if it is to remain faithful to its charter. In the Byzantine East, because of this dual meaning of "synod," the term does not connote, as it frequently does in the West, only an institution or event that is local or relatively minor. Nor are synodal or conciliar restricted to bishops or confined solely to gatherings, ecumenical, provincial, or patriarchal. Synodality, conciliarity, or sobornicity (to use the Slavic equivalent) is a characteristic expected to pervade every expression of ecclesial life. Eastern theologians state that the church expresses communion in Christ through its synodal character. Hence, for Eastern churches, any ecclesial practice that is not conciliar or synodal is judged a distortion.

Theologians and canonists of the East stress that the synodal expression of ecclesial life should be found in every act of communion among all the members of the body of Christ. The church's "order" (*taxis*) is an organic expression of the very nature of the church. Whereas the Roman church in recent times has often extolled "communion" ecclesiology, the Eastern

---

2. Adolf Lumpe, "Zur Geschichte der Wörter *Concilium* und *Synodus* in der Antiken Christlichen Latinität," *Annuarium Historiae Conciliorum* 2 (1970): 1-21; "Zur Geschichte des Wortes Synodus in der antiken Gräzität," *Annuarium Historiae Conciliorum* 6 (1974): 40-53. See also, Gustav Koffmane, *Geschichte des Kirchenlateins*, vol. 1 (Breslau: 1879), 27 ff.

3. Günther Stemberger, "Stammt das synodale Element der Kirche aus der Synagoge?" in *Synodale Strukturen der Kirche: Entwicklung und Probleme*, ed. W. Brandmüller (Donauwörth, F.R.G.: Auer, 1977), vol. 8 (1976) of *Annuarium Historiae Conciliorum*, 1-14.

Orthodox and Eastern Catholics prefer to speak of the church's conciliarity or "sobornicity." Eastern Christians are uneasy about the Roman church not only because of papal prerogatives but because of its seeming neglect of true conciliarity. The following judgment of the Romanian Orthodox theologian Dumitru Staniloae is typical:

> Sobornicity is distinguished from an undifferentiated unity by being of a special kind, the unity of communion. The Roman Catholic Church has lost this sense of catholicity as communion, for the doctrine of papal primacy and the ecclesiastical magisterium make impossible the communion of all the members of the Church in all things. The Roman Catholic Church remains content with the unity which characterizes a body under command, and it has replaced the unity of communion (catholicity or sobornicity properly so-called) with the universality in the sense of geographical extension.[4]

One notable expression of the synodal life of the church for Eastern Christians is the patriarchs and heads of the various autocephalous churches who express the mutual communion among their particular churches. But synodal expression is also manifested, it is judged, in every act of communion between a metropolitan and other bishops in his province, between a bishop and his presbyterate (the priests in his jurisdiction), as well as between presbyter and faithful in a particular parish, and finally even among the faithful themselves. As the Eastern Orthodox metropolitan of Pergamum, the theologian John D. Zizioulas, stressed at the 1988 symposium on episcopal conferences in Salamanca: "Bishops are not to be understood as individuals but as heads of communities."[5] At every level, the church is expected to function as a harmonious symphony of believers who have been gathered in Christ and upon whom the Holy Spirit rests. Conciliarity seeks to fashion ecclesiastical life in a way that will express the church's nature and distinctiveness. This

---

4. Dumitry Staniloae, *Theology and the Church*, trans. Robert Barringer (Crestwood, NY: St. Vladimir's, 1980), 56-57.

5. John D. Zizioulas, "The Institution of Episcopal Conferences: An Orthodox Reflection," in *The Nature and Future of Episcopal Conferences*, ed. Hervé Legrand et al. (Washington, DC: Catholic University of America, 1988), 376-83.

synodal way of life is intended to signify how human beings are called by God's grace to collaborate in the work of redemption and the preservation of the apostolic tradition.

Permanent Synod

Many ecclesiologists have concentrated on the synodal nature of the church as expressed in the patriarchal "permanent synod" (*synodos endemousa*).[6] It is notable that only in the twelfth century was the institution of a permanent synod in the church of Rome replaced by the consistory of cardinals. Eastern theologians ask that the see of Rome recognize as legitimate the synodal structures of the East especially in those regions where historically Rome did not exercise patriarchal jurisdiction. They also expect Rome to admit the contingent character of Vatican I's formulations about papal primacy and infallibility.

How a *synodos endemousa* or a "permanent synod" operates in the life of a patriarchate can be illustrated by noting the genesis of several encyclical letters regarding the ecumenical movement published in this century by Constantinople. A 1902 encyclical, identified as "A Patriarchal and Synodal Encyclical," was signed and published by the Ecumenical Patriarch Joachim II

---

6. Pierre Duprey, "La structure synodale de l'église dans la théologie orientale," *Proche orient chrétien* 20 (1970): 123-45; English translation: "The Synodical Structure of the Church in Eastern Theology," *One in Christ* 7 (1971): 152-82; W. Aymans, *Das synodale Element in der Kirchenverfassung* (Munich, 1970); W. Beinert, "Konziliarität der Kirche: Ein Beitrag zur ökumenischen Epistemologie," *Catholica* 33 (1979): 81-108; Hermenegild Alfons Biedermann, "Die Synoden des 4. und 5. Jahrhunderts und das orthodoxe Verständnis der Ortskirche," in *Ortskirche; Weltkirche*, Festgabe Julius Kardinal Döpfner, ed. H. Fleckenstein and G. Gruber (Würzburg: Echter, 1973), 284-303; H. Biedermann, "Einige Grundlinien orthodoxen Kirchenverständnisses," *Ostkirchliche Studien* 19 (1970): 3-18; René Metz, "L'Institution synodale d'après les canons des synodes locaux (topiques): Étude des sources et application actuelle," in *Kanon, Jahrbuch der Gesellschaft für das Recht der Ostkirchen*, ed. W. M. Plöchl and R. Potz (Vienna: Herder, 1974), Bd. II, 154-76; U. Mosiek, "Der Bischofssynode der lateinischen Kirche und die ständige Synode der unierten Kirchen," *Ex aequo et bono: Willibald M. Plöchl zum 70. Geburtstag*, ed. P. Leisching (Innsbruck: Wagner, 1977); Stanley Harakas, "The Local Church: An Eastern Orthodox Perspective," *Ecumenical Review* 29 (1977): 141-53; Heinrich Fries, "Synoden und Konzilien im Leben der Kirche: Historisch-systematische Aspekte," *Catholica* 34 (1980): 174-93; Michael Kessler, "Das synodale Prinzip: Bemerkungen zu seiner Entwicklung und Bedeutung," *Theologische Quartalschrift* 168 (1988): 43-60.

and eleven other members of the synod. The follow-up document dating from 1904 which summarizes responses of the local Orthodox churches to the preceding encyclical is likewise signed by the ecumenical patriarch and eleven metropolitans of the patriarchate. But surprisingly, the next notable encyclical from the patriarchate of Constantinople on church unity, issued in January 1920, was promulgated during a vacancy in the ecumenical patriarchate (*sede vacante*) and was signed only by the *locum tenens* and members of the synod. Such a procedure would be inconceivable today in the Roman church.

The Eastern churches recognize that throughout history there has been a variety of synodal structures shaped by time and circumstances. These include regional, general, provincial, ecumenical synods, as well as the permanent patriarchal synod that collaborates in the administration of a patriarchate or of an autocephalous church. Such a patriarchal synod is "permanent" (*endēmousa*) in the sense that its bishop members, normally located in Constantinople, can be conveniently convened by the patriarch.

From early centuries, synods became vehicles for electing bishops and for reaching agreements. In a real sense, the ecclesiological and dogmatic justification for these permanent synods is the sacrament of orders. The origins of the so-called *endēmousa* synod are rooted in the practice of having the patriarch of Constantinople summon the bishops residing in the capital city at the time (*endēmountes*) to ponder serious issues. Its historical roots, which go back to Constantinople I (A.D. 381), are linked to convening bishops in the capital in order to elect a bishop. This kind of synod grew in importance especially in the eighth century until it became a permanent institution in the Byzantine church. It grew to concern itself with doctrinal disputes, legislative matters, and disciplinary questions, and came to exceed the limited role of the provincial synod. It did not require the elaborate preparations for an ecumenical synod.

Some brief description of how these permanent synods and other related institutions operate in five Byzantine Orthodox patriarchates is instructive for Western Catholics who are now struggling to understand the role of episcopal collegiality in their own church. I comment only on the patriarchates of Constantinople, Alexandria, Antioch, Jerusalem, and Russia. How these patriarchal synods are structured has been analyzed in a detailed volume published in Greece by B. Tzortzatos.[7] From the summary descriptions that follow, I do not imply necessarily that the ideal or the canonical procedures have always been observed. There have been instances when the role of the primate or presiding hierarch has overshadowed the synod's function. Ultimately these exceptions have come to be judged as nonnormative lapses due to local conditions. In most patriarchal churches there exist both a synod of the hierarchy which meets once or twice a year and a permanent synod meeting on an ongoing basis. The synod of the hierarchy is presided over by the patriarch and is made up of the entire hierarchy. It exercises the highest legislative, administrative, and authority in the local church. The permanent synod is a representative body of hierarchs which executes the decisions of the hierarchy synod. Some of the patriarchates have additional administrative bodies to allow clergy and laity to share in organizational issues of the local church even to the point of recommending the election of hierarchs.

Constantinople

The ecumenical patriarch of Constantinople is elected by the *endēmousa* synod made up of certain metropolitans in Constantinople and other parts of the region, although the opinion (*sympsefon*) of other members of the hierarchy, attached to the see but living abroad, is taken into consideration. The permanent holy synod consists of twelve members and is presided over by the patriarch. Members include metropolitans whose sees belong to the patriarchate and are located nearby. The term of service in the synod is for one year, half the membership being replaced every six months. The synod addresses matters of moment to the patriarchate and, because of the primacy of this patriarchal church, it also discusses many far-reaching matters crucial to the life of Orthodoxy worldwide.

The ecumenical patriarch of Constantinople, acting in association with his synod, has in recent years exercised primatial ministry in a number of

---

7. B. Tzortzatos, *Oi vasikoi thesmoi dioikeseos ton Orthodokson Patriarcheion* (Athens, 1972). In June 1980, at the Orthodox Centre of the Ecumenical Patriarchate located in Chambésy-Geneva, an international symposium was held on the central theme of "Local Church and Universal Church" which among other things commented on the specific contributions of a number of these patriarchates. See the acta published as *Église locale et église universelle*, vol. 1 of *Les études théologiques de Chambésy* (Chambésy: Centre Orthodoxe, 1981).

important ways. First, and most importantly, this ministry has been expressed in the promotion of Orthodox unity and in the encouragement of international pan-Orthodox cooperation. In the last several years, with the approval of the synod, the patriarch has embarked upon a series of visits to other patriarchates and major Christian sees, including Rome. While the patriarch and synod do not claim to have "jurisdiction" over other bishops outside the patriarchate, they do claim responsibility for fostering unity. Second, the ecumenical patriarch and his synod have agreed to hear appeals from other local churches, a practice which has historical precedents as far back as the fifth century. Third, they have assumed ecumenical initiatives through publishing encyclical letters and promoting interchurch dialogues. And finally, they exercise pastoral care for churches of the diaspora, which remain at present under the care of this patriarchate.

Alexandria

During the lengthy period when the patriarchate of Alexandria in Egypt consisted of a very small population of Orthodox members, patriarchal governance tended up to the last century to be exercised in monarchical fashion. Today, however, the patriarch is assisted by a patriarchal synod consisting of all metropolitans of the see of Alexandria. It is considered a "complete" synod and differs from a "temporary" synod which meets only to elect a new patriarch or to address a matter of extraordinary urgency. This "complete" synod is composed of at least seven metropolitans, but if that number cannot be attained for the election, the missing number is filled by hierarchs from the churches of Constantinople, Antioch, Jerusalem, Cyprus, or Greece.

Relations between patriarch and metropolitans within the synod are now governed according to the spirit of canon 34 of the *Canons of the Holy Apostles* (fourth century), which situates the primate's supradiocesan role in a collegial context:

> The bishops of every nation (*ethnous*) must acknowledge him who is first (*protos*) among them and account him as their head, and do nothing of consequence without his consent; but each may do only those things which concern his own diocese and the villages within it. But neither is the *protos* to do anything without the consent of all; for so there will be unanimity, and God will be glorified through the Lord in the Holy Spirit.

Ecclesiastical competence of a complete synod covers administrative, canonical, and judicial matters. Such a synod is convened usually twice a year, in the spring and fall. It may also meet in extraordinary session whenever the patriarch deems necessary. He has the right to suspend publication of any synodal decree whose formulation he deems incomplete, but he must justify his action at the synod's next meeting; if the synod insists upon its publication, the patriarch is then obliged to conform to this decision.

Antioch

The patriarchate of Antioch, third in traditional rank among the Orthodox patriarchates, maintained for centuries the synodal system of administration by convening regular and extraordinary synods of hierarchs. But by the early seventeenth century the patriarch began to administer his church in quasi-monarchical fashion, alone selecting bishops and even choosing his own successor. In more recent times, procedures have been worked out to provide for an assembly of clergy and laity to propose names for a patriarch and to provide for a synod and a mixed council (made up of members of the synod and laypersons). The synod itself consists of the patriarch and the active metropolitans of the patriarchal seat. It meets yearly or on extraordinary occasions when the patriarch or at least five metropolitans deem it necessary. Bishops may be present at the sessions of the synod to give reports but do not have the right to vote. The patriarch is obliged to publish within a month any law, regulation, or decision ratified by the synod. If he fails to do this, the duty thereupon falls to the metropolitan first in rank. If the synod is not convened at the appointed time, one may be convened on its own authority.

In addition to the synod, the church of Antioch makes use of a general "mixed" council. It is composed of the entire synod and of lay representatives from each metropolitanate and meets normally twice a year. The synod is competent to deal with financial, administrative, legal, and educational matters. In preparing for the election of a patriarch, this mixed council selects three candidates among whom the synod elects one as patriarch.

Jerusalem

The church of Jerusalem, elevated to a patriarchate by the Fourth

Ecumenical Synod (A.D. 451), ranks fourth among the ancient Eastern patriarchates. This church follows a monastic system or organization; the Greek Orthodox patriarch of Jerusalem also functions as abbot of the Brotherhood of the Holy Sepulchre. This patriarchate did not formulate a written constitutional charter until the second half of the seventeenth century. Under its current statutes, this patriarchate likewise possesses both a synod and a mixed council. The synod is composed of the patriarch, metropolitans, provincial bishops, as well as the titular bishops and archimandrites appointed by the patriarch. The synod's membership may not exceed eighteen. The patriarch in synod may replace any member of the synod if he judges that this would benefit the patriarchate. All the actions of the patriarch in synod and all matters brought before him are decided by a majority vote of the synod.

The mixed council, made up of lay and clerical representatives, allows for lay input in the decision-making process. This council collaborates with local community councils on which a specific number of married priests represent the local church. The mixed council nominates candidates for the patriarchal see. Their recommendation proceeds to a general council made up of the holy synod, the archimandrites, and *protosyngelloi* who live in the monasteries of Jerusalem, as well as married priests who represent the local community councils. Of the three candidates elected by the general council, the members of the synod elect the patriarch.

Russia

Since 1589 the church of Russia has been accorded the status of patriarchate. But, with the ascension of Czar Peter the Great, the patriarchate was abolished in 1721 and replaced with a "governing synod." This arrangement led to the church's domination by the state. This situation lasted until October 1917 when the patriarchate was restored, paradoxically at a time when the state was hostile to the church. Eventually, a charter of rights was worked out with the government, but the relationship between church and state in this century, as is well known, has often been very inimical.

Today the patriarchal synod of Russia possesses the highest authority in legislative, administrative, and judicial matters of the church. It is convened periodically and made up of bishops, other clergy and members of the laity. Again, based on canon 34 of the *Canons of the Holy Apostles*, the patriarch as primate administers the patriarchate together with a synod. When the need exists to resolve important ecclesiastical matters, the patriarch may convene a synod of bishops, provided he obtains the approval of the civil government. The synod is made up of the patriarch and six member hierarchs who administer dioceses. Of the synod members, three are permanent and three temporary.

Eastern Catholic Churches

In this overview of synodal practices I have touched briefly on only five patriarchates. A complete study would have to include the other Orthodox patriarchal or autocephalous churches such as those in Greece, Serbia, Romania, Bulgaria, etc. My description has restricted itself only to one of the four (albeit the largest) major groupings of Eastern Christians, namely the Orthodox church. A fuller account would also include the practice of synodal life in the three other Eastern Christian families: the Oriental Orthodox (pre-Chalcedonian), the small Assyrian church of the East, and finally the various Eastern Catholic churches, most of which have counterparts in either the Orthodox or Oriental Orthodox groupings.[8]

The synodal practices in the Byzantine churches in communion with Rome have been studied and analyzed in various writings in the last decade, especially by Joseph Hajjar.[9] He has shown how practice has varied widely depending upon local needs and various degrees of intervention into their affairs by the Roman See. After the Union of Brest-Litovsk in 1595, for instance, the synods of the Ruthenians were closely supervised by the Roman ecclesiastical authorities. Also Romanians who entered into communion with Rome held relatively frequent diocesan synods, but not until 1872 with the Synod of Blaj was a truly provincial synod held and this actually was carefully orchestrated by Rome. The Melkites too, who have always claimed autonomy for their patriarchal synods, have had this independence challenged by various papal documents which either contested or flatly rejected their legitimacy. A

---

8. For a short discussion of the Eastern churches, see Michael A. Fahey, "Eastern Churches," in *The New Dictionary of Theology*, ed. Joseph Komonchak et al. (Wilmington: Michael Glazier, 1987), 301-306.

9. Joseph Hajjar, "The Eastern Churches," in *The Church in a Secularised Society*, ed. Roger Aubert et al., vol. 5 of *Christian Centuries* (New York: Paulist, 1978), 439-532.

similar situation happened to other Eastern Catholic churches, such as with the Maronite synods of the sixteenth century and with the synod of Mt. Lebanon in 1736.

During the papacy of Pius IX the non-Byzantine churches in full communion with Rome were asked to adopt a legislative system similar to that which had emerged from the Council of Trent. A synod held by the Chaldeans in 1852 and one held by the Syrians in 1853 reflect these Roman plans for redesigning. The Chaldeans did not openly refuse this legislation but frequently chose rather to ignore it in practice; Syrian Catholics eventually tried to recover their traditional governing practices especially in liturgical matters at a synod which they convoked several years later.

At Vatican I there was a short-lived attempt to unify all the disciplines of the Eastern Catholic churches by suppressing local synodal decisions in favor of Roman uniformity. Thanks especially to the interventions of the Chaldean and Melkite patriarchs at Vatican I, the Latin bishops were informed that in fact only a patriarchal or national synod could legitimately initiate reform in these Eastern churches. The abrupt interruption of Vatican I's proceedings by a military invasion of the city of Rome hindered attempts by the Latin church to bypass Eastern practices of governance.

Under Pope Leo XIII (1878-1903), respect and appreciation for the ecclesiastical traditions of the Christian East increased. However, regarding synods, the pope insisted they be presided over by a papal representative and that their decisions needed Roman approval before promulgation. As early as 1929 the proposed Code of Canon Law for the Oriental Churches began to encroach more and more on the legislative jurisdiction of Eastern Catholic synods. Gradually the Eastern provincial synods came to function as do the various episcopal conferences in the Roman Catholic church, namely as consultative bodies without appreciable legislative authority. Even the permanent synod, although still in existence, possesses, in the eyes of the Roman church, only limited administrative and juridical competence.[10] The

---

10. See Joseph Hajjar, *Le synode permanent (synodos endēmousa) dans l'église byzantine des origines au XIe siècle*, vol. 164 of *Orientalia Christiana Analecta* (Rome: Oriental Institute, 1962); Joseph Hajjar, "The Synod in the Eastern Church," *Concilium* 8 (1965): 55-64; Joseph Hajjar, "Les synodes des Églises Orientales Catholiques et l'évêque de Rome," in *Kanon*, vol. 2 (1974): 53-99; and Joseph Hajjar, *Le Vatican, la France et le Catholicisme oriental (1878-1914): Diplomatie et histoire de l'Église* (Paris: Beauchesne, 1979).

history of gradual Romanization over the Eastern synods is well known to the Eastern Orthodox and naturally makes them very cautious in any dialogue about closer ecclesial *rapprochement* with Rome.

Conclusions

Synodal governance within the Eastern, especially Orthodox ecclesiology may be summarized in the following points:

(1) The point of departure for an Eastern understanding of the church is the Ignatian vision of the local church: The faithful come together as church *epi to auto* (1 Cor 11:17, 20; 14:23, 26), become the body of Christ in the Eucharist, and the bishop signifies this unity, summing up the local church in himself but governing in synodal fashion.

(2) The eucharistic assembly under the presidency of the bishop is completely church in all its fullness, a complete church even if not the total church. The local church is not just a part of the church; the church that dwells in Corinth has the same fullness as the church in Jerusalem, Antioch, or Rome.

(3) This status of all the local churches implies the essential unity and equality of all bishops.

(4) This equality of local churches and of bishops does not mean uniformity, just as unity of essence cannot exclude plurality of unique hypostases. Each local church is unique. Among them some may "preside in love," some may express more completely and perfectly the shared faith. Many factors may have contributed to a church's potential for presiding: antiquity, presumed apostolicity of foundation, martyrdom, geopolitical advantages, size, wealth. In contemporary Orthodox church life there are three types of episcopal primacy: (a) that of the regional primacy of a metropolitan archbishop who presides within the synod of bishops of a particular geographical region, (b) the primacy of the head of an autocephalous church, and (c) the unique and distinctive primacy of the patriarch of Constantinople who is recognized as the ecumenical patriarch.

Catholic ecclesiology in the West, especially since the Council of Trent but in fact much earlier, has operated out of a "two-tiered" model of church: the diocese (an *ecclesia particularis*) and, without intermediary structure, the universal church.[11] Hence in this double-deckered vision there is little room for the autocephalous or autonomous church. This narrower Western vision of church had resulted from the effects of the estrangement between East and West, which culminated in 1054 but which had in fact originated much earlier. In the West, papal and patriarchal jurisdictions merged into one office, thus producing in the mind of the Roman church the conviction that it presided over the universal church. This historical process explains in part why today the Vatican has so much difficulty in accepting the competence of episcopal conferences over many matters, and why the Vatican's central administration holds on firmly to supervising the process by which bishops are appointed in every country. Such a two-tiered ecclesiology has undesirable implications, especially when it promotes an exaggerated sense of the diocesan bishop's responsibility to promulgate the theological opinions or the governing priorities of the pope.

The West needs to reappropriate some form of the three-tiered church in which the "particular church" would be seen to be an intermediate ecclesial unit. Episcopal conferences would be seen not primarily as a convening of bishops but of churches represented by bishops. Whether either the episcopal conference or some other form of intermediate ecclesial governance should be assigned a similar role as that of the historic synodal institutions of the past is a question that needs discussion. But the present centralist situation in the Roman Catholic church is certain to promote tension and to pose serious obstacles to the reestablishment of Rome's full communion with the churches of the East.

---

11. The Society for the Law of the Oriental Churches (an ecumenical association including Oriental, Orthodox, Catholic, and Protestant members) held its fourth congress in 1978 in Regensburg on the theme: "The Church and the Churches—Autonomy and Autocephaly." The communications given at the meeting have been published in two volumes as: *Die Kirche und die Kirchen: Autonomie und Autokephalie*, vols. 4 and 5 of *Kanon* (Vienna: Verlag des Verb. d. Wissenschaft. Ges. Oesterreichs, 1980). For a Catholic critique of the Western Catholic two-tier structure, see George Nedungatt, S.J., "Autonomy, Autocephaly, and the Problem of Jurisdiction Today," *Kanon* 5: 19-35. See also, Hervé Legrand, "La Réalisation de l'Église en un lieu," in *Initiation à la pratique de la théologie*, vol. 3/2, ed. B. Lauret and F. Refoulé (Paris: Cerf, 1983), 143-345.

James H. Provost

Episcopal Conferences as an Expression of the Communion of Churches

JAMES PROVOST is professor of canon law at
The Catholic University of America

Much of the discussion on episcopal conferences takes for granted that as bodies composed of bishops, conferences are somehow related to the college of bishops. The extent to which they can be characterized as an expression of episcopal collegiality is debated, but authors on all sides of this debate accept as a given that this is the most apt frame of reference in which to discuss conferences. The purpose of this study is to suggest that another frame of reference may be appropriate, namely that episcopal conferences are an expression of the communion of churches.[1]

The concept of communion is fundamental. It serves as a basic presupposition, something taken for granted in Vatican II and by the Code of Canon Law as they deal with other issues.[2] "Communion" was not so explicitly developed at the council as, for example, collegiality, with which it is often intertwined, for it was collegiality which focused the debate at the council. Thus an attempt to explore episcopal conferences as an expression of the

---

1. This is not an altogether novel approach. See, for example, the approach of Karl Rahner, "On Bishops' Conferences," in *Theological Investigations* 6 (New York and London: Seabury Press and Darton, Longman & Todd, 1969), 377-79. See also the explicit suggestions with regard to the *communio Ecclesiarum* contained in Winfried Aymans, *Das synodale Element in der Kirchenverfassung* (Munich: Max Hueber, 1970), 334-37, and in Giorgio Feliciani, *Le Conferenze Episcopali* (Bologna: Il Mulino, 1974), 450-51. Angel Antón gives this as a first theological basis for conferences; see "The Theological 'Status' of Episcopal Conferences," *Jurist* 48 (1988): 193-200. See also J. M. R. Tillard, "Conférences épiscopales et catholicité de l'Église," *Cristianesimo nella Storia* 9 (1988): 523-39.

2. Ladislas Orsy numbers it among what he calls the "seminal" concepts emerging from Vatican II; see Ladislas Orsy, "New Era of Participation in Church Life," *Origins* 17 (April 28, 1988): 797.

communion of churches will have to proceed by an indirect route, for here we are dealing with something taken for granted in the course of other debates rather than with a concept fully developed on its own.

The understanding of conferences as an expression of the communion of churches will be explored in four stages. First some theoretical considerations will be developed which, when seen together, help to sketch the significance of the communion of churches. Second, the conciliar texts will be examined to see if presenting episcopal conferences in this framework is consonant with the council's teaching. Third, the provisions of the Code of Canon Law will be discussed to illustrate that this approach is in keeping with canonical tradition, and provides some significant insights into the role and importance of conferences. Finally, the study will conclude with some reflections on tensions and implications related to understanding conferences as communions of churches.

Theoretical Considerations

Several elements support an understanding of conferences of bishops as an expression of the communion of churches. First, bishops are not isolated individuals, but stand in necessary relationship to the church. Second, the church is not some monolithic unit, but is itself fundamentally a communion of churches, including a communion of autonomous churches which have a special importance in the historical development and present organization of the Catholic church. Third, these autonomous churches are themselves communions of particular churches whose very purpose is both communion and mission. Finally, bishops and their conferences exist in necessary relationship to churches in virtue of communion and mission as these are realized in various dimensions of ecclesial life.

Bishops and the Church

Just as Peter was chosen from among the apostles (*LG* 19) for his special role, so the apostles were chosen from among the broader community of the disciples (Luke 6:13). Thus from the very beginning, those to whom the Lord entrusted the *munus pascendi* are presented in Scripture and the magisterium as being within the body of the church, rather than as isolated individuals or as somehow not part of the larger body of the faithful. They exist not by themselves but in relationship to the church, to all of God's people.

The body of bishops succeeds the apostles in the *munus pascendi* (*LG* 20). Bishops are pastors. But a "pastor" implies a body of the faithful whom he serves. In virtue of their function, bishops must be seen as within the church, as in essential relationship to the church. The office of bishop, of *episcopos* ("overseer"), makes sense only in relationship, only as a term which demands of its nature the presence of another term--the church.

What is being raised here is not a question of political theory applied to the church (e.g., the issues of monarchy or democracy), neither is it an attempt at some kind of reductionism such that the church would consist solely or primarily in the *christifideles*. Rather, it is a recognition that pastors and faithful, bishops and the rest of God's people, are intimately connected as church, and that the church is God's. The church is not primarily the work of individuals, bishops or others, but of God who forms and animates this body, who calls it in faith and who sustains it in grace. To speak of bishops, then, is to speak at the same time of the church to which they are committed in service, primarily a service of unity (*LG* 23). A gathering of bishops as bishops includes this essentially ecclesial dimension of who bishops are.

Communion of Autonomous Churches

The church is a mystery which can be presented under a variety of images.[3] It is realized in various dimensions, whether at the most local celebration of the Eucharist under the authority of the bishop (*LG* 26) or in the solemn gathering of bishops at an ecumenical council, representing the diverse local churches (*LG* 23).

The bishops at the Second Vatican Council adopted a pattern of addressing the church in three fundamental dimensions: as the whole church (or church universal), as particular churches, and as groupings of particular churches. This order was followed consistently in such documents as *Lumen Gentium* and *Christus Dominus*, where the issues were initially how to

---

3. *Lumen Gentium* chapters 1 and 2 present a variety of images, by this very fact illustrating that the church can be approached from various angles, no one of which fully expresses the mystery which is the church.

complete the work of Vatican I on the relationship between the primacy and the rest of the bishops.

But when a different problematic was at work, the bishops adopted a different ordering of these dimensions to suit the topic under consideration. Thus in the decree on missions, *Ad Gentes*, consideration is given to the organic development of evangelization, which begins on the most local level and eventually culminates in the particular church. Only in discussing the planning of missionary activity (chapter 5) is the previous order reintroduced, starting with the responsibilities of the church universal, then of the diocese, and finally of bishops' conferences.

When the specific problematic of the Second Vatican Council is set aside for the more living context of Catholic life, it is important to note that there is a fundamental significance given to autonomous churches, the Western and Eastern Catholic churches. For example, a Catholic is baptized into an autonomous church, and in that manner is joined to both the local church and the church universal.[4] This attachment to an autonomous church constitutes the first and fundamental condition of a Christian. This canonical fact reflects the basic ecclesiological reality that the Catholic church is indeed a communion of churches, and in a special way, a communion of autonomous churches.

What are these autonomous churches? At the council they were sometimes characterized as rites, and the Code of Canon Law for the Latin church refers to them as ritual churches *sui iuris* (cc. 111-112). The council characterized them as groupings of churches "organically united, which. . . enjoy their own discipline, their own liturgical usage, and their own theological and spiritual heritage"[5] within the unity of faith and the divine constitution of the whole church. The grouping of local churches in an autonomous church is held together by its own hierarchy (*O* 2), reflecting the reality that all dimensions of the church's communion are linked together by those who serve it in the *munus pascendi*, as will be discussed shortly.

Although historically conditioned, and capable of being revised or even

---

4. See *Code of Canon Law, Latin-English Edition* (Washington, DC: Canon Law Society of America, 1983), c. 111.

5. *Lumen Gentium* 23; translations of conciliar documents are taken from *The Documents of Vatican II*, ed. Walter M. Abbott, S.J., and trans. Joseph Gallagher (New York: America Press, 1966).

multiplied (*O* 11), autonomous churches are a reality which the church takes quite seriously. The validity of the administration of various sacraments, for example, depends upon respect for the rite of the minister or even of the recipient.[6] The Christian people have a right "to worship God according to the prescriptions of their own rite" (c. 214). If the means of salvation are tied to autonomous churches, however much these churches may be historically conditioned they are nevertheless basic to the reality of the church today. The council teaches they are to be held in "high esteem" (*O* 1).

The official position of church authorities is that various autonomous churches are equal within the Catholic communion. "They enjoy the same rights and are under the same obligations, even with respect to preaching the gospel to the whole world (cf. Mk. 16:15) under the guidance of the Roman Pontiff" (*O* 3). This may not always be respected in practice, but it does state a policy position which expresses the reality of the church as a communion of churches. It also places that communion in the context of mission, itself a constitutive dimension of the church's very foundation.

Thus the church to which bishops stand in necessary relationship is a communion of churches. Bishops themselves pertain to a specific autonomous church, and perform a necessary function of unity within that church while at the same time respecting the equality and dignity of other autonomous churches and their own bishops. Thus for bishops to gather as bishops includes a necessary relationship to this dimension of the church as a communion of churches.

Communion and Mission[7]

Autonomous churches are themselves communions of particular churches. Although much in vogue today, and in danger of becoming banal,

---

6. See, for example, c. 1109, where the valid celebration of marriage depends on at least one of the parties being subject to the local ordinary or pastor in whose jurisdiction the marriage takes place. If neither party is of the Latin autonomous church, the wedding would be invalid without further authorization from a hierarch of the appropriate autonomous church.

7. The interrelationship of these two concepts has recently been highlighted by Pope John Paul II in his apostolic exhortation on the laity. See John Paul II, apostolic exhortation *Christifideles Laici*, December 30, 1988, *Origins* 18 (February 9, 1989): 561, 563-95.

"communion" properly understood is not some vague concept.[8] It is richly theological, rooted in our very understanding of God as a communion of three Persons in one Godhead.[9] This divine life is manifested to us in that unique communion of the divine and human natures, the hypostatic union. This divine life of communion dwells within us by the indwelling of the Spirit, so that our life becomes a communion with the divine. Those who share this same divine communion express it in the communion of the Eucharist, where in a Holy Communion we are nourished by Christ's Body and Blood and at the same time express the bond which this divine life forms among us.

So it is that "in any community existing around an altar, under the sacred ministry of the bishop," Christ is present and "by virtue of him the one, holy catholic and apostolic Church gathers together" (*LG* 26). This sacramental community is based on the "sacrament of love, a sign of unity, a bond of charity" (*SC* 47), and is linked in communion with other such communities through the ministry of the bishop, whose function it is to be "the visible principle and foundation of unity in his particular church" (*LG* 23).

Communion through a hierarch is one dimension of the hierarchical communion by which all dimensions of the church are bonded together. That is, the function of bishops is especially to be the source of unity within their diocese, and to be the link of communion for their particular church with other particular churches (*Lumen Gentium* 23). The college of bishops is thus at the service of the communion of churches, for it is "in and from such individual churches" that "there comes into being the one and only Catholic Church" (*LG* 23). The Vatican Council fathers addressed this unifying role of bishops in terms of "representation" in *Lumen Gentium*: "each individual bishop represents his own church, but all of them together in union with the

---

8. See for example the following studies: Jerome Hamer, *The Church is a Communion* (London: Geoffrey Chapman, 1964); Oskar Saier, *"Communio" in der Lehre des Zweiten Vatikanischen Konzils: Eine rechtsbegriffliche Untersuchung* (Munich: Max Hueber, 1973); Antonio Acerbi, *Due Ecclesiologie: Ecclesiologia giuridica ed ecclesiologia di comunione nella "Lumen gentium"* (Bologna: Dehoniane, 1975); various authors in the special issue, "The Church as Communion," *Jurist* 36 (1976): 1-245; various authors in the special conference, "La Communion dans l'Église," *L'Année Canonique* 25 (1981): 19-259; J. M. R. Tillard, *Église d'Églises: L'écclesiologie de communion* (Paris: Cerf, 1987). The "Final Report" of the 1985 extraordinary Synod of Bishops highlighted communion as central to the conciliar teaching on the church; cf. Extraordinary Synod 1985, "The Final Report," II, C, 1, *Origins* 15 (December 19, 1985): 448.

9. *Christifideles laici*, n. 18.

Pope represent the entire Church joined in the bond of peace, love, and unity."[10]

Representation is not to be taken in this context as some social or political theory, such that the bishop would be considered a "representative sample" of the Catholics in a particular church, or serve as that church's "delegated representative" in the broader communion. Representation has a much richer meaning when it is used in the context of the magisterium's teaching on the church. Bishops "represent" Christ in their churches; they "in an eminent and visible way undertake Christ's own role as Teacher, Shepherd, and High Priest" so that "they act in his person" (*LG* 21). So, too, they "act in the person" of the particular church and not in their own name when they represent that church in the communion of churches. They make present (re-present) the joys and sorrows, hopes and aspirations of the particular church they serve; they make present the faith of that church within the communion, just as "acting in the person of Christ" within the particular church they are to proclaim the gospel and nourish the faith of the people.

Communion, therefore, is a rich and complex reality. It has important theological roots and finds important expression through the collegiality of bishops as making present the communion of the churches. Thus a gathering of bishops as bishops includes this communion dimension, for that is what the church itself is.

Communion, however, is necessarily related to mission.[11] "Mission" is not just some activity of the church, something it *does*. Mission is a dimension of what the church *is*, and thus participates in the mystery which we profess the church to be.[12] Mission is rooted in God's coming to us; it is in terms of the divine mission that we come to glimpse the mystery of the Trinity. Jesus comes to us on mission, keenly aware that he has been sent (missioned) by his Father. Jesus sends the Spirit to be our strength and advocate. And

---

10. *Lumen Gentium* 23; see discussion on "representation" in Tillard, *Église d'Églises*, 243-51.

11. *Christifideles laici*, n. 32: "Communion and mission are profoundly connected with each other. . . : Communion gives rise to mission, and mission is accomplished in communion."

12. See M. J. Le Guillou, *Mission et Unité: Les exigences de la communion*, 2 vols., *Unam Sanctam* 33-34 (Paris: Cerf, 1960); various authors in "The Church as Mission," *Jurist* 39 (1979): 1-288; Severino Dianich, *Chiesa in missione: Per una ecclesiologia dinamica* (Turin: Edizioni Paoline, 1985); Giuseppe Colombo, "Communion, Mission, and Episcopal Conferences," *Jurist* 48 (1988): 107-110.

empowered by the coming of that Spirit, the Apostles undertook the mission on Pentecost to spread the gospel to all lands. In virtue of the indwelling of the Spirit within each of the baptized, we ourselves are sent to proclaim the gospel in keeping with our talents and charisms (*AG* 3).

So to be church is to be on mission, for the church is missionary by its very nature (*AG* 2). The mission is carried out not in isolation, for "it has not pleased God to call men to share his life merely as individuals without any mutual bonds. Rather, he wills to mold them into a people in which his sons, once scattered abroad, can be gathered together" (*AG* 2). The mission of the church is not limited to the work of specialists, or of church officials; it "is fulfilled by that activity which makes her fully present to all men and nations" (*AG* 5), by implanting the church among all peoples. Thus even the most local grouping of Christians, planted in a given time and place, bears witness to the one, holy, catholic, and apostolic church when, in communion with the successors of the Apostles, it professes the one apostolic faith.

The mission of the church encompasses the preaching of the gospel, the celebration of the sacraments, and as the bishops at the 1971 synod of bishops taught, "action on behalf of justice and participation in the transformation of the world."[13] To be planted among all peoples, the church is to exercise its mission in such a way as to touch the various dimensions of the realities which make up their lives. Thus the church's mission touches human conditions at a most intimate and local level, but also in light of the various groupings of people ranging from the local community, to larger communities, and even to states and nations. Indeed, the Catholic church proclaims its mission to be a light to all the peoples, to address their concerns even in their worldwide dimensions.

Bishops have the special function of promoting, directing, and coordinating the church's mission. They do this in various ways, united with one another and with the bishop of Rome as their head, relating to the various dimensions of the church's communion and to the various dimensions of human reality. Thus a gathering of bishops as bishops includes this mission dimension, for that is also what the church itself is.

---

13. 1971 Synod of Bishops, declaration on Justice in the World, November 30, 1971, *Acta Apostolicae Sedis* 63 (1971): 923.

Nature of Episcopal Conferences

In light of the above considerations, what can be said of episcopal conferences as an expression of the communion of churches? First, conferences of bishops cannot be understood as only a congenial support group for bishops personally. By their nature, and by the nature of bishops as bishops, these conferences have a necessary relation to the churches their members serve.

Second, the role of episcopal conferences is episcopal; that is, it is related to service, for hierarchical authority itself is service.[14] The service they provide is directed toward building up communion and fostering mission. Both of these dimensions are found in the particular churches served by the bishops who make up a conference. Their service as a conference promotes the realization of communion and mission in the human dimension appropriate to a conference--the nation--as well as in support of the realization of communion and mission within the particular churches or in various groupings of them (e.g., provinces, regions, etc.).

Third, it is appropriate for episcopal conferences to be concerned with both inner church issues, which relate to building up and fostering the communion of the church, and church-world issues where the church engages in witnessing to the gospel and calling all persons of good will to a life of value and meaning. Episcopal conferences address issues of faith, worship, church discipline and structure; they organize and support the missionary works of Catholics at home and abroad; they engage in or sponsor activities which are intended to foster the unity of Christians; they are to be concerned with the social conditions of human society, with issues of justice and peace, with the welfare of the poor.[15] In other words, as expressing the communion of churches the agenda for episcopal conferences arises from their nature as communion and mission, recognizing that pastoral, missionary, and ecumenical

---

14. John Paul II, apostolic constitution *Sacrae disciplinae leges*, January 25, 1983, *Acta Apostolicae Sedis* 75/2 (1983): xii.

15. For listings of episcopal conferences' competencies see Joseph Listl in *Handbuch des katholischen Kirchenrechts*, ed. Joseph Listl et al. (Regensburg: Pustet, 1983), 313-20; G. Melguizo Y. et al., "Las conferencias episcopales en el nuevo Código de Derecho Canónico," *Universitas Canonica* 3/7 (1983): 41-61; James H. Provost in *The Code of Canon Law: A Text and Commentary*, ed. James A. Coriden et al. (New York/ Mahwah, NJ: Paulist, 1985), 370-72.

concerns are rooted in the same basic charge to preach the gospel to all creatures.

Vatican II

The question must now be asked whether this view of conferences of bishops as expressions of the communion of churches is in keeping with official church teaching at the Second Vatican Council. It is already evident that several of the elements of the discussion in the previous section were drawn from conciliar teaching. Now, however, it is a question of turning to the conciliar documents themselves and rereading them to determine more exactly whether such a view of episcopal conferences is consonant with the conciliar texts. Attention here will focus on two texts in which the Second Vatican Council dealt directly with the nature and purposes of episcopal conferences: *Lumen Gentium* 23 and *Christus Dominus* 36-38.

Lumen Gentium 23[16]

This text is located within the constitution's third chapter, where the bishops developed one of the central themes of the council. The immediately preceding section, *Lumen Gentium* 22, addresses collegiality; there Vatican II was completing the work of Vatican I. *Lumen Gentium* 22 teaches the existence of the college of bishops and the various expressions of the full college, especially in an ecumenical council and in the nonconciliar collegial action of bishops around the world.

Lumen Gentium 23 then turns to other expressions of the collegial union of bishops with one another and with the pope. It begins with the relationship between the pope and individual diocesan bishops. These latter are said to be "the visible principle and foundation of unity" in the particular churches. *Lumen Gentium* 23 then states an important teaching on the reality of the church as a communion of churches: "In and from such individual churches there comes into being the one and only Catholic Church."

Addressing the role of individual bishops, the constitution affirms that

---

16. For an analysis of this text with special reference to our topic, see Tillard, "Conférences épiscopales et catholicité de l'Église," 523-30.

their governing power is limited to their respective churches. The document then moves to a broader perspective on the episcopal role. Moving from a limited concern for governing power, it expands on that solicitude by which bishops express their concern for the welfare of the whole church. This leads to a discussion of the responsibility bishops have "to enter into a community of effort among themselves and with the successor of Peter" to promote the mission of the whole church, applying the resources of their respective dioceses for missions elsewhere. The section concludes with a strong plea to "extend their fraternal aid to other churches, especially to neighboring and more needy dioceses, in accordance with the venerable example of antiquity."

The "venerable example of antiquity" is then discussed not in terms of charitable acts by individual bishops, as might be expected if the only term of reference were the college of bishops, but in terms of the communion of churches. This also forms the context for the next concept, the council's treatment of the development of groupings of churches. *Lumen Gentium* 23 opens this topic by addressing the historical development of ritual churches, teaching that the variety of "churches with one common aspiration is particularly splendid evidence of the catholicity of the undivided Church." It then turns to modern-day *Coetus Episcopales*, a term which elsewhere is used to designate episcopal conferences (cf. *SC* 22, 128; *LG* 29; *CD* 38, 1º), for which the official nomenclature was still being developed when this text was drafted. These are said to be able to render "manifold and fruitful assistance" so that the collegial sense may bear fruit in practice.

Such a "collegial sense" was historically manifested in the ritual churches which had just been described. These are clearly communions of particular churches. Moreover, the text follows upon the important discussion of solicitude by which bishops bring the resources of their particular churches to bear for the welfare of other churches, and foster the mission which is the work of all the church. These activities are not the work of private individuals who happen to be bishops, but of bishops representing their particular churches and fostering the participation by the people of their church. The context points toward the communion of churches at work when bishops join together to bring their collegial sense to bear on practical concerns in episcopal conferences.

If a more explicit reference is lacking in this context, the opening observation of this study should be recalled. It is very difficult to separate collegiality from the communion of churches; the college of bishops does not exist as an isolated group but in relation to the churches, for which it has the important function of serving as the link of hierarchical communion assuring the unity of the whole church.

Christus Dominus 36-38

The context for these sections is also significant. *Christus Dominus* follows the schema discussed earlier: the first chapter deals with the relationship of bishops to the whole church (church universal); the second chapter concerns bishops and their particular churches or dioceses; now the third chapter moves to the intermediate dimension of church life, "concerning the cooperation of bishops for the common good of many churches." *Christus Dominus* 36-38 are the opening sections of this chapter, and are grouped under the heading of "Synods, Councils, and Especially Episcopal Conferences."

Christus Dominus 36 summarizes briefly the historical practice of regional gatherings of bishops ("synods, provincial councils, and plenary councils"). The council teaches that this practice sprang from the bishops' "fellowship of fraternal charity" and "zeal for the universal mission entrusted to the apostles." In them, "a common pattern to be followed in teaching the truths of faith and ordering ecclesiastical discipline" was legislated for various churches.

In other words, the history of what church law now terms "particular councils" is rooted in concern for the welfare of churches, and in that sense is a reflection of the communion of churches linked together by the solicitude and collegial spirit of their respective bishops. This is not some historical fossil to be admired but not continued. Quite the contrary, *Christus Dominus* 36 states that the "sacred Ecumenical Synod" of Vatican II "earnestly desires that the venerable institution of synods and councils flourish with new vigor" so that "faith will be spread and discipline preserved more fittingly and effectively in the various churches." The communion of churches within a province (provincial council) or nation (plenary council) has a distinct importance here.

To promote the communion of churches within a regional area, the council turns to episcopal conferences. *Christus Dominus* 37 presents these as "associations" of bishops within the same nation or region which have already evidenced their worth by the fruits they have produced in the harmony and close working together of bishops in their respective offices.

In itself, this view could be seen as presenting conferences as a sort of bishops' support group ("association"), rather than an expression of the communion of churches. But the description concludes with a distinctly ecclesial perspective: "when the insights of prudence and experience have been shared and views exchanged, there will emerge a holy union of energies *in the service of the common good of the churches*" (emphasis added). This is clearly in keeping with what was developed above concerning the necessary relation of bishops and their churches. The focus of episcopal conference concerns is on the service of the churches, reflecting the fact that when bishops act as bishops, they "represent" their churches and thus articulate the communion of churches.

Christus Dominus 37 concludes by introducing *Christus Dominus* 38, where specific norms are set forth concerning episcopal conferences. Several of these provisions reflect the conferences' dimension as expressing the communion of churches.

a. A conference is a kind of *coetus* in which the bishops of a nation or territory exercise their pastoral function *coniunctim* for the purpose of promoting that greater good which the church offers humankind, especially through forms and programs of the apostolate adapted to current circumstances (*CD* 38, 1º). Here a distinctly mission perspective is given to conferences. Their agenda is not limited to internal or strictly institutional concerns; primarily, they are to address how the church can be a light to the peoples of their place and time. Moreover, it is not just what the bishops can offer humankind, but what the *church* can offer. The necessary connection of bishops with church is quite evident.

The joint (*coniunctim*) exercise of their pastoral function goes beyond their governing power within their particular churches, and looks to this greater effort which the church--the communion of their churches as well as the whole church itself--is called to make for humankind. This is a specific expression of solicitude, not just the general one discussed in *Lumen Gentium* 23, for it is to be expressed in "forms and programs of the apostolate" which the bishops determine jointly to pursue. The text does not limit the pursuit of such apostolic programs to individual churches, although this is where the apostolate may be most effectively carried out. The joint efforts of several particular churches, under the joint leadership of their bishops, can also be necessary to relate to broader dimensions of human reality.

The joining here of communion and mission concerns is a practical expression of the insight the council developed in discussing missions, where it affirmed the close connection between missionary work, pastoral activity, and ecumenical concern (*AG* 6). The pastoral function of bishops extends to working for the unity of Christians, in order that the world may believe. It is especially fitting that churches cooperate in this work of Christian unity, which looks to the fullness of that unity which these particular churches already express through their bishops working together, including their working together in episcopal conferences.

b. Membership in episcopal conferences pertains to those who have a pastoral responsibility in the area. This includes "all local ordinaries of every rite, coadjutors, auxiliaries, and other titular bishops who perform a special work entrusted to them by the Apostolic See or the episcopal conferences" (*CD* 38, 2º). Local ordinaries clearly "represent" the particular church. Coadjutor and auxiliary bishops must also be given pastoral responsibility within the particular church; coadjutors are always to be appointed vicars general, whereas auxiliaries are to be either vicars general or episcopal vicars (*CD* 26). The other titular bishops mentioned in the decree also perform some special work on behalf of the church, whether at the behest of the Apostolic See or the episcopal conference itself.

In effect, the membership of an episcopal conference according to *Christus Dominus* 38 is primarily related to the service of the church. Those bishops must be members who are in some manner missioned to serve the church within this area. Other bishops are not *de iure* members. The criteria for membership indicate a concern for the churches of the area, not just the personal welfare of the bishops there. These criteria point in a special way to an understanding of episcopal conferences as expressing the communion of churches.

c. Certain decisions of the conference can have the force of law for the churches in the territory (*CD* 38, 4º). The decision must have been taken in a matter for which the conference has competence to make a binding decision, as determined in law or by mandate of the Apostolic See; it must have been passed by a two-thirds majority; and it must have received the *recognitio* of the Apostolic See.

These conditions are not unlike those which bound a provincial or plenary council at the time.[17] However, in the case of councils the matters subject to its deliberation are stated in broad terms rather than the restrictive ones which apply to conferences, and the required vote is only a simple majority rather than two-thirds. In both cases, the decisions must receive the *recognitio* of the Apostolic See.

This provision of *Christus Dominus*, together with the many responsibilities given to episcopal conferences elsewhere in conciliar documents and in postconciliar directives for implementing the council,[18] make it clear that they are at the service of the particular churches and in this sense express the communion of churches within an area. A diocesan bishop, as the center and source of unity for that particular church, has the "right and duty" to legislate for what concerns its welfare (*LG* 27). If conferences can exercise a similar right for several churches, this reflects the fact that they are an expression of the communion of those churches.

These conciliar texts reflect several dimensions of the doctrinal foundation for episcopal conferences. Not only are conferences an expression of the collegial spirit among bishops; they are also an expression of the communion of the churches the bishops represent. As indicated at the beginning, these two dimensions are intimately connected and thus difficult to distinguish. But it does seem that the conciliar texts themselves reflect an unspoken presumption that conferences do express the communion of churches.

1983 Code of Canon Law

The revised Code of Canon Law deliberately proposes to express in juridical language the council's teaching on the church, even if this mystery can only find imperfect expression in law.[19] Thus the conciliar teaching controls the interpretation of the code and at the same time provides an important source for the 1983 legislation.

---

17. See 1917 code, cc. 290-291.

18. See analysis of the pre-1983 code competence of episcopal conferences in Raymond W. Kutner, *The Development, Structure, and Competence of the Episcopal Conference*, vol. 480 of *Canon Law Studies* (Washington, DC: Catholic University of America, 1972), 139-73.

19. John Paul II, *Sacrae disciplinae leges*, xi.

The 1917 code dealt with episcopal conferences only as provincial gatherings of bishops.[20] The context for this canon indicated that episcopal conferences were a participation in the supreme power of the church, rather than an expression of what that code termed "subordinate episcopal power."[21] The perspective is completely changed in the new code.

The 1983 code organizes its treatment of the hierarchical constitution of the church into two sections, the first dealing with "Supreme Church Authority" and the second with "Particular Churches and Their Groupings." Title two of this second section contains the canons on "Groupings of Particular Churches." It is here that the canons on episcopal conferences are found. So from the very context of the law, episcopal conferences are presented as an expression of the grouping of particular churches, hence of the communion of those churches.[22]

Conferences, however, are not the first item in the title. The organization of ecclesiastical provinces and regions sets the stage, then the canons on metropolitans, followed by those on particular councils, and finally the thirteen canons on episcopal conferences. The organization of the topics integrates conferences into the more traditional forms of intermediary church structures.[23]

Taking up the council's expressed desire to revitalize provincial and plenary councils, the code provides a renewed approach to particular councils.[24] Their membership is expanded to include a broader cross-section of the laity, religious, and clergy from the particular churches involved, making particular councils more clearly assemblies in which the communion of

---

20. See 1917 code, c. 292.

21. See Titles VII and VIII of Book II, First Part, Section II, of the 1917 code.

22. A proper interpretation of the law relies on understanding the meaning of the words of the law in their text and context (c. 17). The present context in which episcopal conferences are treated in the 1983 code takes on a special significance, therefore, in the perspective of this paper.

23. In earlier drafts of the code, conferences were given first treatment; some may view the present arrangement as an attempt to downgrade conferences, but from the perspective of the issues dealt with in this paper it would seem actually to strengthen the understanding of conferences in light of the communion of particular churches.

24. See cc. 439-446. As will become apparent, the new canons present creative opportunities for episcopal conferences, and the possibility for renewed synodal activity on a supradiocesan scale involving broader participation by the Catholic community.

churches will be visible (c. 443). The canons focus the competence of a particular council on the pastoral needs of the people of God in its own territory and clarify the legislative power which is exercised in it (cc. 443, §§1 and 2; 445).

Perhaps most striking is the prominence given to episcopal conferences in the functioning of plenary councils. Plenary councils are held "for all the particular churches belonging to the same conference of bishops."[25] While formerly it was the right of the Apostolic See to convoke plenary councils and to name their presiding officer, it is now up to the conference of bishops to do this, although with the subsequent approval of the Apostolic See. The conference also selects where the council shall meet, determines its agenda, sets the time and place for its meeting, and determines its closing. The episcopal conference can also transfer, prolong, or dissolve the council. And the rules on voting membership in a plenary council can be the same as those for the episcopal conference itself.[26]

In effect, a plenary council is an episcopal conference meeting in more solemn session, with the participation of other members of the people of God from the particular churches involved. Such councils are traditionally understood as an expression of the communion of the churches involved. The presumption in the law is that these will be the legislative sessions of conferences of bishops, for the legislative power of plenary councils is affirmed, limited only by due regard for the universal law of the church.[27] It is evident in this setting that episcopal conferences are an expression of the communion of churches.

Although the specific provisions on episcopal conferences in the new code (cc. 447-459) express some hesitation and qualifications on the conciliar

---

25. Canon 439, §1. Translation of canons is taken from *Code of Canon Law, Latin-English Edition.*

26. Compare c. 443, §§1 and 2, with c. 450.

27. See c. 445: "A particular council sees to it that provision is made for the pastoral needs of the people of God in its own territory, and it possesses the power of governance, especially legislative power, so that with due regard always for the universal law of the Church it can decree what seems appropriate. . . ." Contrast this with the limited legislative power acknowledged for episcopal conferences acting only as conferences, in c. 455, §1: "The conference of bishops can issue general decrees only in those cases in which the common law prescribes it, or a special mandate of the Apostolic See . . . determines it."

material,[28] these must not be taken as rejecting the conciliar teaching. As the pope indicated in promulgating the code, the teaching of the council remains the controlling source of interpretation for the law.

The code describes conferences as exercising *coniunctim* "certain pastoral functions on behalf of the Christian faithful of their territory in view of promoting that greater good which the Church offers humankind" (c. 447). The comments above on *Christus Dominus* remain valid here; underlying the description in canon 447 remains the perspective of a communion of churches.

This becomes more explicit in the criteria for membership (c. 450), drawn on the conciliar norms and envisioning conferences as related to the pastoral good of the churches rather than a support group for members of the college. Moreover, only those who head up diocesan churches (e.g. diocesan bishops and coadjutors) can determine the conference's statutes (c. 454, §2). Since the statutes govern how the conference is organized and operates, this restriction is understandable when conferences are understood to express the communion of those churches.

A recent authoritative interpretation of the code reaffirms this sense of conferences being based on a communion of churches, by restricting to diocesan bishops the position of president or vice-president ("pro-president" in the European sense). In an explanation by Cardinal Castillo Lara, who heads up the commission which interprets church law, the point is emphasized that conferences are rooted in the exercise of the pastoral function in an area, not just in the collegiality of the bishops there.[29]

As with the conciliar teaching on which they are based, the canons of the 1983 code reflect various bases for episcopal conferences. A major presupposition is that they in some way express the communion of churches within the territories for which the conferences are established.

---

28. For a detailed analysis of the reservations about conferences which affected the drafting of the new code, see Angel Antón, *Conferencias Episcopales: Instancias Intermedias?* (Salamanca: Ediciones Sigueme, 1989), 142-56, 202-203.

29. Cardinal Rosalio Castillo Lara, "The Presidency of Episcopal Conferences," *L'Osservatore Romano* [English edition], March 20, 1989, 11.

Tensions and Implications

Approaching episcopal conferences from the perspective of the communion of churches may shed some light on contemporary tensions related to these conferences. Here it will be possible only to sketch some reflections on three of these tensions: maintaining communion in a world-wide church; promoting the church's mission; relating conferences and plenary councils.

Maintaining the Communion

One might expect that the major tensions for episcopal conferences in regard to communion would relate to the diocesan churches represented in the conference. There are some instances of this, but they are so few as to make the existing communion all the more remarkable. Despite differences in style, personality, and pastoral outlook among the bishops, the various conferences generally reflect a living and effective communion among the diocesan churches in the Catholic church.

The major tension has been between conferences and the Apostolic See: how to maintain communion in a church which is now worldwide, and in which the local hierarchies are more numerous and organized than ever before.[30] The encyclical *Humanae Vitae* serves as a watershed in this regard. Prior to 1968 there was a general openness at the Apostolic See toward conferences, despite some reservations expressed by various interventions at Vatican II.[31] Conferences responded in varying ways to *Humanae Vitae*,[32] leading to the convocation of the first extraordinary session of the synod of bishops in 1969 to discuss precisely the relationship between episcopal conferences and the Apostolic See. A frank exchange is reported to have

---

30. For an analysis of the canonical framework for this relationship, see Peter Krämer, "Episcopal Conferences and the Apostolic See," *Jurist* 48 (1988): 134-45; and Antonio Acerbi, "The Development of the Canons on Conferences and the Apostolic See," ibid., 146-52.

31. See the various views discussed in Remigius Sobanski, "The Theology and Juridic Status of Episcopal Conferences at the Second Vatican Council," *Jurist* 48 (1988): 68-106.

32. See review and analysis in *Humanae Vitae and the Bishops: The Encyclical and the Statements of the National Hierarchies*, compiled by John Horgan, analysis by Austin Flannery (Shannon, Ireland: Irish University Press, 1972).

taken place at that session, but in the end the results were quite minimal.[33] A conscious pulling back in regard to conferences has been evident since that time on the part of the Apostolic See, whether in the process of revising the Code of Canon Law, or in statements and positions adopted by various officials. There is a reluctance to explore the extent to which communion admits of diversity, and a preference to assure communion by uniformity and direct dealing with individual bishops instead of conferences and the communion of churches they express.

One of the traditional canonical instruments of communion has been the *recognitio* required for decisions of particular councils, now extended to similar decisions of episcopal conferences.[34] This can be considered a technical application of the ancient practice of exchanging conciliar decisions as an expression of sharing a common faith and discipline, even with accepted diversities. But the actual practice of *recognitio* raises questions as to whether communion is understood as a dynamic reality among appropriately autonomous particular churches, or the extension of central authority assuring communion only on its own terms.[35]

---

33. See the extensive report on the discussions, proposals, and voting at the 1969 synod in Edmundus Farhat, "De primo extraordinario synodi coetu (1969)," *Monitor Ecclesiasticus* 97 (1972): 3-23. In some ways this also marked a turning point for the synod of bishops, which has failed to make such specific proposals in subsequent synods, particularly the parallel extraordinary synod of 1985.

34. The *recognitio* of conciliar decisions was first mandated by Sixtus V as part of his reorganization of the Roman Curia; see constitution *Immensa aeterni Dei*, January 22, 1588, in *Bullarum, diplomatum et privilegiorum Sanctorum Romanorum Pontificum, Taurinensis editio*, t. 8 (Turin: S. Franco and H. Almazzo, 1863), 991. For a discussion of its application to particular councils, see Francis J. Murphy, *Legislative Powers of the Provincial Council: A Historical Synopsis and a Commentary*, vol. 257 of *Canon Law Studies* (Washington, DC: Catholic University of America, 1947), 47-58; and James H. Provost, "Particular Councils," in *The New Code of Canon Law. Proceedings of the Fifth International Congress of Canon Law* (Ottawa: Saint Paul University, 1986) 1: 553-54. Applications to episcopal conferences are discussed in Heribert Schmitz, "Erwägungen zur Gesetzgebungstechnik der Bischofskonferenzen," *Trier theologische Zeitschrift* 73 (1964): 285-96; Winfried Aymans, "Ab Apostolica Sede recognitum," *Archiv für katholisches Kirchenrecht* 139 (1970): 405-427; Marianne Pesendorfer, *Partikulares Gesetz und partikularer Gesetzgeber in System des geltenden lateinischen Kirchenrechts* (Vienna: Herder, 1975), 99; Georg May, "Verschiedene Arten des Particularrechts," *Archiv für katholisches Kirchenrecht* 152 (1983): 31-45.

35. For a presentation of this latter perspective, see Gianfranco Ghirlanda, "*Hierarchica Communio*," vol. 216 of *Analecta Gregoriana* (Rome: Università Gregoriana Editrice, 1980).

This exemplifies that Vatican II provides general principles, the Code of Canon Law supplies a general framework, but it is only in practice that the reality of communion will be discovered in our times. History teaches that this discovery is not something which is achieved once and for all. Since it arises out of practice it needs to be grasped anew as practical issues change.[36]

Communion Completed in Mission

It is not enough for episcopal conferences to express the communion of the particular churches represented in them. Conferences, by their nature and historical development, are designed to promote the church's mission.

Conferences have a key role in the inculturation of Catholic faith and practice. For example, they are the agencies responsible for the translation of liturgical books into the vernacular and to make appropriate adaptations in keeping with local culture and customs (*SC* 39-40; c. 838, §3). The inculturation of the gospel lies at the heart of effective evangelization.

Historically, episcopal conferences have played a key role in addressing church-world issues, whether these relate to social and economic conditions, or to political realities that affect peace. The recent efforts of the National Conference of Catholic Bishops in the United States illustrate a continuation of this traditional role. The NCCB's method of preparing pastoral letters also incorporates elements of consultation typical of the Code of Canon Law's vision of the functioning of conferences in the context of a plenary council.

Inculturation, consultation, and applying the church's social teaching to local realities are not without tension. Some of this tension has been experienced in conference relations with the Apostolic See, particularly over liturgical questions. Tension with individuals over social teaching has been evident within the United States, and in some other parts of the world (e.g., some of the tensions in Latin America over the positions adopted by CELAM at Medellín and Puebla). Here again, the Second Vatican Council provides principles, the law supplies structures and procedures, but it is only through

---

36. Historical precedents are developed by Hermann J. Sieben, "Episcopal Conferences in Light of Particular Councils During the First Millennium," *Jurist* 48 (1988): 30-56; and Antonio García y García, "Episcopal Conferences in Light of Particular Councils During the Second Millennium," ibid., 57-67; and Brian Daley in this volume.

experience that the conferences will work out the implications of their commitment to mission.

Conferences and Councils

Tensions related to communion and mission were addressed in the early church through regular meetings of bishops in councils. The decline in conciliar activity, and the actual prohibition of holding councils in recent centuries in certain parts of the world, paved the way for the development of episcopal conferences in the last century and their further expansion since the middle of the twentieth century.[37]

While expressing the communion of their churches, the gatherings of bishops by themselves in conferences suffers from the absence of other witnesses of the Spirit who are also present in their churches. This is why the code presents councils as the full expression of the communion of churches in the area. In councils the legislative activity of episcopal conferences takes place in a context of dialogue and consultation with representatives from all the people of God, and thus is not so restricted as when conferences act on their own. In councils there is a greater opportunity for the wisdom of the Spirit resident in the entire community to be more clearly expressed.

Conciliar activity, however, has not marked recent stages of the church's life. Even the synodal life of individual dioceses has just now begun to revive. The possibility of returning to the active conciliar life of the last century in the United States, but with the expanded participation envisioned by the new code, is scarcely considered today. Why? If it is mainly because of the technical difficulties in holding a nationwide meeting, there are various models from which Catholics can learn. The practicalities of such meetings are not unique to Catholics, nor should the experience of consultative gatherings at the national level be viewed as solely a non-Catholic tradition.[38] From the regular

---

37. See discussion in Bernard Franck, "La conférence épiscopale et les autres institutions de collégialité intermédiaires," *L'Année Canonique* 27 (1983): 69-71. For a history of the difficulties in holding plenary councils in recent centuries, see Eugenio Corecco, *La formazione della Chiesa cattolica negli Stati Uniti d'America attraverso l'attività sinodale, con particolare riguardo al problema dell'amministrazione dei beni ecclesiastici* (Brescia: Morcelliana, 1970), 65-84.

38. See Hervé M. Legrand, "Synodes et conseils de l'après-concile," *Nouvelle revue*

national gatherings of Episcopal, Lutheran, and other churches Catholics could learn the practical processes these other Christians have tested and revised over the years, even as Catholics should continue to draw on their own church's rich conciliar tradition.[39]

The agenda for plenary councils can be developed from the implications of the church as a communion in mission. The procedures adopted for such meetings should themselves reflect a sensitivity to the Spirit and the theological realities expressed in communion and mission, drawing on the basic structure of the communion of particular churches to focus the energies of God's people in mission. But most of all, the spirit and tone for such meetings will determine, as does the practice of communion and mission, whether they are sources of light for all the nations. Episcopal conferences have a key role in determining all of these matters. Whether they are willing and prepared to take up such a challenge could be one test of whether conferences are truly expressions of the communion of churches in our day.

---

théologique 98 (1976): 193-216; James H. Provost, "Preparing for Particular Legislation to Implement the Revised Code," *Jurist* 42 (1982): 348-82.

39. See Earl Kent Brown, "Co-responsibility in Church Governance: Some Protestant Experiences," *Jurist* 31 (1971): 187-222; John E. Lynch, "Church Governance: The Protestant Experience," in *The Ministry of Governance*, ed. James K. Mallett (Washington, DC: CLSA, 1986): 56-79.

Index